DISTURBED IRELAND

A Clachan Reprint

http://clachanpublishing-com.webs.com/

Clachan Publishing,
Ballycastle   : Glens of Antrim,   2014

DISTURBED IRELAND:

BEING THE LETTERS
WRITTEN DURING THE WINTER OF 1880-81.

BY

BERNARD H. BECKER

SPECIAL COMMISIONER OF THE 'DAILY NEWS."

WITH ROUTE MAP

London :
MACMILLAN AND CO.
1881.

The Rights of Translation and Reproduction is Reserved[1]

---

[1] Facsimile of original title page

Disturbed Ireland,

Being the Letters Written During the Winter of 1880-81

Author: BERNARD H. BECKER,

Clachan Publishing

3 Drumavoley Park, Ballycastle, BT54 6PE, County Antrim.
Email; info@clachanpublishing.com
Website: http://clachanpublishing-com.
This edition first published 2014

IBSN 978-1-909906-24-2

Original edition London:
MACMILLAN AND CO. 1881.
London: R. Clay, Sons, and Taylor, Bread Street Hill

Clachan
Publishing

Contents

Acknowledgements

We are grateful to Google books and the Project Gutenberg for making this book available on the web.

Editor's Foreword

Clachan Publishing is a printing service dedicated to the preservation and promotion of print material related to Irish local and family histories. We publish material that may be of local or family interest such as memoires, articles, collections of old photographs, old letters, papers, newspaper cuttings, brochures, scrapbooks. We rely on materials given or lent to us by members of the public as well as commentaries and reports written by contemporaries of historic events.

The present publication, *Disturbed Ireland, Being The Letters Written During The Winter Of 1880-81,* is a reproduction of letters by Bernard H. Becker commissioned in the 1880s by the Daily News. Being in the public domain, we are happy to reproduce it in print form and extend its readership in accordance with our mission to promote historic material of interest to local and family historians.

We are particularly keen that the material be edited in a manner that makes it more accessible to the modern reader. We have therefore added explanatory footnotes to the text to throw light on obsolete and obscure references and turn of phrase. Also, some currency symbols, paragraphing and punctuation have been modernised. Furthermore, we have added an index to the original in order to help the reader navigate the text easily,

As this is a copy of an earlier publication, we cannot take responsibility for errors that may have occurred in the original. We do, however, take responsibility for any that may have resulted from the formatting and printing processes.

We make no claim to ownership of present or future copyright, but request that anyone who uses materials from this publication acknowledge both the original publication and this reproduction.

Seán O'Halloran

EDITOR, Clachan Publishing, September 24th, 2012.

Author's Preface

Having been most cordially granted permission to republish these letters in a collected form, it is my duty to mention that my mission from the Daily News was absolutely unfettered, either by instructions or introductions. It was thought that an independent and impartial account of the present condition of the disturbed districts of Ireland would be best secured by sending thither a writer without either Irish politics or Irish friends - in short, one who might occupy the stand-point of the too-often-quoted "intelligent foreigner." Hence my little book is purely descriptive of the stirring scenes and deeply interesting people I have met with on my way through the counties of Mayo, Galway, Clare, Limerick, Cork, and Kerry. It is neither apolitical treatise, nor a dissertation on the tenure of land, but a plain record of my experience of a strange phase of national life. I have simply endeavoured to reflect as accurately as might be the salient features of a social and economic upheaval, soon I fervently hope, to pass into the domain of history; and in offering my work tithe public must ask indulgence for the errors of omission and commission so difficult to avoid while travelling and writing rapidly in a country which, even to its own people, is a complex problem.

B.H.B.

ARTS' CLUB, January 6th, 1881.

Map of Ireland, showing author's route

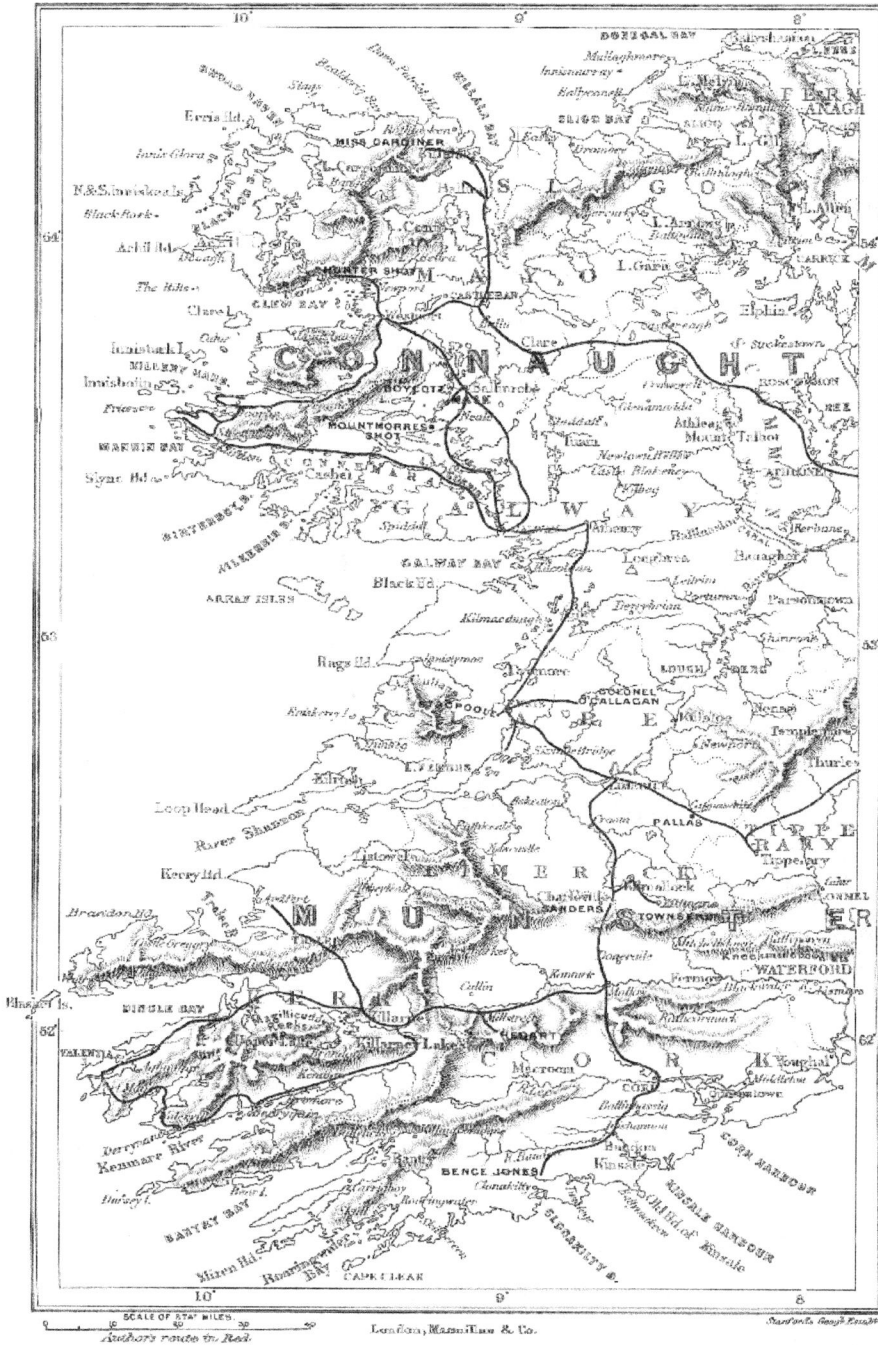

Detailed map of western Ireland, showing author's route

I - AT LOUGH MASK

WESTPORT, CO. MAYO, Oct. 24th

The result of several days' incessant travelling in county Mayo is a very considerable modification of the opinion formed at the first glance at this, the most disaffected part of Ireland. On reaching Claremorris in the heart of the most disturbed district, I certainly felt, and not for the first time, that as one approaches a spot in which law and order are supposed to be suspended the sense of alarm and insecurity diminishes, to put it mathematically, "as the square of the distances." Even after a rapid survey of this part of the West I cannot help contrasting the state of public opinion here with that prevailing in Dublin. In the capital - outside of "the Castle," where moderate counsels prevail - the alarmists appear to have it all their own way. I was told gravely that there was no longer any security for life or property in the West; that county Mayo was like Tipperary in the old time, "only more so;" and that if I would go lurking about Lough Mask and Lough Corrib it was impossible to prevent me; but that the chances of return were, to say the least, remote. It was in vain that I pointed out that every stone wall did not hide an assassin, and that strangers and others not connected either directly or indirectly with the land were probably as safe, if not safer, on a high road in Mayo than in Sackville-street, Dublin. It was admitted that, theoretically, I was quite in the right; but that like many other theorists I might find my theory break down in practice. I was entertained with a full account of the way in which assassinations are conducted in the livelier counties of Ireland, and great stress was laid upon the fact that the assassins were always well primed with "the wine of the country," that is to say whisky, of similar quality to that known in New York as "fighting rum," "Jersey lightning," or "torchlight procession." It was then impressed upon me that half-drunken assassins, specially imported from a distant part of the county to shoot a landlord or agent, might easily mistake a stranger for the obnoxious person and shoot him accordingly, just as the unlucky driver was hit in Kerry the other day instead of the land agent. Furthermore, I was taken to a gunsmith's in Dawson Street, where I was assured that the sale of firearms had been and was remarkably brisk, the chief demand being for full-sized revolvers and double-barrelled carbines. The weapon chiefly recommended was one of the latter, with a large smooth bore for carrying buck-shot and spreading the charge so much as to make the hitting of a man at thirty yards almost certain. The barrels were very short, in order that the gun might be convenient to carry in carriage or car. This formidable weapon was to be carried in the hand so as to be ready when opportunity served; a little ostentation as to one's habit of going armed being vigorously insisted on as a powerful deterrent.

To any person unacquainted with the humorous side of the Irish character a morning spent in such converse as I have endeavoured to indicate might have proved disquieting enough; but those who know Irishmen and their ways at once enter into the spirit of the thing, and enjoy it as much as the untamable jokers themselves. Nothing is more amazing to serious people than the light and easy manner in which everybody takes everything on this side of the Irish Sea. This is perfectly exemplified by the tone in which the Kerry murder is discussed. I have heard it talked over by every class of person, from a landholding peer to a not very sober car-driver, and the view taken is always the same. No horror is expressed at the commission of such a crime, or at the state of society which makes it possible. Nothing of the kind. A little sympathy is expressed for the poor man who was shot by mistake, and then the humour of the situation overrules every other consideration. That poor people resenting what they imagine to be tyranny should shoot one of their own class instead of the hated agent is a fact so irresistibly comic as to provoke a quantity of hilarious comment. As laughter dies away, however, another expression of feeling takes place, and the slackness of the master in not being ready with his pistol, and his want of presence of mind to pursue the murderer and avenge his servant's death, are spoken of with the fiercest indignation. But nobody appears to care about the general and social aspect of the case.

Beneath all this humour and a curious tendency to exaggerate the condition of the West, there undeniably lurked very considerable uneasiness. It was known that "the Castle" was hard at work, and that, before proceeding to coercive measures, Mr Forster was getting together all the trustworthy evidence that could be obtained as to the state of the country. As an instance of the absurd rumours flying about, I may mention that I was in the presence of two Irish peers solemnly assured that a "rising in the West" was imminent, and not only imminent, but fixed for the 31st October. Now, who has not heard at any time within the memory of man of this expected "rising in the West"? It is the *spectre rouge*, or, to be more accurate as to local colour, the *spectre vert* of the Irish alarmist, and a poor, ragged, out-at-elbows spectre it is, altogether very much the worse for wear. Flesh and blood could not bear the mention of this shabby, worn-out old ghost with calmness, and I conveyed to the gentlemen who volunteered the information my opinion that the *spectre vert* was, in American language, "played out." Will it be believed that I was the only person present who ridiculed the "poor ghost"? I soon perceived that my scornful remarks were not at all in accordance with the feeling of the company, who did not see anything impossible in a "rising in the West," and refused to laugh at the Saxon's remark that things did not "rise," but "set" in that direction. County Mayo and parts of county Galway were beyond the law, and could only be cured by the means successfully employed in Westmeath a few years ago - coercion. It was of no avail to say that very few people had been shot in the disaffected counties during the last ten years. The answer was always the same. The minds of the people were poisoned by agitators, and they would pay nobody either rent or any other just debt except on compulsion.

Beyond Athlone the tone of public opinion improved very rapidly, and in Roscommon, once a disturbed county, I found plenty of people ready to laugh with me at the *spectre vert*. There was nothing the matter in that county. A fair price had been obtained for sheep and cattle, the harvest had been good, everything was going on as well as possible. There was some talk, it was true, about disturbances in Mayo, but there was a great deal of imagination and exaggeration, and the trouble was confined to certain districts of the county, the centre of disturbance being somewhere about Claremorris, a market town, on the railway to Westport, and not very far from Knock, the last new place of pilgrimage. At Claremorris I accordingly halted to look about me, and was surprised at the extraordinary activity of the little place. Travellers in agricultural England, either Wessex or East Anglia, often wonder who drinks all the beer for the distribution of which such ample facilities are afforded. A church, a public house, and a blacksmith's shop constitute an English village; but there is nobody on the spot either to go to church or drink the beer. At Claremorris a similar effect is produced on the visitor's mind. The main street is full of shops, corn-dealers, drapers, butchers, bakers, and general dealers in everything, from a horse to a hayseed; but out of the main track there are no houses - only hovels as wretched as any in Connaught. It is quite evident that the poor people who inhabit them cannot buy much of anything. Men, women, and children, dogs, ducks, and a donkey, are frequently crowded together in these miserable cabins, the like of which on any English estate would bring down a torrent of indignation on the landlord. They are all of one pattern, wretchedly thatched, but with stout stone walls, and are, when a big peat fire is burning, hot almost to suffocation. When it is possible to distinguish the pattern of the bed-curtains through the dirt, they are seen to be of the familiar blue and white checked pattern made familiar to London playgoers by Susan's cottage as displayed at the St. James's Theatre. The chest of drawers is nearly always covered with tea-things and other crockery, generally of the cheapest and commonest kind, but in great plenty. House accommodation in Claremorris is of the humblest character. At the best inn, called ambitiously Hughes's Hotel, I found that I was considered fortunate in getting any sort of bedroom to myself. The apartment was very small, with a lean-to roof, but then I reigned over it in solitary grandeur, while a dozen commercial travellers were packed into the three or four other bedrooms in the house. As these gentlemen arrived at odd hours of the night and were put into the rooms and beds occupied by their friends, sleep at Claremorris was not a function easily performed, and it was some foreknowledge of what actually occurred that induced me to sit up as late as possible in the eating, dining, reading, and commercial room, the only apartment of any size in the house, but full of occupants, most of whom were very communicative concerning their business. Here were the eagles indeed, but where was the carcass? To my amazement I found that Mike this and Tim that, whose shops are very small, had been giving large orders, and that the credit of Claremorris was in a very healthy condition. Equally curious was it to find that the gathering of "commercials" was not an unusual occurrence, but that the queer townlet was a genuine centre of business activity.

We sat up as late as the stench of paraffin from the lamps - for there is no gas - would allow us. Lizzie, literally a maid of all work, but dressed in a gown tied violently back, brought up armful after armful of peat, and built and rebuilt the fire over and over again. There was in the corner of the room a huge receptacle, like half a hogshead, fastened to the wall for holding peat - or "turf," as it is called here - but it never occurred apparently to anybody to fill this bin and save the trouble of eternal journeys up and down stairs. It may be also mentioned, not out of any squeamishness, but purely as a matter of fact, that in the intervals of bringing in "arrumfuls" of "torrf" Lizzie folded tablecloths for newcomers so as to hide the coffee-stains as much as possible, and then proceeded to set their tea for them, after which she went back to building the fire again. In the work of waiting she was at uncertain intervals assisted by Joe, a shock-headed, black-haired Celt, who, when a Sybarite asked at breakfast for toast, repeated "Toast!" in a tone that set the table in a roar. It was not said impudently or rudely. Far from it. Joe's tone simply expressed honest amazement, as if one had asked for a broiled crocodile or any other impossible viand.

There are, of course, people who would like separate servants to build up peat fires and to cut their bread and butter; but this kind of person should not come to county Mayo. To the less fastidious all other shortcomings are made up for by the absolutely delightful manner of the people, whose kindness, civility, good humour, and, I may add, honesty, are remarkable. At Hughes's Hotel the politeness of everybody was perfect; and I may add that the proprietor saved me both time and money by giving up a long posting job, to his own obvious loss. But if a visitor to Mayo wants anything done at once, then and there, he had better do it himself. I ventured to remark to Joe that he was a civil-spoken boy, but not very prompt in carrying out instructions, and asked whether everybody in Connaught conducted himself in the same way. He at once admitted that everybody did so. "Divil the bad answer ye'll iver get, Sorr," said he. "We just say, 'I will, Sorr,' and thin go away, and another gintleman says something, and ye're forgotten. Dy'e see, now?" And away he went, and forgot everything.

Being at Claremorris, I tried to see a "lister," that is, a landowner and agent on the "black list." I was obliged to make inquiries concerning his whereabouts, and this investigation soon convinced me that there was something wrong in Mayo after all; not the *spectre vert* exactly, but yet an unpleasant impalpability. All was well at Claremorris. Trade was good "presently now," potatoes were good and cheap, poverty was not advancing arm-in-arm with winter. It was cold, for snow was already on the Nephin; but turf had been stored during the long, fine, warm summer, and nobody was afraid of the frost. But the instant I mentioned the name of the gentleman I wanted to find not a soul knew anything about him. Farming several hundred acres of land on his own account, a resident on Lough Mask for seven years, and agent to Lord Erne, he seemed to be a man concerning whose movements the countryside would probably be well informed. But nobody knew anything at all about him. He might be at the Curragh, or he might be in Dublin, and then would, one informant thought, slip over to England and get out of the trouble, if he were wise.

In one of the larger stores I saw that the mention of his name drew every eye upon me, and that the bystanders were greatly exercised as to my identity and my business. In this part of the country everybody knows everybody, and a stranger asking for a proscribed man excited native curiosity to a maddening pitch. Presently I was taken aside, led round a corner, and there told that most assuredly the man I sought had not come home from Dublin *via* Claremorris. Having a map of the county with me, I naturally suggested that he might have reached Lough Mask by way of Tuam, and, moreover, that, having a shrewd notion he would be shot at when occasion served, he would most likely try to get home by an unusual route on which he would hardly be looked for. "Is it alone ye think he'd be going, Sorr?" asked my informant in astonishment. "Divil a fut does he stir widout an escort." This was news indeed. "He came here, sure, Sorr, wid two constables on the kyar and two mounted men following him." I was also recommended to hold my tongue, for that Mr Boycott's friends would certainly not tell whether he was at home or not, and his enemies would probably be kept in ignorance or led astray altogether.

But it was necessary for me to find out his whereabouts. To go and see whether he was at Lough Mask involved a ride of forty miles, enlivened by the probability of being mistaken for him, slipping quietly home, and cheered by the risk of hearing at his house that he had gone to England. Telegraphing to him appeared useless, as communications were said to be cut off on the five Irish miles between Ballinrobe, the telegraph station, and Lough Mask House. As time wore on, I learned that he had had cattle at Tuam Fair, but that he had not come home that way for certain. In despair I came on to this place, where information reached me yesterday morning that, contrary to all expectations, he had gone on the other line of railway to

Galway, and taken the steamboat on Lough Corrib to Cong, after having telegraphed to his escort to meet him there.

From Westport to Lough Mask is a long but picturesque drive. I was lucky enough to secure an intelligent driver and an excellent horse and car. Thirty Irish miles is not in this part of the country considered an extravagant distance to drive a horse. I believe, indeed, that under other circumstances the unfortunate animal would have been compelled to carry me the entire distance; but I remarked that when I suggested a change of horses at Ballinrobe I was not only accommodated with a fresh horse, but with a fresh car and a fresh driver, who declared that the road to Lough Mask was about the safest and best that he had ever heard of. Now from Westport to Ballinrobe we had met nobody but a very few people going into town either riding on an ass or driving one laden with a pair of panniers or "cleaves" of turf, for which some four pence or five pence would be paid. All seemed thinly clad, despite the fearfully cold wind sweeping down from the Nephin, the Hest, and other snow-clad mountains. Crossing the long dreary peat-moss known as Mun-a-lun, we found the cold intense; but on approaching Lough Carra came into bright broad sunshine. At Ballinrobe the sun was still hotter, and as I approached Lough Mask the heat was almost oppressive. I was not, however, allowed to inspect Lough Mask House and the ruins of the adjacent castle in the first place. I had but just passed a magnificent field of mangolds, many of which weighed from a stone to a stone and a half, when I came upon a sight which could not be paralleled in any other civilised country at the present moment.

Beyond a turn in the road was a flock of sheep, in front of which stood a shepherdess heading them back, while a shepherd, clad in a leather shooting-jacket and aided by a bull terrier, was driving them through a gate into an adjacent field. Despite her white woollen shawl and the work she was engaged upon, it was quite evident, from her voice and manner, that the shepherdess was of the educated class, and the shepherd, albeit dressed in a leather jacket, carried himself with the true military air. Both were obviously amateurs at sheep-driving, and the smart, intelligent bull terrier was as much an amateur as either of them, for shepherd, shepherdess and dog were only doing what a good collie would achieve alone and unaided. Behind the shepherd were two tall members of the Royal Irish Constabulary in full uniform and with carbines loaded. As the shepherd entered the field the constables followed him everywhere at a distance of a few yards. All his backings and fillings, turnings and doublings, were followed by the armed policemen. This combination of the most proverbially peaceful of pursuits with carbines and buckshot was irresistibly striking, and the effect of the picture was not diminished by the remarks of Mr and Mrs Boycott, for the shepherd and shepherdess were no other than these.

The condition of Mr Boycott and his family has undergone not the slightest amelioration since he last week wrote a statement of his case to a daily contemporary. In fact, he is in many respects worse off. It will be recollected that about a month ago a process-server and his escort retreated on Lough Mask House, followed by a mob, and that on the following day all the farm servants were ordered to leave Mr Boycott's employment. I may mention that Mr Boycott is a Norfolk man, the son of a clergyman, and was formerly an officer in the 39th Regiment. On his marriage he settled on the Island of Achill, near here, and farmed there until he was offered some land agencies, which occupied so much of his time, that he, after some twenty years' residence in Achill, elected to take a farm on the mainland. For seven years he has farmed at Lough Mask, acting also as Lord Erne's agent. He has on his own account had a few difficulties with his workpeople; but these were tided over by concessions on his part, and all went smoothly till the serving of notices upon Lord Erne's tenants. All the weight of the tenants' vengeance has fallen upon the unfortunate agent, whom the irritated people declare they will "hunt out of the country." The position is an extraordinary one. During his period of occupation Mr Boycott has laid out a great deal of money on his farm, has improved the roads, and made turnips and other root crops to grow where none grew before. But the countryside has struck against him, and he is now actually in a state of siege. Personally attended by an armed escort everywhere, he has a garrison of ten constables on his premises, some established in a hut, and the rest in that part of Lough Mask House adjacent to the old castle.

Garrisoned at home and escorted abroad, Mr Boycott and his family are now reduced to one female domestic. Everybody else has gone away, protesting sorrow, but alleging that the power brought to bear upon them was greater than they could resist. Farm labourers, workmen, herds-men, stablemen, all went long ago, leaving the corn standing, the horses in the stable, the sheep in the field, the turnips, swedes, carrots, and potatoes in the ground, where I saw them yesterday. Last Tuesday the laundress refused to wash for the family any longer; the baker at Ballinrobe is afraid to supply them with bread, and the butcher fears to send them meat. The state of siege is perfect. When the strike first began Mr Boycott went bravely to work with his family, setting the young ladies to reaping and binding, and looking after the beasts and sheep himself. But the struggle is nearly at an end now. Mr Boycott has sold some of his stock; but he can neither sell his crop to anybody else, nor, as they say in the North of England, "win" it for himself. There remains in the ground at least five hundred pounds worth of potatoes and other root crops, and the owner has no possible means of doing anything with them. Nor, I am assured on trustworthy authority, would any human being buy them at any price; nor, if any such person were found, would he be able to find any labourer to touch any manner of work on the spot under the ban. By an impalpable and invisible power it is decreed that Mr Boycott shall be "hunted out," and it is more than doubtful whether he will, under existing circumstances, be able to stand against it. He is unquestionably a brave and resolute man, but there is too much reason to believe that without his garrison and escort his life would not be worth an hour's purchase.

There are few fairer prospects than that from the steps of Lough Mask House, a moderately comfortable and unpretending edifice, not quite so good as a large farmer's homestead in England. But the potatoes will rot in the ground, and the cattle will go astray, for not a soul in the Ballinrobe country dare touch a spade for Mr Boycott. Personally he is protected, but no woman in Ballinrobe would dream of washing him a cravat or making him a loaf. All the people have to say is that they are sorry, but that they "dare not." Hence either Mr Boycott, with an escort armed to the teeth, or his wife without an escort - for the people would not harm her - must go to Ballinrobe after putting a horse in the shafts themselves, buy what they can, and bring it home. Everybody advises them to leave the country; but the answer of the besieged agent is simply this: "I can hardly desert Lord Erne, and, moreover, my own property is sunk in this place." It is very much like asking a man to give up work and go abroad for the benefit of his health. He cannot sacrifice his occupation and his property. There is very little doubt that this unfortunate gentleman has been selected as a victim whose fate may strike terror into others. Judging from what I hear, there is a sort of general determination to frighten the landlords. Only a few nights ago a man went into a store at Longford and said openly, "My landlord has processed me for the last four or five years; but he hasn't processed me this year, and the divil thank him for that same."

II - AN AGRARIAN DIFFICULTY

"Tiernaur, Sorr, is on the way to Claggan Mountain, where they shot at Smith last year, and - if I don't disremember - is just where they shot Hunter last August eleven years. Ye'll mind the crossroads before ye come to the chapel. It was there they shot him from behind a sod-bank." This was the reply I received in answer to my question as to the whereabouts of a public meeting to be held yesterday morning, with the patriotic object of striking terror into the hearts of landlords and agents. It was delivered without appearance of excitement or emotion of any kind, the demeanour of the speaker being quite as simple as that of Wessex Hodge when he recommends one to go straight on past the Craven Arms, and then bear round by the Dog and Duck till the great house comes in sight.

Tiernaur, I gathered, was about fifteen miles to the north-west along Clew Bay towards Ballycroy. It is called Newfield Chapel on the Ordnance map, but is always spoken of here by its native name. It is invested with more than the mere transient interest attaching to the place of an open-air meeting, for it is the centre of a district subject to chronic disturbance, and is just now the scene of serious trouble, or what would appear serious trouble in any less turbulent part of the country. It is necessary to be exact in describing what occurs here, as a phrase may easily be construed to imply much more than is intended. When it is said that the country between Westport and Ballycroy is disturbed, and that law and order are set at defiance, it must not be imagined that the roads are unsafe for travellers, or that any ordinary person is liable to be shot at, beaten, robbed, or insulted. I have no hesitation in stating that a stranger may go anywhere in the county, at any hour of the day or night, alone and unarmed, and that even in country inns he need take no precautions against robbery. Mayo people do not steal, and if they shot a stranger, it would only be by mistake for a Scotch farmer or an English agent. And I am sure that the accident would be sincerely deplored by the warm-hearted natives.

I have thought it well to master all the details of the Tiernaur difficulty, because it is a perfect type of the agrarian troubles which agitate the West. In the first place the reader will clearly understand that English and Scotch landlords, agents, and farmers, are as a rule abhorred by the Irish population. It is perhaps hardly my province to decide who is to blame. Difference of manner may go for a great deal, but beyond and below the resentment caused by a prompt, decisive, and perhaps imperious tone, lies a deeply-rooted sense of wrong - logically or illogically arrived at. The evictions of the last third of a century and the depopulation of large tracts of country have filled the hearts of the people with revenge, and, rightly or wrongly, they not only blame the landlord but the occupier of the land. If, they argue, there had been no Englishmen and Scotchmen to take large farms, the small holders would not have been swept away, and "driven like a wild goose on the mountain" to make room for them. Without for the present discussing the reasonableness of this plea, I merely record the simple fact that an English or Scotch farmer is unpopular from the beginning. Here and there such a one as Mr Simpson may manage to live the prejudice down; but that he will have to encounter it on his arrival is absolutely certain.

This being the case, it is not to be wondered at that when the late Mr Hunter, a Scotchman, took a large grazing farm at Tiernaur, his arrival was at once regarded in a hostile spirit. The land he occupied was let to him by two adjoining proprietors, Mr Gibbings, of Trinity College, Dublin, and Mr Stoney, of Rossturk Castle, near at hand. There was a convenient dwelling-house on the part of the farm looking over Clew Bay towards Clare Island, and all was apparently smooth and pleasant. No sooner, however, was Mr Hunter established there than a difficulty arose. The inhabitants of the surrounding country had been in the habit of cutting turf and pulling sedge on parts of the mountain and bog included within the limits of Mr Hunter's farm. It is only fair to the memory of the deceased gentleman to state that such rights are frequently paid for, and that he had not taken the farm subject to any "turbary" rights or local customs. Accordingly he demanded payment from the people, who objected that they had always cut turf and pulled sedge on the mountain; that they could not live without turf for fuel and sedge to serve first as winter bedding for their cattle and afterwards as manure; that except on Mr Hunter's mountain neither turf nor sedge could be got within any reasonable distance; and, finally, that they had always enjoyed such right. And so forth. As this was, as already intimated, not in the bond, Mr Hunter, not very unnaturally, insisted that if the people would not pay him his landlord must, and asked Mr Gibbings to allow him ten pounds a year off his rent. The latter offered him, as I am informed, five pounds. The matter was referred to an umpire, who awarded Mr Hunter twelve pounds, an assessment which Mr Gibbings declined to take into consideration at all.

After some further discussion Mr Hunter warned the people off his farm and declared their supposed "turbary" rights at an end. It is of course difficult to arrive at any conclusion on the merits of the case. All that is certain is, that the people had long enjoyed privileges which Mr Gibbings declared to be simple trespass. Finally he told Mr Hunter he had his bond and must enforce it himself. The unfortunate farmer, thus placed, as it were, between the upper and nether millstone, endeavoured to enforce his supposed rights. It is almost needless to remark that the people went on cutting turf just as if nothing had happened. In an evil hour Mr Hunter determined to see what the law could do to protect him in the enjoyment of his farm, and he sued the trespassers accordingly. I will not attempt to explain the intricacies of an Irish lawsuit farther than to note that, owing to some deficiency in their pleas, the trespassers underwent a nonsuit, or some analogous doom, and went gloomily away without having even the satisfaction of a fair fight in court. At the instance of Mr Hunter, execution for damages and costs was issued against the most solvent of the trespassers, one John O'Neill, of Knockmanus - his next-door neighbour, so to speak. On Friday the execution was put in, and, on its being found impossible to find anybody to act as bailiff, Mr Hunter himself asked the sub-sheriff to put in his name, and he would see himself that the crops were not removed. This was done, and on the following Sunday Mr Hunter went with his family to attend Divine service at Newport. Leaving Newport in the evening, he had gone not half-way to Tiernaur when his horse's shoe came off. This circumstance, ominous enough in the disturbed districts of Ireland, was not heeded by Mr Hunter, who put back to Newport and had his horse shod. As he set out for the second time, the evening was closing in, and as he reached the road turning off from the main track towards his own dwelling he was shot from the opposite angle. The assassin must have been a good marksman, for there were four persons in the dog-cart - Mr Hunter, his wife, his son, and a servant lad. The doomed man was picked out and shot dead. It is obviously unnecessary to add that the assassin escaped, and has not been discovered unto this day.

Immediately on the commission of the crime the widow of the murdered man was afforded "protection," as it is called, in the manner usual during Irish disturbances - that is, four men and a sergeant of the constabulary were stationed at her house. In course of time, however, Mrs Hunter felt comparatively safe, and the constables removed to a hut about two miles on the Newport road, opposite to some very good grouse-shooting. There the five men dwell in their little iron-clad house, pierced with loopholes in case of attack - a very improbable event. At the moment of writing, four constables are also stationed at Mr Stoney's residence, Rossturk Castle, although it is not quite certain what the owner has done to provoke the anger of the people. This being the situation, a very short time since Mrs Hunter elected to give up the farm and leave this part of the country. The property is therefore on the hands of the landlord, and is "to let." How bright the prospect of getting a tenant is may be estimated by the remark made to me by a very well-instructed person living close by - "If the landlord were to give me that farm for nothing, stock it for me, and give me a cash balance to go on with, I would gratefully but firmly decline the generous gift. No consideration on earth would induce me to occupy Hunter's farm." In the present condition of affairs it would certainly require either great courage or profound ignorance on the part of a would-be tenant to impel him to occupy any land under ban. A rational being would almost as soon think of going to help Mr Boycott to get in his potatoes. For the people of Tiernaur are now face to face - only at a safe distance for him - with Mr Gibbings. The cause of the new difficulty is as follows: Mrs Hunter having given up the farm, it was applied for by some of the neighbours, who offered a similar rent to that paid by her. Either because the landlord did not want the applicants as tenants, or because he thought the land improved, he demanded a higher rent. This is the one unpardonable crime - an attempt to raise the rent. For his own reasons the landlord does not choose to let what is called Hunter's farm to the Tiernaur people on the old terms, and the stranger who should venture upon it would need be girt with *robur et aes triplex*.

Within the last few days this proprietary deadlock has been enlivened by an act which has caused much conversation in this part of Ireland. A house on Glendahurk Mountain has been burned down, and the cattle of the neighbouring farmers have been turned on to the mountain to pasture at the expense of Mr Gibbings. Moreover the bailiff has been warned not to interfere, or attempt to scare the cattle and drive them off. Thus the tenant farmers are grazing their cattle for nothing, and, what is more, no man dare meddle with them. The sole remedy open to Mr Gibbings is civil process for trespass. Should he adopt this course he will probably be safe enough in Dublin, but I am assured that the life of his bailiff will not be worth a day's purchase.

III - A LAND MEETING

WESTPORT, CO. MAYO, Oct. 27th

The way from this place to Tiernaur is through a country, as a Mayo man said to me, "eminently adapted to tourists." Not very far off lies Croagh Patrick, the sacred mountain from which St. Patrick cursed the snakes and other venomous creatures and drove them from Ireland. I was assured by the car-driver that the noxious animals vanished into the earth at the touch of the Saint's bell. "He just," said this veracious informant, "shlung his bell at 'um, and the bell cum back right into his hand. And the mountain is full of holes. And the snakes went into 'um and ye can hear 'um hissing on clear still days." Be this as it may, the line of country towards Newport is delightfully picturesque. The great brown cone of Croagh Patrick soars above all, and to right and left rise the snow-covered Nephin and Hest. Evidences of careful cultivation are frequent on every side. Fairly large potato-fields occur at short intervals, and mangolds and turnips are grown for feeding stock. Cabbages also are grown for winter feed, and the character of the country is infinitely more cheerful than on the opposite side of Westport. Inquiring of my driver as to the safety of the country, I received the following extraordinary reply, "Ye might lie down and sleep anywhere, and divil a soul would molest ye, barring the lizards in summer time; and they are dreadful, are lizards. They don't bite ye like snakes, or spit at ye like toads; but if ye sleep wid ye'r mouth open, they crawl, just crawl down ye'r throat into ye'r stommick and kill ye. For they've schales on their bodies, and can't get back; and they just scratch, and bite, and claw at your innards till ye die." There was nothing to be done with these terrible lizards but to drink an unmentionable potion, which, I am assured, is strong enough to rout the most determined lizard of them all, and bring him to nought. It is, however, noteworthy that stories of persons being killed by lizards crawling down their throats are widely distributed. There is one of a young Hampshire lady who, the day before she was married, went to sleep in her father's garden, and was killed by a lizard crawling down her throat. And, my informant said, the lizard is carved on her tomb - a fact which makes it appear likely that the story was made for the armorial bearings of the lady in question.

By a pleasant road lined with cabbage gardens we came on to Newport - a port which, like this, is not one of the "has beens," but one of the "would have beens." There is the semblance of a port without ships, and warehouses without goods, and quays overgrown with grass. Beyond Newport the country grows wilder. There is less cultivation, and behind every little shanty rises the great brown shoulder of the neighbouring mountain covered with rough, bent grass - or sedge, as it is called here. Grey plover and curlew scud across the road, a sign of hard weather, and near the rarer homesteads towers the hawk, looking for his prey. Now and again come glimpses of the bay, of the great island of Innisturk, of Clare Island, and of Innisboffin. Wilder and wilder grows the scenery as we approach Grace O'Malley's Castle, a small tenement for a Queen of Connaught. It is a lone tower like a border "peel," but on the very edge of the sea. The country folk show the window through which passed the cable of a mighty war ship to be tied round Grace O'Malley's bedpost, whom one concludes to have been, in a small way, a kind of pirate queen. As we approach Tiernaur the road becomes lively with country folk going to and from chapel, and stopping to exchange a jest - always in the tongue of the country - by the way. In this part of the wild road the Saxon feels himself, indeed, a stranger - in race, in creed, and in language. Now and then he sees the Irishman of the stage, clad in the short swallow-tailed coat with pocket-flaps, the corduroy breeches, the blue worsted stockings and misshapen caubeen[2], made familiar by a thousand novels and plays. These articles of attire are becoming day by day as rare as the red petticoats formerly worn by the peasant women. On the latter, however, may still be seen, now and then, the great blue cloth cloaks which once formed a distinctive article of costume, and a very necessary one in this severe climate. Presently jog by a few men on horseback, very ill-mounted on sorry beasts, and riding in unison with the quality of their animals. Men, women and children are in their Sunday best, and to all outward appearance scrupulously clean. I am constrained to believe that among the very lowest class - that which comes under prison regulations - the preliminary washing is counted as the severest part of the punishment; but the evidence of my own eyesight is in favour of the strict personal cleanliness of Sunday folk in this part of the country.

Near Tiernaur I find bands of men marching to the gathering, which is a purely local affair, not regularly organized by the Land League. But the men themselves appear to be very strictly organized, to march well, and to obey their bugler promptly. They are all in Sunday clothes, wear green scarves, and carry green banners. The latter are inscribed with various mottoes proper to the occasion. On the Kilmeena banner appears,

No prison cell nor tyrant's claim
Can keep us from our glorious aim.

The Glendahurk men proclaim on another green banner, bearing the harp without the crown, that "Those who toil Must own the soil;" and the Mulrawny contingent call upon the people to "Hold the Mountain," to cry "Down with the Land Grabbers," and "God save Ireland." The musical arrangements are of the humblest kind, and not a single man is armed, at least outwardly, and not one in twenty carries a stick. All is quiet and orderly,

[2] Irish beret formerly worn by peasants, now the headdress of the Irish British regiments, [Clachan ed.].

and the same tranquil demeanour obtains at Tiernaur, or rather at Newfield Chapel, appointed as the trysting-place after morning service. In accordance with recent regulations there is no ostentatious display of police, but everybody knows that a strong detachment is posted in Mrs Hunter's house, and that on any sign of disturbance they will promptly put in an appearance. On the side of the Government, as on that of the people, there is an obvious desire to avoid any semblance of an appeal to force.

The scene at Newfield Chapel is both interesting and beautiful. Tiernaur lies between the brown mountains and a sapphire sea, studded with islands rising precipitously from its level. In front lies the lofty eminence of Clare Island, below which appears to nestle the picturesque castle of Rossturk. The bay - which is said to hold as many islands as there are days in a year and one over - presents a series of magnificent views. One might be assisting at one of the meetings of the Covenanters held amid the seas and mountains of Galloway, but with the difference that the faith of the meeting is that of the Church of Rome, and that the scenery is far grander than that of Wigton and Kirkcudbright. It is a natural amphitheatre of sea and mountain, perfect in its beauty, but for one dark spot, just visible - the place where Hunter was shot. The chapel, modest and unpretending, is a simple, whitewashed edifice, surrounded by a white wall, over which gleam, in the already declining sun, the red and black plaid shawls of the peasant women who have remained after mass to witness the proceedings. Not a dozen bonnets are present, and hardly as many hats, for nearly all the women and girls wear the shawl pulled over their heads, Lancashire fashion. In appearance the people contrast favourably with those of the inland towns of county Mayo. The men look active and wiry, and the women are well grown and in many cases have an air of distinction foreign to the heavy-browed, black-haired Celt of the interior. Altogether the picture is well worthy of a master of colour, with its masses of black and green, relieved by patches of bright red, standing boldly out against the background of brown moor and azure sea.

The proceedings are hardly in consonance with the dignity of the surroundings. Many marchings to and fro occur before the various deputations are duly ushered to their place near the temporary hustings erected in front of the chapel. When the meeting - of some two thousand people at most - has gathered, there is an unlucky fall of rain, advantage of which is taken by a local "omadhaun,[3]" or "softy" as they call him in Northern England, to mount the stage and make a speech, which elicits loud shouts of laughter. Taking little heed of the pelting shower the "omadhaun," who wears a red bandanna like a shawl, and waves a formidable shillelagh, makes a harangue which, so far as I can understand it, has neither head nor

[3] Irish fool, idiot, simpleton, [Clachan ed.].

tail. Delivered with much violent gesticulation, the speech is evidently to the taste of the audience, who cheer and applaud more or less ironically. At last the rain is over, and the serious business of the day commences. The chair is taken by the parish priest of Tiernaur, whose initial oration is peculiar in its character. The tone and manner of speaking are excellent, but alack for the matter! A more wandering, blundering piece of dreary repetition never bemused an audience. In fairness to the priest, however, it must be admitted that a Government reporter is on the platform, and that the presence of that official may perhaps exercise a blighting influence on the budding flowers of rhetoric. All that the speaker - a handsome man, with a very fine voice - said, amounted to a statement, repeated over and over again with slight variations, that the people of Tiernaur were placed by the Almighty on the spot intended for them to live upon; that they were between the mountains and the sea; that all that the landlords could take from them they had taken; "the wonder was they had not taken the salt sea itself." This was all the speaker had to say, and he said it over and over again. He was succeeded by his curate, who insisted with like iteration on the duty of supporting the people imposed upon the land. Out of the fatness thereof they should, would, and must be maintained. Other sources of profit there were, according to this rev. gentleman, absolutely none. The land belonged to the people "on payment of a just rent" to the landlords. "Down wid 'em!" yelled an enthusiast, who was instantly suppressed. And the people had a right to live, not like the beasts of the field, but like decent people. And *da capo*[4].

Now among many and beautiful and picturesque things Ireland possesses some others altogether detestable. The car of the country, for instance, is the most abominable of all civilised vehicles. Why the numskull who invented the crab-like machine turned it round sidewise is as absolutely inconceivable as that since dog-carts have been introduced into the West the car should survive. But it does survive to the discomfort and fatigue of everybody, and the especial disgust of the writer. There is another thing in Connaught which I love not to look upon. That is the plate of a diner at a *table d'hote*, on which he has piled a quantity of roast goose with a liberal supply of stuffing, together with about a pound of hot boiled beef, and cabbage, carrots, turnips, and parsnips in profusion - the honour of a separate plate being accorded to the national vegetable alone. It is not agreeable to witness the demolition of this "Benjamin's mess" against time; and when the feat is being performed by several persons the effect thereof is the reverse of appetising. But I would rather be driven seventy miles - Irish miles - on a car, and compelled to sit down to roast goose commingled with boiled beef and "trimmings," than I would listen to a political speech from the curate of Tiernaur.

---

[4] A musical term meaning 'back to the beginning', [Clachan ed.].

By degrees I felt an utter weariness and loathing of life creeping over me, and I turned my face towards the sun, setting in golden glory behind Clare Island, and lighting up the rich ruddy brown of the mountain, behind which lay the invaded pastures of Knockdahurk. By the way this invasion of what are elsewhere deemed the rights of property was barely alluded to by the reverend speakers, the latter of whom, after making all kinds of blunders, finally broke down as he was appealing to the "immortal and immutable laws of - of - of" - and here some wicked prompter suggested "Nature," a suggestion adopted by the unhappy speaker before he had time to recollect himself. After this lame and impotent conclusion, a gentleman in a green cap and sash, richly adorned with the harp without the crown, infused some vitality into the proceedings by declaring that the only creature on God's earth worse than a landlord was the despicable wretch who presumed to take a farm at an advanced rent. This remark was distinctly to the point, and was applauded accordingly. It was indeed a significant, but in this part of the country quite unnecessary, intimation that safer, if not better, holdings might be found than "Hunter's Farm." As most of the persons present had come from a long distance, some as much as fifteen or twenty Irish miles, the subsequent proceedings, such as the passing of resolutions concerning fixity of tenure and so forth, were got through rapidly, and the meeting dispersed as quietly as it assembled. The organized bodies marched off the ground in good order, without the slightest sign of riot or even of enthusiasm. Men and women, the latter especially, were almost sad and gloomy - for Irish people. I certainly heard one merry laugh as I was making for my car, and it was at my own expense. A raw-boned, black-haired woman, "tall, as Joan of France or English Moll," insisted that I should buy some singularly ill-favoured apples of her. As I declined for the last time she fired a parting shot, "An' why won't ye buy me apples? Sure they're big and round and plump like yerself, aghra" - a sally vastly to the taste of the bystanders. It struck me, however, that the people generally seemed rather tired than excited by the proceedings of the day - the most contented man of all being, I take it, Mike Gibbons, who had been driving a brisk trade at his "shebeen," the only house of business or entertainment for miles around.

As I drove homewards on what had suddenly become a hideously raw evening, my driver entertained me with many heartrending and more or less truthful stories of evictions. He showed me a vast tract of land belonging to the Marquis of Sligo, from which the original inhabitants had, according to his story, been driven to make way for one tenant who paid less rent for all than they did for a part. One hears of course a great deal of this kind of thing from the poorer folk, - car-drivers, whose eloquence is proverbial, not excepted. My driver had assuredly not been corrupted by reading inflammatory articles in newspapers, for, although he speaks English as well as Irish, "letter or line knows he never a one" of either, any more than did stout William of Deloraine. His statements, however, are strictly of that class of travellers' tales told by car-drivers, and must be taken with more than the proverbial grain of seasoning. I find him as a rule very quiet until I have administered to him a dose of "the wine of the country," and then he mourns over the desolation of the land and the ravages of the so-called "crowbar brigade" as if they were things of yesterday.

Whether the local Press reflects the opinion of the peasants of Mayo, or the peasants only echo the opinion of the Press as reproduced to them by native orators, I am at present hardly prepared to decide. One thing, however, is certain. Not only that professional "deludher," the car-driver, but tradesmen, farmers, and all the less wealthy part of the community still speak sorely of the evictions of thirty and forty years ago, and point out the graveyards which alone mark the sites of thickly populated hamlets abolished by the crowbar. All over this part of the country people complain bitterly of loneliness. According to their view, their friends have been swept away and the country reduced to a desert in order that it might be let in blocks of several square miles each to Englishmen and Scotchmen, who employ the land for grazing purposes only, and perhaps a score or two of people where once a thousand lived - after a fashion. It is of no avail to point out to them that the wretchedly small holdings common enough even now in Connaught cannot be made to support the farmer, or rather labourer, and his family decently, even in the best of years, and that any failure of crop must signify ruin and starvation. Any observation of this kind is ill received by the people, who cling to their inhospitable mountains as a woman clings to a deformed or idiot child. And in this astonishing perversion of patriotism they are supported in unreasoning fashion by their pastors, who seem to imagine that because a person is born on any particular spot he must remain there and insist on its maintaining him and his.

Now, it is not inconceivable that a landlord should take a very different view of the situation. Whether his estate is encumbered or not, he expects to get something out of it for himself. It was therefore not unnatural that advantage should have been taken of the famine and the Encumbered Estates Act to get the land into such condition that it would return some ascertainable sum. The best way of effecting this was thought to be the removal of the inhabitants who paid rent or not as it suited them, and in place of a few hundred of these to secure one responsible tenant, even if he paid much less per acre than the native peasant. I draw particular attention to the latter fact, as one of the popular grievances sorely and lengthily dwelt upon is that the oppressor not only took the land from the people, evicted them, and demolished their cabins with crowbars, but that he let his property to the hated foreigner for less than the natives had paid and were willing to pay, or promised to pay, him. He let land by thousands of acres to

Englishmen and Scotchmen at a pound an acre, whereas he had received twenty-five and thirty shillings from the starving peasants of Connaught. This was deliberate cruelty, framed to drive the people away who were willing to stay and pay their high rents as of old. But the fact unfortunately was that Lord Lucan, Lord Sligo, and other great landowners in county Mayo had found it so difficult to get rent out of their tenants that they determined to let their land to large farmers only, at such a price as they could get, but with the certainty that the rent, whatever it was, would be well and duly paid, and there would be an end to the matter. This, I hear, is the true history of the eviction of the old tenants and the letting of great tracts of land to tenants like Mr Simpson on favourable terms. The landlord knew that he would get his rent, and he has got it, that is, hitherto.

The story of the great farm, colossal for this part of the country, leased by Mr Simpson from Lord Lucan, and now on that nobleman's hands, is a curious one as revealing the real capacity of the soil when properly handled. Twenty-two hundred Irish acres at as many pounds sterling per annum represent in Mayo an immense transaction. The tenant came to his work with capital and ripe experience, farmed well, and, I am assured on the best authority, fared well, getting a handsome return for his capital. So satisfied was he with his bargain, that he offered to renew his agreement with Lord Lucan if he were allowed a deduction for the false measurement of the acreage of the farm, which had been corrected by a subsequent survey. As I am instructed, there were not 2,200 acres, but the tenant was quite willing to pay a pound per acre for what was there. Now, an Irish acre is so much bigger than an English acre that thirty acres Irish measurement make forty-nine English. Lord Lucan consequently thought the farm cheaply let, and hesitated to make any allowance. This negotiation began last spring, but soon became hopeless. The country about Hollymount and Ballinrobe grew disturbed. Proprietors, agents, and large farmers required "protection" from the constabulary, and there was no longer anything to attract capital to the neighbourhood in the face of a deterrent population. Hence one of the largest and most popular farmers in Mayo has retired from the field with his capital, and has left his landlord to farm the land himself. Apparently Lord Lucan can do no better; for it would be difficult to find a stranger of sufficient substance to rent and farm twenty-two hundred acres of land, endowed with sufficient hardihood to bring his money and his life hither under the existing condition of affairs.

The incident just narrated, moreover, appears to prove that one object at least of the party of agitation has been achieved. To politico-economists it will appear a Pyrrhic victory. Capital is effectually scared from this part of Ireland, and those who have invested money on mortgage and found themselves at last compelled to "take the beast for the debt" are bitterly regretting their ill-judged promptitude. A large farm between this and Achill, or near Ballina on the north, or in the country extending from the spot where Lord Mountmorres was shot, towards Ballinrobe, Hollymount, Claremorris, or Castlebar, could hardly be let now at any price, even where the neighbours have not actually taken possession, as at Knockdahurk. Landlords have apparently the three proverbial courses open to them. They cannot sell their land, it is true; but they can let it lie waste, they can farm it themselves "if," as a trustworthy informant said to me just now, "they dare," or they can let it directly, as of old, to small tenants, who will come in at once and perhaps pay what they consider a fair rent in good years. It is folly to expect them to pay at all when crops are bad. And then there is the inevitable delay and uncertainty at all times which has led to the system of "middlemen" of which so much has been said and written. The middleman is that handy person, to the landlord, who assures him of a certain income from his property by buying certain rents at a deduction of 30 or 40 per cent., and collecting them as best he can. To the landlord he is a most useful man of business, thanks to whom he can count upon a certain amount of ready money. To the peasant he appears as a fiendish oppressor.

Touching this word "peasant," a great deal of misconception concerning the condition of the people of the West and their attitude towards their landlords will be got rid of by substituting it for the word "farmer." It is absurd to compare the tenant of a smallholding in Mayo with an English farmer - properly so called. The latter is a man engaged in a large business, and must possess, or, as I regret to be obliged to write, *have been* possessed of capital. The misuse of the word farmer and its application to the little peasant cultivators here can only lead to confusion. The proper standard of comparison with the so-called Mayo farmer is the English farmer's labourer. In education, in knowledge of his trade, in the command of the comforts of life, a Mayo cultivator of six, eight or ten acres is the analogue of the English labourer at fourteen shillings per week. The latter has nearly always a better cottage than the Mayo man, and, taking the whole year round, is about as well off as the Irishman. The future of neither is very bright. The Wessex hind may jog on into old age and the workhouse; the Irishman may be ruined and reduced to a similar condition at once by a failure of his harvest. Neither has any capital, yet the Irishman obtains an amount of credit which would strike Hodge dumb with amazement. He is allowed to owe, frequently one year's, sometimes two years' rent. Indeed, I know of one particularly tough customer who at this moment owes three years' rent - to wit, £24 - and will neither pay anything nor go. Now for an English labourer to obtain credit for a five-pound note would be a remarkable experience. His cottage and his potato patch cost him from one to two shillings per week; but who ever heard of his owing six months', let alone three years', rent? But this is the country of credit; and, so far as I have seen, nobody is in a violent hurry either to pay or to be paid, barring those who have lent money on mortgage. And even they are not in a hurry to foreclose just now.

The marked - I had almost written ostentatious - absence of weapons at the meetings of the last two Sundays has attracted great attention. From perfectly trustworthy information I gather that appearances are in this matter more than usually deceitful. It is impossible to doubt that the large population of this country is armed to the teeth. Since the expiration of the Peace Preservation Act the purchase of firearms has been incessant. At the stores in Westport, where carbines are sold, more have been disposed of in the last five months than in the ten previous years, and revolvers are also in great demand. The favourite weapon of the peasantry, on account of its low price and other good qualities, is the old Enfield rifle bought out of the Government stores, shortened and rebored to get rid of the rifling. The work of refashioning the superannuated rifles and adapting them for slugs and buckshot has, I hear, been performed for the most part in America, whence the guns have been re-imported into this country in large quantities. It is believed that the suppression of arms on the occasion of large gatherings is due to the judgment of popular leaders, who are naturally averse to any display which would afford the Government a pretext for disarming the inhabitants. There is, however, no doubt that the people of this district are more completely armed than at any previous period of Irish history. A ten-shilling gun license enables any idle person to walk about anywhere with a gun on his shoulder, but this privilege is rarely exercised. Two mornings ago four men passed in front of the Railway Hotel at Westport with guns on their shoulders, but such occurrences are very rare, the only individuals who carry weapons ostentatiously being landlords, agents, and the Royal Irish Constabulary affording them "protection." This protection is always granted when asked for, but many landlords have an almost invincible repugnance to go everywhere attended by armed police. Lord Ardilaun, I hear, has organised a little bodyguard of his own people, in preference to being followed about by the tall dark figures now frequent everywhere in county Mayo from Achill to Newport, from Ballina to Ballinrobe, and from Claremorris to Westport. Still, anything like a "rising in the West" is regarded here as chimerical; and the arming of the people as aimed only at the terrifying of landlords. No apprehension of any immediate outbreak or collision with the authorities is entertained in the very centre of disturbance. It may be added that, owing to the firm yet gentle grip of the Resident Magistrate, Major A.G. Wyse, late of the 48th Regiment, a veteran of the Crimea and of the war of the Indian Mutiny, the Government has this district well in hand, and is kept perfectly informed as to every occurrence of the slightest importance. Meanwhile, the possibility of armed resistance to the serving of civil-bill and other processes is averted by the presence of an overwhelming body of armed constabulary. Fifty men and a couple of sub-inspectors attended the serving of some civil-bill processes towards Newport only a few days ago, and a similar body attended to witness an abortive attempt at eviction on Miss Gardiner's property near Ballina.

From all that I can ascertain, the position of the Lord-Lieutenant of the country is by no means enviable. Having succeeded in losing his chief tenant and been compelled, in order to farm his own land in safety, to ask for "protection," he is now embroiled with a portion at least of the Castlebar people, who think, rightly or wrongly, that the lord of the soil and collector of tolls and dues has something to do with providing the town with a market-place. Into the merits of the question it is hardly necessary to enter. Suffice it to say that the local Press has taken advantage of the occasion to renew the popular outcry against "this old exterminator." Perhaps it does not hurt anybody very much to be called an "exterminator," especially when the extermination referred to occurred thirty years ago. The instance is merely worth citing as showing the undying hatred felt in this part of the country towards those who, acting wisely or unwisely, after the famine, determined to get rid of a population which the soil had shown itself unequal to support. There is no doubt that Lord Lucan brought "a conscience to his work" and made a solitude around Castlebar. "On the ruins of many a once happy homestead," continues the local scribe, "do the lambs frisk and play, a fleecy tribe that has, through landlord tyranny, superseded the once happy peasant." It is also urged as an additional grievance that the sheep, cattle, and pigs raised by "the old exterminator" are sent from the railway station "to appease the appetite of John Bull." Thus Lord Lucan and in a minor degree John Bull are shown up as the destroyers of the Irish peasant and devourers of that produce which should have gone to support him in that happiness and plenty which he enjoyed - at some probably apocryphal period. Be this, however, as it may, the personal hatred of the "exterminator" is a fact to be taken into account in any attempt to reflect the public opinion of this part of Ireland.

Those able to look more impartially on the matter than is possible to the children of the soil can perceive that the decay only too visible in many parts of Mayo is due in great measure to causes far beyond the control of exterminators, or even of the arch-devourer John Bull himself. In the old time, before the famine and before railroads and imported grain, this far western corner of Ireland had a trade of its own. I am not prepared to believe that the enormous warehouses of Westport were ever filled to overflowing with merchandise, being inclined rather to assign their vast size to that tendency towards overbuilding which is a permanent characteristic of a generous and hopeful people. Perhaps the trade of Westport might have expanded to the dimensions of the gaunt warehouses which now look emptily on the sea, but for adverse influences. At the period of the old

French war Westport was undoubtedly a great emporium for grain, especially oats, for beef, pork, and military stores, which were shipped thence to our army in the Peninsula. But other sources of supply and improved means of communication have left the little seaport on the Atlantic, as it were, on one side, and such vitality as exists in the coasting trade of this part of the country is rather visible at Ballina than at Westport. It is quite possible that under the old condition of affairs the peasant whose oats were in brisk demand for cavalry stores fared better than his son who fell on the evil days of the famine; but there can be no doubt that the decline of Mayo as an exporting county can hardly be laid to the charge of the depopulators of the land. So far as can be descried through the cloud of prejudice which involves the entire question, the land was no longer able to feed its inhabitants, much less afford any surplus for sale or export.

The Marquis of Sligo, whose agent, Mr Smith, was shot at - and missed - last year, is almost as unpopular as Lord Lucan, for not only have most of the people been swept from his country, but the rent was raised on the remainder no longer ago than 1876. It is probably this nobleman who was in the mind of the humourist who pointed out that the shooting of an agent was hardly likely to intimidate that "distant Trojan," the landlord. The Lucan and Sligo lands in Mayo have, therefore, been managed on nearly parallel lines, and it is curious to contrast with them the management of Sir Robert Blosse's estate. This is another very large property, and has been conducted on the exactly opposite principle to that pursued by Lords Sligo and Lucan. The people have been let alone; they retain the holdings their fathers tilled, and they have tided over bad times so well that their April rents have, to my certain knowledge, been all paid. What will occur in November it is unnecessary to predict, but it may be remarked, by the way, that the Irish landlord, whose rents do not overlap each other, is in an exceptionally fortunate position.

When I was at Ballinrobe the other day I was much struck with the unanimity with which everybody had agreed to leave that unfortunate gentleman, Mr Boycott, in the lurch. That his servants should revolt, that his labourers should go away, that strangers should be bribed or frightened away from taking their place, are things by no means unparalleled even in the most manufacturing town in England. But that his butcher and baker should strike against their customer was a new experience hardly to be explained on any ready-made theory. I confess that I was so much astonished that I preferred waiting for facts before committing myself to any explanation. At this moment I have no hesitation in stating that the trades people of the smaller towns in the west are neither strong enough to resist the pressure put upon them by the popular party nor very much disposed to defend their right to buy and sell as they please. On the same principle apparently that a great nobleman of the Scottish Lowlands has, since the last election, made his sovereign displeasure known to his tenants, have the party of agitation made "taboo" any tradesmen who have dared to run counter to the current of present opinion. When a baker is told he must not do a certain thing he obeys at once, and, with a certain quickness and suppleness of intellect, casts about to see how he can best represent himself as a martyr. "Pay rint, Sorr," said a well-to-do shopkeeper to me two days ago; "and how are thim poor divils to pay rint that cannot pay me? And how am I to pay any one when I can't get a shillin' ov a soul?"

This little incident will explain how the opportunity of shirking responsibility is seized upon by many. To begin with, the advantage is with the assailant, for the custom of any one farmer or agent is a small matter compared with that of the countryside. It is therefore manifestly to the interest of the little shopkeeper to curry favour with the populace rather than with those set in authority over them. Again, the petty trader would fain, after the example laid down by Panurge[5], pray to God for the success of the peasant in order that he might *"de terre d'aultruy remplir son fosse"* - that the till might be filled if the agent's book remained empty. As I have previously explained, everybody owes to somebody, or is owed by somebody, in this island of weeping skies and smiling faces. The peasant owes his landlord, who owes the mortgagee or the agent. And the peasant has another creditor - the little trader who works on the credit extended to him from Dublin or Belfast. Beyond a certain limit the little shopkeeper cannot go. So he likes to be threatened, to be made "taboo," to be a martyr, and then presses the tenants who have paid no rent to the landlord to pay him "as they can afford to, begorra, if they hould the harvest." This advice of Mr Parnell's is keenly relished by many, and has gained him, from a poet, whose Hibernian extraction speaks in his every line, the incomprehensible title of "Young Lion of the Fold."

> *Young Lion of the Fold,*
>   *Says the Shan Van Vocht[6],*
> *Young Lion of the Fold,*
>   *Says the Shan Van Vocht;*
> *Young Lion of the Fold,*
> *Bade us the harvest hold——*
> *We'll do as he has told,*
>   *Says the Shan Van Vocht.*

> *We'll pay no more Rackrents,*

---

5 an exceedingly crafty knave, libertine, and coward found in Rabelais' Pantagruel, [Clachan ed.].

6 *An tSeanbhean Bhocht* (The Poor Old Woman), a traditional Irish song of the United Irishmen of 1798, [Clachan ed.].

Says the Shan Van Vocht,
We'll pay no more Rackrents,
Says the Shan Van Vocht;
We'll pay no more Rackrents,
To upstart shoneen gents,
Whose hearts are hard as flints,
Says the Shan Van Vocht.

Then glory to Parnell,
Says the Shan Van Vocht,
Then glory to Parnell,
Says the Shan Van Vocht,
Oh, all glory to Parnell,
Whom the people love so well,
And his foes may go to - - ,
Says the Shan Van Vocht.

There is an American humourist who once said that "if the lion ever did lie down with the lamb it would be with the lamb inside of him." Mayhap this is what the indigenous "pote" dimly shadows forth from the mist-land of verse. Or has he mixed up the lion with the eagle in a dovecot?

IV - MISS GARDINER AND HER TENANTS

WESTPORT, CO. MAYO, Nov. 1st.

A trip into the northern part of this county, which has occupied me for the last three days, has hardly reassured me as to the condition of the country around Ballina and Killala. The last-named place is famous for its round tower and that invasion of the French in '98, which led to "Castlebar Races." Ballina is a town of about six thousand inhabitants, situate on the river Moy - an excellent salmon stream which debouches into Killala Bay, the most important inlet of the sea between Westport and Sligo. Perhaps Ballina is the principal town in county Mayo; certainly it seems to be the most improving one. It is, however, a considerable distance from the sea. Just now it is the seat of a species of internecine war between landlord and tenant, waged under conditions which lend it extraordinary interest. Exacting "landlordism" and recalcitrant "tenantism" seem here to have said their last word. Between a considerable landholder and her tenants a fight is being fought out which throws a lurid light on the present land agitation in Ireland.

The landholder referred to is the Miss Gardiner whose name is familiar in connection with more or less successful attempts at eviction. This lady, who many years ago inherited a large property from her father, the late Captain Gardiner, has become a by no means *persona grata* to "the Castle," the sub-sheriff, the Royal Irish Constabulary, and her tenants. She is doubtless a resolute and determined woman, and possessed by a vigorous idea of the rights of property. If not descended from the celebrated Grace O'Malley[7], Queen of Connaught, she has at least equally autocratic ideas with that celebrated ruler of the West.

For years past Miss Gardiner has been famous as a raiser of stock, equine and bovine, but unfortunately she has been most frequently before the public as the strong assertor of territorial rights. She dwells far beyond Killala, near the village of Kilcun, at a house called Farmhill. From Westport to Farmhill the country is as picturesque as any in the West of Ireland. The snow-clad hills of Nephin and Nephin Beg are in sight all the way from Manulla Junction - the chief railway centre hereabouts, and the line past Loughs Cullen and Conn to Ballina, and the car-drive beyond Ballina, reveal a series of magnificent views. There is, however, something very "uncanny" to the Saxon eye about Farmhill. The first object which comes in sight is a

---

[7] *Gráinne Ní Mháille*, Queen of Umaill, Irish Chieftain, pirate, trader and seafarer of the 1500s, [Clachan ed.].

police barrack, with a high wall surrounding a sort of "compound," the whole being obviously constructed with a view to resisting a possible attack. This stiff staring assertion of the power of the law stands out gaunt and grim in the midst of a landscape of great beauty. Autumn hues gild the trees, the wide pastures are of brilliant green, and on the rough land the reddening bent-grass glows richly in the declining sun, which throws its glory alike over snowy hills and rosy clouds. The only blot, if a white edifice can be thus designated, is the stern, angular police barrack. In the front enclosure the sergeant is drilling his men; and those not under drill are watching the domain immediately opposite, to the end that no unauthorised person may approach it. Like most of the dwellings in a country otherwise sparsely supplied with trees, Farmhill is nestled in a grove. But the surroundings of the house are not those associated in the ordinary mind with a home. The outer gate is locked hard and fast, and the little sulky-looking porter's lodge is untenanted. Its windows are barred, and all communication with the house itself is cut off, except to adventurous persons prepared to climb a stone wall. From the lodge onward the private road passes through a poor kind of park, and subsides every now and then into a quagmire. It is vile walking in this park of Farmhill, and as the house is approached there is a barking of dogs. Oxen are seen grazing, and peacocks as well as turkeys heave in sight. The house itself is barred and barricaded in a remarkable manner. The front door is so strongly fastened that it is said not to have been opened for years. Massive bars of iron protect the windows, and the solitary servant visible is a species of shepherd or odd man, who comes slinking round the corner. No stranger gentlewoman's dwelling could be found in the three kingdoms. The spot reeks with a dungeon-like atmosphere. It is, according to the present state of life in Mayo, simply a "strong place," duly fortified and garrisoned against the enemy.

It must be confessed that the proprietress who has a police detachment opposite to her gate, and lives in a house defended by iron bars and chains, has some reason for her precautions against surprise. She was shot at through the window of her own house not very long ago. Now this experience of being shot at acts variously on different minds. Mr Smith, the Marquis of Sligo's agent, whose son returned fire and killed the intending assassin, took the matter as an incident of business in the West, and is not a whit less cheery and happy than before the attack at Claggan Mountain. It is also true that Miss Gardiner is not an atom less personally brave than Mr Smith. It is said that she carries a revolver in the pocket of her shooting-jacket, and only asks for an escort of armed constabulary when she goes into Ballina. But she, nevertheless, thinks it well to convert her home into a fortress - perhaps the only one of the kind now extant in Europe. Here she dwells with a lady-companion, Miss Pringle, far out of range of such social life as remains in the county, occupied nearly exclusively with the management of her estate; a matter which, far from concerning herself alone, entails great vexation, embarrassment, and expense upon others. The sending of bodies of constabulary half a hundred strong to protect the officers of the law serving writs on Miss Gardiner's tenantry is a troublesome and costly business, and has the effect of stirring up strife and exciting public opinion to no small degree. As her property is widely scattered over Northern Mayo, there is generally something going on in her behalf. One day there is an ejectment at Ballycastle; the next an abortive attempt to evict at Cloontakilla. In the opinion of the poorer peasantry this eccentric lady is a malevolent fiend, an "extherminathor," a tyrant striving to make the lives of the poor so wretched as to drive them off her estate. "A sthrange lady is she, Sorr," cried one of her tenants to me. "Och, she's a divil of a woman, entoirely. All she wants is to hunt the poor off the face of the wor-r-rold." There are, however, to this question, as to every Irish question, two sides - if not more. If Miss Gardiner "hunts" her tenants off her estate, Lord Erne's people are just now trying their best to perform the same operation upon Captain Boycott.

It is not all at once that Farmhill has become a sort of dreary edition of Castle Rackrent, oppressing the mind with almost inexpressible gloom. The owner's feud with her tenants began long before the Land League was known. It is said in Northern Mayo that her father was the first of the "exterminators," justly or unjustly so called, and that the traditions of the family have been heartily carried out by his heiress. There is perhaps very little doubt that Miss Gardiner, like Lord Lucan and the Marquis of Sligo, prefers large farmers as tenants to a crowd of miserable peasants striving to extract a living for an entire family from a paltry patch of five acres of poor land; but whatever her wish may be she has undoubtedly a large number of small tenants on her estate at the present moment. It is therefore probable that she is somewhat less of an exterminatrix than the exasperated people represent her to be. In their eyes, however, she is guilty of the unpardonable crime of insisting upon her rent being paid. Her formula is simple, "Give me my rent, or give me my land." In England and in some other countries such a demand would be looked upon as perfectly reasonable; but "pay or go" is in this part of Ireland looked upon as the option of an exterminator. Miss Gardiner merely asks for her own, and judged by an English standard would appear to be a strange kind of Lady Bountiful if she allowed her tenants to go on quietly living on her property without making any show of payment. But this is very much what landlords are expected to do in county Mayo, except in very good seasons. The majority of the people in the islands of Clew Bay have given up the idea of paying rent as a bad job altogether, and these advanced spirits have many imitators on the mainland. To the request, "Give me my rent, or give me my land," is made one eternal answer, "And how can I pay the rent when the corn is washed away and the pitaties rot in the ground? And if I give ye the land, hwhere am I to go, and my wife and my eight childher?" This answer, long used as an *argumentum ad misericordiam*, is now defended by popular orators. No longer ago than yesterday I heard it averred that the failure of the crop by the visitation of God absolved the tenant from the payment of rent. The assumption of the speaker was that landlord and tenant were in a manner partners, and that if the joint business venture produced nothing the working partner could pay over no share of profit to the sleeping partner. Such doctrine is naturally acceptable to the tenant. It signifies that in bad years the landlord gets nothing; in good years, what the tenant pleases to give him, after buying manure and paying up arrears of debt all round. It is, however, hardly surprising that the landlords see the question through a differently tinted medium. They entertain an idea that the land is their property, and, like any other commodity, should be let or sold to a person who can pay for it. Strict and downright "landlordism," as it is called, as if it were a disease like "Daltonism," [8] does not see things through a medium charged with the national colour, and Miss Gardiner is a true type of downright landlordism such as would not be complained of in England, but in Ireland is viewed with absolute abhorrence.

As a proof how utterly an exacting landlord puts himself, if not outside of the law, yet beyond any claim to public sympathy, I may cite the conduct of Mr James C. MacDonnell, the sub-sheriff of this county. I have the story from an intimate friend of that gentleman, on whose veracity I can implicitly rely. I say this because I did not in the first place pay much attention to the story, but have since been enabled to verify it in every particular.

Last spring Mr MacDonnell, in his capacity as sub-sheriff, was required by Miss Gardiner to serve notices of ejectment against about a score of her tenants who had not paid up. There was great excitement when it became known that twenty families would be evicted from their holdings, and a breach of the peace appeared very probable. In England the public voice would possibly be in favour of executing the law at all hazards. Some of the tenants owed two years' rent. The patience of the landlord was exhausted. The tenants would neither pay nor take themselves off. There was no option but to evict them; the sub-sheriff must do his duty, backed by as large a body of constabulary as might be necessary. Law and order must be enforced. This would be the view taken in any other place but this, but in Ireland the matter appeared in a totally different light. To begin with, the idea of blood being shed in order that Miss Gardiner might get in her rents appeared utterly preposterous. Secondly, the two past crops had completely failed in Mayo. Thirdly, the bad crops of 1878 and 1879 in England had prevented the Mayo men from earning the English harvest money on which they entirely depend for their rent, and much more than their rent. Finally,

---

[8] Colour-blindness of the red-green type [Clachan ed.].

29

the sub-sheriff himself, who, despite his being at once a proprietor, a middleman, and an officer of the law, has won popularity by sheer weight of character, felt a natural reluctance to enforce his authority. Compelled to execute the law, he determined to make a personal appeal to the tenants before evicting them. Accordingly, he adjured them to get together a little money to show that they really meant to act well and honestly, and that he would then help them himself. The matter ended in his advancing them about £140 out of his own pocket, on their notes of hand, and paying Miss Gardiner, who observed that "he had done well for her tenants, but not so well for her." To the credit of the tenants helped by Mr MacDonnell it must be added that all have met their notes save two or three, who among them owe but £15 This little story is entirely typical of the kindliness and honesty of Mayo men, and of their peculiar ideas of right and justice. Miss Gardiner's tenants would not pay her a shilling; they were prepared to resist eviction by force, and would have been backed by the whole countryside, but they paid the sub-sheriff with the first money they got. He had stood their friend, and they could not act meanly towards him.

As a contrast to this pleasant picture I am compelled to draw one not altogether so agreeable. I mentioned in a previous letter a particularly "tough customer" who, owing £24 for three years' rent, would part neither with a single shilling nor with the land. I thought this champion of the irreconcilables must be worth a visit, and foregoing the diversion of a call on Tom Molloy, a noted character in the Ballina district, I drove out in the direction of Cloontakilla. On the way to that dismal spot by a diabolical road I passed a homestead, so neat and trim, standing on the hillside clear of trees, that I at once asked if it were not owned by a Scotchman, and was answered that Mr Petrie was indeed a Scot and a considerable tenant farmer. On one side of his farm was a knot of dismantled houses, telling their story plainly and pathetically enough, and on the further side stood a row of hovels, only one of which was uninhabited. The locked-up cabin had a brace of bullet-holes in the door, those which caused a great deal of trouble some time since. A Mr Joynt it seems, in a wild freak, fired his gun through the door of the cabin occupied by Mistress Murphy, who with her children is now about to join her husband in America. Instead of being frightened, the courageous matron opened the door, issued there from armed with a fire-shovel and administered to the delinquent "the greatest batin' begorra" my informant had ever heard of. Afterwards the law was invoked against Mr Joynt, who was esteemed very lucky in escaping punishment on account of his ill-health. A little further on, still to the right of the road, branched off suddenly a narrow bridle-path, or "boreen," as it is called in this part of the country. It was my car-driver, a teetotaller, opined on this "boreen," that the irreconcilable tenant, one Thomas Browne, dwelt. There were doubts in his mind; but, nevertheless, we turned on to the wretched track, and tried to get the car over the stones and mud-lakes which formed it. It could not be strictly called a road of any kind, but was rather a space left between two deep ditches of black peat-oozings from the bog. Finding progress almost impossible, we at last forsook the car. I can quite imagine an impatient reader asking why we did not get out and walk at first; but the option was hardly a simple one. By walking the horse and letting the car swing and jolt along one experienced the combined agonies of sea-sickness and rheumatism, with the additional chance of being shot headlong into the inky ditch on either side. By taking to what the driver called "our own hind legs," we accepted an ankle-deep plod through filth indescribable and treacherous boulders, which turned over when trust and sixteen stone were reposed on them. It was at this part of the journey that I saw for the first time the Mountain Sylph. Some women and children, who looked very frightened, cleared away towards their wretched dwellings, and the place would presently have been deserted had not my driver roared at the top of his voice, "Hullo, the gyurl!" Presently, out of the crowd of frightened people sprang a "colleen" of about twelve years, as thinly and scantily clad as is consistent with that decency and modesty for which Irishwomen of the poorer classes are so justly celebrated. Her legs and feet were bare, as a matter of course; a faded red petticoat, or rather kilt, and a "body" of some indescribable hue, in which dirt largely predominated, formed all her visible raiment and adornment, except a mass of fair hair, which fluttered wildly in the cutting wind. Skipping from stone to stone she neared us swiftly, and stood still at last perched on a huge boulder - an artist's study of native grace and beauty - with every rag instinct with "wild civility."

An inquiry whether "Misther Browne" was at home was met by the polite answer that he was from home "just thin," almost instantly supplemented by "Oi know hwhere he is, and will fetch him to ye, sorr." And away went the Sylph dancing from spot to spot like the will-o'-the-wisp of her native bog. She had also indicated the dwelling of Thomas Browne, and I pushed on in that direction through a maze of mud. At last I came to a turning into a path several degrees worse in quality than the "boreen," and concluded that, as it was nearly impassable, it must lead to the home of the Irreconcilable. As a change it was pleasant to step from deep slippery mud and slime on to stones placed with their acutest angles upwards, but a final encounter with these landed me literally at Mr Browne's homestead.

It has been my lot at various times to witness the institution known as "home" in a state of denudation, as my scientific friends would call it. It is not necessary to go far from the site of Whitechapel Church to find dwellings unutterably wretched. Two years ago I saw people reduced to one "family" pair of boots in Sheffield, and without food, or fire to cook it with if they had had it; and I have seen a Cornish woman making turnip pie. But for general misery I think the home of the Browne family at Cloontakilla equals, and more than equals anything I have seen during a long experience of painful sights. The road to it as already described, is a quagmire, and the dwelling, when arrived at, exceeds the wildest of nightmares. Part of the stone wall has fallen in, and the two rooms which remain have the ground for a carpet and miserable starved-looking thatch for a roof. The horses and cattle of every gentleman in England, and especially Mr Tankerville Chamberlayne's Berkshire pigs, are a thousand times better lodged than the family of the irreconcilable Browne. The chimney, if ever there were one, has long since "caved in" and vanished, and the smoke from a few lumps of turf burning on the hearth finds its way through the sore places in the thatch. In a bed in the corner of the room lies a sick woman, coughing badly; near her sits another woman, huddled over the fire.

Now, I have been quite long enough in the world to be suspicious, and had it been possible for these poor people to have known of my coming I should certainly have been inclined to suspect a prepared scene. But this was impossible, for even my car-driver did not know where he was going till he started. And as we could not find the house without the Mountain Sylph, the inference must be in favour of all being genuine. There are no indications of cooking going on, and, barring[9] an iron pot, a three-legged stool, a bench, half a dozen willow-pattern dishes, and a few ropes of straw suspended from the roof with the evident object of supporting something which is not there, no signs of property are visible. And this is the outcome of a farm of five acres - Irish acres, be it well understood. There is nothing at all to feed man, wife, sister-in-law, son, and daughter during the winter, and the snow is already lying deep on Nephin.

While my inspection of the Browne domicile has been going on, the Mountain Sylph has vanished, never more to be seen. Whether she disappeared in the peat-smoke or sank gracefully into the parent bog it is impossible to decide; but it is quite certain that she has faded out of sight. Poor Mountain Sylph! When she grows older, and goes out to earn money as a work-girl in Ballina, she will no longer appear picturesque, but ridiculous. She will wear a cheap gown, but of the latest fashion, and a knowing-looking hat flung on at a killing angle; and she will don smart boots while she is in Ballina, and will take them off before she is far on her way to Cloontakilla, and trudge along the road as barefooted as of old. But she will never more be a Mountain Sylph - only a young woman proudly wearing a bonnet and mantle at which Whitechapel would turn up its nose in disdain. But the Sylph has gone, and in her place stands the Irreconcilable himself - a grey-haired man with bent shoulders and well-cut features, which account for the good looks of the Sylph. He is a sorrowful man; but, like all Irishmen, especially when in trouble, is not wanting in loquacity. He shows

---

[9] 'bating' in original , [Clachan ed.].

me his "far-r-rum," as he calls it, and it is a poor place. He has had a good harvest enough; but what does it all amount to? An acre (English) of oats, mayhap a couple of acres of potatoes and cabbages, and the rest pasture, except a little patch on which, he tells me, he grew vetches in summer for sale as green feed for cattle. Of beasts he has none, except dogs of some breed unknown either to dog-fanciers or naturalists, and an ass - the unfortunate creature who is made to drink the dregs of any sorrow falling upon Western Ireland. Put to work when not more than a year old, the poor animal becomes a stunted, withered phantasm of the curled darlings of the London costermongers which excited the kindly feelings of Lord Shaftesbury and the Baroness Burdett-Coutts.

A Mayo donkey is a wretched creature, and Mr Browne has a very poor specimen of an under-fed, overworked race. But there is a cow browsing in the field, and the tenant hastens to explain that she is not his own, but the absolute property of his sister-in-law. I must confess that I cool somewhat after this - inwardly that is - towards the Irreconcilable in battered corduroys who amuses me with a string of stories more or less veracious. I am required to believe that "baring the ass," no living beast on the five-acre farm belongs to the tenant. The turkeys belong to a neighbour, as do the geese, and there is neither hen nor egg left on the premises. "And where is everything?" I naturally ask.

"And the neighbours is good to me, sorr, and they reaped my oats for me in a day, and carried 'um in a night. And my pitaties they dug for me, and carried all clane away before the sheriff could come. And when Mr MacDonnell did come my wife was sick in bed, and the house was full of people, and all he could do was to consult the doctor and go away."

Now, as the basis for a burlesque or Christmas pantomime, in which the Good Fairy warns the tenant to remove his crops lest the Demon Landlord should seize upon them - the tenant being of course transmuted into Harlequin and the landlord into Clown - this would be funny enough; but it is difficult to see how the everyday business of life could be carried on under such conditions. The case of Miss Gardiner against Thomas Browne is one purely of hide and seek. When he owed two years' rent he begged for time on account of two bad crops. When he was threatened with eviction he begged time to get in his crop. It was given to him. It is quite easy to understand that a tenant who has been thirty years on a little holding thinks himself entitled to great lenity, especially if his rent has been raised during that period, and, as this man asserts, his "turbary" rights restricted, and every kind of privilege reduced. But it has been said by a great literary and social authority that there are such things as limits. Now this man, Browne, feeling that he had an execution hanging over him, contrived to temporise until his grain and potatoes were secured, and then, aided by the accident of a sick wife, defied the law. The house was full of people, a doctor said that the woman could not be removed, and the sub-sheriff, backed by fifty policemen, could make nothing of the business without incurring the odium of tearing a sick woman from her bed. He offered the irreconcilable Browne the offer of accepting the ejectment and remaining in the house as "caretaker," but the tenant was staunch and would make no terms. The consequence is that when Miss Gardiner again attempts to evict him she must incur the considerable cost of a new writ. The condition of affairs now is that a tenant owing three years' rent, and not having paid a shilling on account, simply defies the landlord and remains in his wretched holding, having possibly - for the Irish are an intelligent as well as good-humoured people - the proceeds of his miserable little harvest to live upon through the winter months. Mr Browne is, I doubt me, not very rigid as to his duties, and takes but an imperfect view of financial obligations; but he is horribly poor, nevertheless, and is as much a type of his class as Miss Gardiner of hers.

V - FROM MAYO TO CONNEMARA

LEENANE, Tuesday, Nov 2

The meeting which took place on Sheehane Hill was only remarkable as affording an additional proof of the extraordinary faculty of selection possessed by Western Irishmen. Whether they intend to shoot a landlord or merely to hold a meeting to bring him to his bearings, they choose their ground with equal discrimination. In the former case a spot is selected at the descent or ascent of a hill, so that the carriage of the victim cannot be going at a sufficient pace to defeat the marksman's aim, and a conveniently protected angle, with facilities for escape, is occupied by the ambuscade. In the latter, either a natural amphitheatre or a conspicuous hill is pitched upon for the gathering. To the picturesque Mayo mind a park meeting on a dead flat would be the most uninteresting affair possible unless vitality were infused into the proceedings by a conflict with the police, which would naturally atone for many shortcomings. The meeting at Tiernaur was held in the midst of magnificent scenery, and that on Sheehane was equally well selected.

From the top of the hill, which is crowned by a large tumulus, the country around for many miles lay spread like a map; and, what was of more immediate importance, the small additional hill afforded a convenient spot for posting the orators and displaying the banners of the various organizations represented at the meeting. The demonstration, however, could hardly be represented as successful - not more than a thousand persons being present. It was weary waiting until the proceedings commenced, the only diversion being provided by a hare which got up in an adjacent field. In a moment greyhounds, bull-dogs, terriers, and mongrels were in pursuit, followed by the assembled people. The hare, however, completely distanced both dogs and spectators, and was in comparative safety several fields away from the foremost greyhound, when she doubled back in an unaccountable manner, and ran into the midst of the crowd, who set upon her with sticks, and killed her in the most unsportsmanlike manner. A man next held poor puss over his head as if she were a fox, and a voice went up "That's the way to serve the landlords." This ebullition was followed by shouts of "Down wid 'em!" and the meeting on Sheehane became more cheerful. It was recollected that O'Connell once held a meeting on the same spot, and that the hare and the meetings were both mentioned by the prophet Columbkill[10].

---

[10] Saint Columba —also known as Colum Cille was a Irish missionary monk who spread Christianity to Scotland during the Early Medieval Period, [Clachan ed.].

Of the speeches it need only be said that what they lacked in elegance was made up in violence. The speeches made in the North were oddly designated "seditious," and every kind of reprisal was hinted at in the event of Mr Parnell being arrested. If he were seized, not a landlord in Ireland would be safe except in Dublin Castle. This kind of thing, accompanied by shouts of "Down wid 'em!" at every mention of the abhorred landlords, became very tedious, especially in a high wind and drifting rain. The meeting gradually became thinner and thinner, and finally faded out altogether. It is quite true that such gatherings may have a powerful effect upon the vivacious Celt, but if so, it is quite beneath the surface, for the people seemed to take little interest in the proceedings. To all outward show the oratory at Sheehane produced no more serious impression than that at Tiernaur on the preceding Sunday. Yet there is something in the air, for the first thing I heard on returning to Westport was that Mr Barbour's herdsman, who lives at Erriff Bridge, had been warned to leave his master's service. The "herd" (as he is called here, as well as on the Scottish border) is in great alarm. He cannot afford to leave his place, for it is his sole means of subsistence, and if turned out in the world the poor fellow might starve. Now it is a disagreeable thing to think you will starve if you leave, and be shot if you remain at your work; but I hear that the "herd" has asked for protection and will try to weather it out. His master, Mr Barbour, and Mr Mitchell hold each about half of the great farm formerly held of Lord Sligo by Captain Houstoun, the husband of the well-known authoress[11]. Large numbers of black-faced sheep and polled Galloways are raised by Mr Barbour, who lives at Dhulough, in the house formerly occupied by Captain Houstoun.

I have just come from Westport to this place, the mountain scenery around which is magnificent. On the lofty heights of "the Devil's Mother," a famous mountain of this country, the sheep are seen feeding almost on the same level as the haunt of the golden eagles who breed here regularly. I believe that the valley of the Erriff was once well populated, but that after the famine the people were cleared off nearly 20 square miles of land to make way for the great grazing farm now divided between two occupants. As I have stated in previous letters, the resentment of the surrounding inhabitants at this depopulation of a vast tract of country is ineradicable. In the wretched huts which appear at wide intervals on the sea-shore the miserable people sit over the fire and talk of the old times when they might go from Clifden to Westport and find friends nearly everywhere on the road, while now from the last-named place to this - a distance of 18 Irish miles - the country is simply wild mountain, moor, and bog, barring[12] the little

[11] Mrs Houstoun (Matilda Charlotte) author of 'Recommended to Mercy', 'To Sink or Swim', among others.

Ulster Protestant village, not far from Westport (a curious relic of '98), a few herds-men's huts, and the police-station at Erriff Bridge.

To those who, like myself, love animals, the drive is by no means uninteresting. As the car jolts along past "Hag's Valley," a dozen curlews take wing, and a little further on the shrill cry of the redshank strikes on the ear. Now and then a hare will start among the bent-grass, while aloft the falcon rests poised on her mighty wing. But saving these wild animals, the beautiful blackfaced sheep, and black Galloway calves, the country has no inhabitants. What little was once cultivated has reverted to rough pasture, covered with bent or sedge and a little grass, or to bog impassable to man or any creature heavier than the light-footed fox, who attains among these mountains to extraordinary size and beauty. But hares and grouse, and even stray pheasants from Mr Mitchell Henry's woods at Kylemore, will not convince the fragment of population around the great grazing farms that things are better now than of yore; and there is some reason for believing that disturbance is to be apprehended in this part of the country. The warning to Mr Barbour's unfortunate herd can hardly be a separate and solitary act of intimidation and oppression. The work of one herd is of no great matter. But the distinct warning given to the poor man at Erriff Bridge to give up his livelihood on the first instant is possibly part of a settled scheme to reduce great grazing farmers to the same condition as landlords. They are to be frightened away, in order that squatters may pasture their cattle on "the Devil's Mother," as the Tiernaur people have done theirs on Knockdahurk. Nothing would surprise me less than a strike against anybody in this neighbourhood.

If one may judge by the language used yesterday at Westport Fair, at which I was glad to discover more outward evidence of prosperity than had yet come under my observation in this part of Ireland, the landlords and their agents are determined to make another effort to get in their rents in January. Their view of the case is that the law must assist them: but whatever abstract idea of the majesty of the law may exist elsewhere is obviously foreign to those parts of Connaught which I have visited. It is urged day after day upon me by high as well as low, that if Sir Robert Blosse and Lord De Clifford can get in their rents without "all the king's horses and all the king's men," other landlords must try to do the same. To prevent misconception, I will aver, even at the risk that I may seem to "protest too much," that this argument is not thrust upon me by the Land League, but by persons who are proprietors themselves. It is held ridiculous, in this section of the country, that enormous expense should be thrown upon the county in order that the rents of certain landlords may be collected. There is, it must be admitted, a rational indisposition in the West to ascribe any particularly

---

sacred character to rent as distinguished from any other debt. This is an agreeable feature in the Irish character. In some other countries there prevails a preposterous notion that rent must be paid above and before all things, as a species of solemn obligation. Until the other day there prevailed in Scotland the almost insane law of hypothec, which allowed a landlord to pursue his tenant's goods even into the hands of an "innocent holder." But there is no argument in favour of the landlord which any other creditor might not advance with equally good reason. The butcher, the baker, the clothier, as well as the farmer, the dealer in feeding-cake and manure, have claims quite as good as that of the landlord, and, as they think, a great deal better. Tradesmen who have fed and clothed people, and others who have helped them to fatten their land and their cattle, think their claims paramount. It is of the nature of every creditor to think he has the right to be paid before anybody else. But the landlord, probably because landlords made the law, such as it is, has a claim which he can enforce, or rather just now seeks to enforce, by the aid of armed intervention. The civil bill creditor can only levy execution where anything exists to levy upon; but the landlord can turn his tenants out of doors and put the key in his pocket - that is, theoretically. But, it is argued, if this cannot be done without the aid of an army, it would be better for the majority of peaceable inhabitants if it were left alone. It is not easy to predict the state of popular feeling here in January next; but it is quite certain that attempts to evict, if made now, would be met by armed resistance. I have already stated that Mayo is armed to the teeth, and I have good reason for believing county Galway to be in a similar condition. This being fairly well known on the spot, it is quite easy to understand how any resolution to commence a landlords' crusade is received by the public.

LETTERFRACK, CONNEMARA, Wednesday.

At this pretty village, in the most beautiful part of the West of Ireland, I hear that the disinclination to pay rent and the desire to "hunt" grazing farmers out of the country have spread to the once peaceful region of Connemara. Three years ago crime and police were alike unknown. The people were poor, and preserved the sense of having been wronged. But theft and violence, saving a broken head now and then, were unknown.

Within the last two years a great change has come over this remote corner of Ireland. Police barracks have made their appearance, and outrages of the agrarian class have become disagreeably frequent. Formerly cattle and sheep were as safe on the mountain as oats in the stackyard. Now nobody of the grazing farmer class is entirely free from alarm. At any moment his animals may be driven into the sea or his ricks fired. The population, if not so fully armed as that of Mayo, is arming rapidly. To my certain knowledge revolvers and carbines are being distributed among the peasantry of Connemara proper. This district - which including within its limits the pretty village I write from, as well as Clifden and Ballynahinch, lies mainly between the seashore and a line drawn from Leenane to Carna - has, during the last twelve months become disturbed in such wise that it is impossible to shut one's eyes to the fact that here, as in Mayo, a sort of dead set is being made against grazing farmers. It is true that life is not taken, and, it may be added, not even threatened in Connemara proper, but outrages of a cowardly and destructive kind are common. During last winter an epidemic of destruction broke out, the effect of which may be seen in the large amount added to the county cess to give compensation to the injured persons. The grand jury has levied altogether between seven and eight hundred pounds more than usual. So ignorant or reckless are the destroyers, that they take no heed of what is well understood in other places; to wit, that the amount of the damage done is levied upon the adjacent townlands. Thus the addition to the county cess in Lettermore is 10s. 11½ in the £1; in Carna, 8s. 9 1/2d.; and in Derryinver, 8s. 7 1/2d. - a cruel additional burden on the ratepayer. Some of the items are very large. To George J. Robinson was awarded £181 for seventy-six sheep and two rams "maliciously taken away, killed, maimed, and destroyed." To Hamilton C. Smith three separate awards were made - £28 for four head of cattle driven or carried out to sea and drowned; £21 for fourteen sheep maliciously driven off and removed; and again £17 10s. for fourteen sheep similarly treated. Houses and boats have been burned, and even turf-ricks destroyed. The object in all cases seems to have been to "hunt" the injured persons out of the country in order that the neighbours might turn their cattle on to his grazing land, as has been done in Mayo. In one conspicuous case these tactics have proved successful. Michael O'Neil was awarded £120 "to compensate him for ninety-six sheep, his property, maliciously taken or carried away and destroyed, at Tonadooravaun, in the parish of Ballynakill." This sum is levied off the fourteen adjacent townlands, among which is the unlucky Lettermore, just quoted as paying an enormous addition to the county cess. Michael O'Neil, who appears to have been a respectable man, not otherwise objectionable than as the tenant of more grazing land than was considered his share by his neighbours, has received his £120, and is so far reimbursed; but he thought it better to obey the popular will than to attempt to stand against it, and gave up his farm accordingly. Such deeds as the frightening of "decent people" out of Connemara by maiming cattle and burning houses, which must be paid for by the offending districts, speak more distinctly than any words could do of the ignorance of this part of the wild West.

So wild is it that although the Roman Catholic clergy of Connemara adhere to the elsewhere-obsolete practice of holding "stations" for confession, there are many dwellers on the mountain who have never received any religious instruction. Chapels are few and remote from each other, and even the "stations" kept for the purpose of getting at the scattered population only attract those dwelling within reasonable distances. The poor mountaineers in the neighbourhood of the Recess Valley and away over the hills seldom go far enough from home to rub shoulders with civilisation. Many of them have never seen bigger places than Letterfrack and Leenane, and those perhaps not fifty times in their lives.

The islanders of Clew Bay are almost as difficult to assist and to improve as the highlanders of Joyce's country, Southern Mayo, and Great and Little Connemara; but for an opposite reason. The latter are thinly scattered on the fringe of the grazing farms, while the former are crowded together on islands inadequate to support them. This question of space assumes a curious importance in Ireland owing to the want of other industry than such as is intimately connected with the land. With the exception of a few manufacturing districts in Ulster, which is altogether another country from Connaught, there are no industries in Ireland independent of the produce of arable land and pasture. What is to be enjoyed by the people must be got out of the land, and this in a country where nobody will turn to and work hard as a cultivator so long as he can graze, "finish," or "job" cattle, sheep, or horses. I was citing to a Mayo-man this defect of the so-called farmer, and was at once met by a prompt reply. The tendency to graze cattle, which is not hard work, and to "gad" about to cattle fairs, which are esteemed the greatest diversion the country affords, is an indication of the distinct superiority of the quick-witted Celt to the dull Saxon hind. An Irish peasant cultivator is a being of greater faculty of expansion than Wessex Hodge. He is profoundly ignorant and absurdly superstitious, but he is naturally keen-witted, and his innate gifts are brightened by contact with his fellow man. He is not a ploughman, for he often cultivates with the spade alone, and he has, besides his oats, his potatoes, his cabbages, and mayhap a few turnips, and a variety of animals, all of which he understands - or misunderstands. If a holder of twenty or thirty, or, still better, forty acres, he will have a horse, a cow, a beast or two, a few sheep, and some turkeys and geese. It is possible to have all these on fifteen acres or less of fairly good land, and then the Western peasant cultivator becomes a many-sided man by dint of buying and selling stock - that is, he acquires the sort of intelligence possessed by a smart huckster. This is held to be cleverness in these parts, and undoubtedly gives its possessor a greater "faculty of expansion" than the career of an Essex or Wessex ploughman or carter.

But what is peculiarly pertinent to the burning question of peasant cultivators and proprietors is the tendency, perpetually visible in the Western Irishman, to fly off at a tangent from agriculture to grazing. According to an ancient and indurated belief in all this section of the country, animals ought to get fat on the pasture provided by nature. I am told that thirty years ago there was not a plough in existence from Westport to Dhulough, and that the turnip was an unknown vegetable in Connemara. The notion of growing turnips and mangolds in a country made for root crops was at first not well received. "Bastes" had done hitherto on the rough mountain pasture "well enough;" which signified that no properly fatted animal had ever been seen around the Twelve Pins.

Now that the Connemara man here and there has been taught to grow root crops for cattle he begins to yield, and feeds his beasts, sometimes, on roots instead of sedge. Thus far he has become a cultivator; but I have my doubts whether the hard work of tillage suits him well. To get good crops off a little farm is an undertaking which requires "sticking to work." It is not so pleasant by a great deal as looking at cattle and taking them to market. Hence the tilled part of an Irish farm in the West nearly always bears a very small proportion to that under pasture. It is only quite recently that artificial feeding for cattle has been resorted to, and compelled the farmer to grow root crops. Perhaps, in the present condition of the market for beasts and grain the nimble-minded Celt is hitting the right nail on the head, and cattle and dairy farms are the future of the agriculturist, who will compete against American meat with English produce fed upon English grass and roots, and upon maize imported from the New World. I prefer, however, to leave this possibility for the discussion of Mr Caird and Mr Clare Read, and to confine myself to the fact that the Western cultivator is far less a farmer than a cattle-jobber or gambler in four-legged stock.

The poor inhabitants of the islands between this place and Achill Point cannot certainly be accused of a tendency to gad about. Almost everybody blames their dull determination to remain at home. They are, I doubt, neither good fishermen nor good farmers - at least, I know that they neither catch fish nor pay their rent. Neither on Clare Island, Innishark, Innisbofin, nor Innisturk is there any alacrity in making the slightest attempt to satisfy the landlord. That these little tenants are only removed by a hairsbreadth from starvation at the best of times will be gathered from the facts that Clare Island with 4,000 acres, some of which is let at 10s. per acre, with common grazing rights "thrown in," is called upon to support nearly seven hundred souls. A glance at the picturesque outline of the island will tell of the proportion of "mountain," that is moor and bog, upon it, and it is at once seen that unless there is either good fishing or some other source of supply the land cannot keep the people. No better proof can be given than that of the greatest tenant, who pays £55 a year for some five hundred acres. In Innisbofin and Innishark are at least 1,500 individuals, nearly all very small tenants, either on the brink of starvation or pretending to be so. It is nearly as impossible to extract any rent from them as from the twenty-three families on Innisturk, an island belonging to Lord Lucan, whose rents are farmed, so far as Innisturk is concerned, by Mr MacDonnell, the sub-sheriff, who is said to have a bad bargain. Lord Lucan, of course, receives his £150 yearly from his "middleman," who is left to fight it out with the people, and get £230, the price at which the land is let, out of them, if he can. Just now he is getting nothing, and the situation is becoming strained. The people pay no rent, the sub-sheriff, is not only losing his margin of profit but cannot get £150 a year out of them. They said they liked him well enough but would not pay a "middleman's" profit, whereupon he offered to take the exact amount he contracts to pay to Lord Lucan, and forego his profit altogether; but this proposition, after being received with some amusement, was not declined exactly, but, in American language, "let slide." And nothing has been or can be done. For if it were attempted to evict the Inisturk people the evictors would be accused of hurling an entire population into the sea.

The more that is seen of the people of far Western Connaught the more distinct becomes the conviction that the present difficulty is rather social and economic than political. It is far more a question, apparently, of stomach than of brain. The complaints which are poured out on every side refer not in the least to politics. Very few in Mayo, and hardly anybody at all in Connemara, seem to take any account of Home Rule, or of any other rule except that of the Land League. The possibility of a Parliament on College-green affects the people of the West far less than the remotest chance of securing some share of the land. If ever popular disaffection were purely agrarian, it is now, so far as this part of Ireland is concerned. Orators and politicians from O'Connell until now have spoken of Repeal and Reform; but it is more than probable that the Connaught peasant always understood that he was to be emancipated from some of his burdens. All his ideas are dominated by the single one of land. He knows and cares for very little else. He is superstitious to an astounding degree, and his ignorance passes all understanding - that is, on every subject but the single one of land. And the land he knows of is that in his own county, or home section of a county. But his knowledge of this is singularly and curiously exact. Either by his own experience or by tradition he is perfectly acquainted with the topography of his own locality and with the history of its present and former proprietors and occupants. With perfect precision he will point out a certain tract of country and tell how, in the old, old time, it was, "reigned over" by the O'Flahertys, and then was owned by the Blakes, who disposed of part of their country to the present possessors. He knows perfectly well how the great Martin country came first into the hands of the Law Life Insurance Company, and then into those of Mr Berridge, and how the latter gentleman came down to Ballynahinch, of the traditional avenue, extending for forty miles to Galway. More than this, he knows how an island was bought by its present owner with so much on it due to the above-named society. Moreover, he knows the site and size of the villages depopulated by famine, emigration, or the "exterminator," and in many cases the very names of the former tenants. He is a man of one idea - that the country was once prosperous and is now wretched, not in consequence of natural causes but of oppression and mismanagement. When he shouted in favour of Repeal he meant Land. When he applauded Disestablishment and Denominational Schools he meant Land, Land, nothing but Land. At last his dominant feeling is candidly expressed when he cries out against landlords, "Down wid 'em!"

In one of those neat remarks, distracting attention from the real point at issue, for which Lord Beaconsfield is justly famous, he expressed an opinion that "the Irish people are discontented because they have no amusements." Like all such sayings, it is true as far as it goes. Despite dramatists, novelists and humorists, Ireland is singularly barren of diversion. In a former letter I pointed out that the only relaxation from dreary toil enjoyed in Mayo is found at the cattle-fairs, and little country races to which they give rise. There are no amusements at all at Connemara. One ballad-singer and one broken-legged piper are the only ministers to public hilarity that I have yet seen. Nothing more dreary can be imagined than the existence of the inhabitants. When by rare good luck a peasant secures road-work or other employment from a proprietor at once sufficiently solvent and public-spirited to undertake any enterprise for the improvement of the country, he will walk for a couple or three hours to his work and then go on with it till dinner-time. But it is painfully significant that the word "dinner" is never used in this connection. The foreman does not say that the dinner hour has arrived, but "Now, boys, it is time to eat your bit o' bread." The expression is painfully exact; for the repast consists of a bit of bread and perhaps a bottle of milk. Indian corn meal is the material of the bit of bread, a heavy square block unskilfully made, and so unattractive in appearance that no human being who could get anything else would touch it. Then the man works on till it is time to trudge over the mountain to the miserable cabin he imagines to be a home, and meet his poor wife, weary with carrying turf from a distant bog, and his half-clad and more than half-starved children. Luckily the year has been a good one for drying peat, and one necessity for supporting human life is supplied. What the condition of the people must be when fuel is scarce is too terrible to think of.

I esteem myself fortunate in being enabled to describe what the life of the Connemara peasant is under favourable circumstances. His abject misery in years of famine and persistent rain, when crops fail and peat cannot be dried, may be left to the imagination. Potatoes raised from the "champion" seed introduced during the distress last year are, if not plentiful, yet sufficient, perhaps, for the present, in the localities to which a good supply of seed was sent; but I should not like to speculate on the probable condition of affairs in March next. I have also spoken of such a peasant as has been fortunate enough to obtain work at nine shillings a week, esteemed a fair rate hereabouts. But in truth there is very little work to be had; for the curse of absenteeism sits heavily on the West. Four great landed proprietors, who together have drawn for several years past about £70,000 from their estates in Mayo, Galway, and Clare, have not, I am assured, ever spent £10,000 a year in this country. As with the land itself, crop after crop has been gathered and no fertiliser has been put in. The peasant is now aware of as many of such facts as apply to his own locality, and this knowledge, coupled with hard work and hunger, has aroused a discontent not to be easily appeased. To him his forefathers appear to have led happy lives. It would be beyond my purpose to discuss whether the good old times ever existed, either here or anywhere else. My object just now is simply to reflect the peasant's mind, after having endeavoured, so far as is possible in this place, to verify the facts adduced by him, and I may add generally admitted by others.

The peasant looks lovingly on the tradition of the old time when the native proprietors dwelt among their people, without reflecting that it was the almost insane recklessness and extravagance of the hereditary lords of the soil which led to the breaking up of their estates among purchasers who had no kind of sympathy with the inhabitants. But good or bad, as they may have been, the names of the Martins, the O'Flahertys, the Joyces, and the Lynches are still held in honour, although their descendants may have disappeared altogether, or remained on a tenth or twentieth part of the vast possessions once held by their family. Some of the present representatives, however, are unpopular from no fault of their own. To cite a typical case. There is a large estate between this place and Clifden, the present holders of which should hardly be held responsible for the faults of their ancestors. A very large part of it has been sold outright and is in good hands. The remainder is strictly settled on a minor, and is mortgaged, in the language of the country, "up to the mast-head." Naturally the guardians of the minor are unwilling that the estate should be sold up, all possibility of improvement and recovery sacrificed, and themselves erased from the list of the county gentry. Landlords have as much objection to eviction and compulsory emigration as tenants, and are as much inclined to cling to their land, hoping for better things. Thus arises a state of affairs against which the peasant at last shows signs of revolt. Physically and mentally neglected for centuries by his masters, he has found within the last fifty years neglect exchanged for extortion and oppression. To prevent the sale of the property, the owners or trustees must pay the interest on the encumbrances. Moreover, they, being only human, think themselves entitled to a modest subsistence out of the proceeds of the property. To pay the interest and secure this "margin" for themselves there are only two ways - to wring the last shilling out of the wretched tenants, to first deprive them of their ancient privileges, and then charge them extra dues for exercising them, or to let every available inch of mountain pasture to a cattle-farmer, whose herds take very good care that the cottier's cow does not get "the run of the mountain" at their master's expense.

This "run of the mountain" appears to have been the old Irish analogue of the various kinds of rights of common in England, which have for the most part been lost to the poorer folk, not always without a struggle with the neighbouring landlord or lord of the manor. I hear from almost every place a complaint that within thirty or forty years the "run of the mountain" has been taken from the people and let to graziers. On the legal merits of the case I cannot at this moment pretend to decide, but inasmuch as this addition to an ordinary holding survives on some estates, there appears strong ground for believing that the practice was general. Where the cattle-run remains it is mapped out as a "reserve" for a certain townland, and is greatly prized by the peasants. It may therefore be imagined that those from whom it has been taken by the strong hand are bitterly resentful, and even where the change was made so long as twenty-five or thirty years ago nourish a deeply-rooted sense of wrong. It is absurd to suppose that when the act of spoliation took place village Hampdens could spring up on every hill-side in Connemara. Owing to the neglect of those who were responsible for their condition, they were the most ignorant and superstitious people in the British Islands. Landlords were not yet awakened to a sense that their tenants should at least be taught to read; and Connemara was esteemed, I am told, as a kind of penal settlement for priests who had not proved shining lights in more civilised communities. The latter reproach can no longer be brought, for the zeal and activity of the local clergy are conspicuous; and where the children are within any reasonable distance of a school they come readily to it, and prove bright and apt scholars. But when the "run of the mountain" was seized upon by many proprietors, the people were mentally, if not bodily, in a swinish condition. The idea of any right which a landlord was bound to respect had not dawned upon them, and, if it had, prompt vengeance would have descended on the village Hampden in the shape of a notice to quit, and he whose conception of the world was limited to his native mountains would have been turned out upon them with his wife and children to die.

I hear on very good authority that the purchaser of part of one of the old estates has acquired an unpleasant notoriety in his management of the land. I am compelled to believe that in the old period the peasants enjoyed their little holdings at a very low rent. Moreover these holdings were not all "measured on 'um," as one of my informants phrased it, but were often composed of two or more patches, bits of productive land, taken here and there on the rough mountain. Doubtless this arrangement had its inconveniences, but the people were accustomed to it, and also set great store by the run of the mountain, which they had, it seems, enjoyed without let or hindrance from time immemorial. The first act of the new management was to "sthripe the land on 'um," that is to mark it out into five-pound holdings, each in one "sthripe" or block. This arrangement, which to the ordinary mind hardly appears unreasonable, was considered oppressive by the tenants, who submitted, however, as was then the manner of their kind. They had still the mountain, and could graze their cow or two, or their half-dozen sheep upon it, and they naturally regarded this privilege as the most valuable part of their holding, inasmuch as it paid their rent, clothed them, and supplied them with milk to drink with their potatoes. In these days of alimentary science it is needless to remind readers that, humble as it appears, a dinner of abundant potatoes and milk is a perfect meal, containing all the constituents of human food - fat, starch, acids, and so forth.

Thus many of the tenants were, as they call it, "snug." Satisfied with little, they rubbed on contentedly enough, only the more adventurous spirits going to England for the harvesting. Then came serious changes. The rent of the five-pound holdings was raised to seven pounds, and the mountain was taken away. The poor people protested that they had nothing to feed their few animals upon on the paltry holdings of which a couple of acres might be available for tillage, a couple more for grass, and the remaining two or three good for hardly anything. An answer was given to them. If they must have the mountain they must pay for it - practically another rise in the rent. To this they agreed perforce, and even to the extraordinary condition that during a month or six weeks of the breeding season for grouse they should drive their tiny flocks or herds off the mountain and on to their holdings, in order that the game might not be disturbed at a critical period. I hear that for the last year rents have fallen into arrear, and that the beasts of those who have not paid up have just been driven off the mountain.

I have cited this case as one of the proofs in my hands that the country is not overpopulated, as has been so frequently stated. I drove over part of the estate mentioned, and questioned some of the people as to the accuracy of the story already told to me, and the agreement was so general that I am obliged to give credence to it. To talk of over-population in a country with perhaps half-a-dozen houses per square mile, is absurd. What is called over-population would be more accurately described as local congestion of population. The people who in their little way were graziers and raisers of stock have been deprived of their cattle run, and having no ground to raise turnips upon, cannot resort to artificial feeding. What was originally intended to serve, as a little homestead to raise food on for themselves is all they have left, and it is now said that they are crowded together. It would be more correct to say that they have been driven together like rats in the corner of a pit. As one steps out of one of their cabins the eye ranges over a vast extent of hill, valley, and lake - as fair a prospect as could be gazed upon. Yet the few wretched inhabitants are cooped within their petty holdings, and allowed to do no more than look upon the immense space before them. Where there is so much room to breathe they are stifled.

On the long dreary road from Clifden to this place, the greater part of which is included in the vaunted "avenue" to Ballynahinch, there is visible at ordinary times very little but mountain, bog, and sky. Of stones and water, and of air marvellously bright and pure, there is no lack, and some of the scenery is of surpassing grandeur, especially on a day like yesterday, so fair and still that mountain and cloud alike were mirrored on the surface of a legion of lakes. It was only when one reached the clump of trees which in these wild districts denotes the presence of a house of the better sort that any symptoms of disturbance were seen. All was calm and bright on Glendalough itself, but no sooner had I entered the grounds of the hotel than I became aware of the presence of an armed escort. Presently Mr Robinson, the agent for Mr Berridge, the purchaser of the "Martin property" from the Law Life Insurance Company, came out, jumped on his car with his driver, and was immediately followed by the usual escort of two men armed with double-barrelled carbines. A few minutes later I heard that Mr Thompson's "herd" over at Moyrus, near the sea-coast, had been badly beaten on Sunday night, or rather early yesterday morning; and there were disquieting rumours of trouble impending at Lough Mask. If the Moyrus story be true, it is noteworthy as marking a new line of departure in Connemara. Hitherto actual outrages have been confined to property; persons have only been threatened, and few but agents go in downright bodily fear. I have not heard why Mr Thompson is unpopular; but can easily understand that Mr Robinson has become so. The management of 180,000 acres of poor country, in some parts utterly desolate, in others afflicted with congested population, can hardly be carried on without making some enemies. Moreover, I have no reason to believe that the vast "Law Life" property has, since it passed out of the hands of its ancient insolvent owners, been either more wisely or liberally administered than in the wild, wicked days when the Martins "reigned" at Ballynahinch, and boasted that the King's writs did not run "in their country."

Before leaving Connemara I resolved to give a detailed account of the condition of the peasants of the sea-coast at the conclusion of a phenomenally good season followed by a fair harvest, thinking that a better impression would be obtained now than in periods of distress. I regret to say that the effect of several excursions from Letterfrack and Clifden has been almost to make me despair of the Connemara man of the sea-coast. I hesitate to employ the word "down-trodden," because it has been absurdly misused and ignorantly applied to the whole population of Ireland. I may be pardoned for observing in this place, once for all, that my remarks are always particularly confined to the place described, and by no means intended to apply to districts I have not yet visited, still less to Ireland generally - if a country with four if not five distinct populations should ever by thoughtful persons be spoken of "generally." What I say of the inhabitants of the sea-coast of Connemara does not, I hope most sincerely, apply to any other people in the British Islands. They are emphatically "down-trodden" - bodily, mentally, and in a certain direction morally. They do not commit either murder, adultery, or theft, but they are fearfully addicted to lying - the vice of slaves. Their prevarication and procrastination are at times almost maddening. I have seen men and women actually fencing with questions put to them by the excellent priest who dwells at Letterfrack, Father McAndrew, who was obliged to exercise all his authority to obtain a straight answer concerning the potato crop grown on a patch of conacre land. Did they have any "champion" seed given to them at the various distributions of that precious boon? "Was it champions thin?" was the reply. "'Deed, they had the name o' champions." The woman who said this in my hearing only confessed under very vigorous cross-examination that "the name o' champions" signified four stone weight of the invaluable seed which has resisted disease in its very stronghold. Now in very poor ground the yield of this quantity should have been twelvefold, or about 5 cwt. of potatoes. "'Deed, and it wasn't the half of it. The champions was planted too thick, sure; and two halves of 'um was lost." Taken only mathematically this statement would not hold water, but it was not till after a stern allocution that the fact was elicited that much champion seed had been wasted by over-thick planting - a habit acquired by the people during successive bad years. As these poor people prevaricate, so do they procrastinate. The saddened man who said, in his wrath, all men are liars, would have found ample justification for his stern judgment on the Connemara sea-coast at the present moment; but the Roman centurion immortalised in Holy Writ would make a novel experience. He might say "Go," but he would have to wait a while before the man went, and if he cried "Come" would need to possess his soul with patience. Yet the people are not dull. In fact the dull Saxon is worth a hundred of them in doing what he is told, and in doing it at once. This simple fact goes far to explain the unpopularity of English land-agents. Prepared to obey their own chief, Englishmen, especially if they have served in the army, expect instant obedience from others. Now that is just what they will not get in Clifden or elsewhere in the neighbourhood. Almost everybody is as fearfully deliberate in action as in untruth, and the Saxon who expects instant attention and a straightforward answer, and is apt to storm at procrastinators and shufflers, appears to the poor native as an imperious tyrant. Now the native is always as civil as he is deceptive. About the middle of my journey yesterday, I discovered that the pair of horses who were to bring me twenty-six Irish miles from Clifden to Oughterard had been driven ten miles before they began that long pull. Of course the poor creatures dwindled to a walk at last, and I sank into passive endurance lest the driver might inflict heartless punishment upon them. My remarks on arriving at Oughterard, where an excellent team awaited me, were vigorous in the extreme; but I am bound to admit that they were accepted in a thoroughly Christian spirit.

My long car-drives from Letterfrack and Clifden were directed mainly towards the spots mentioned in a former letter as of specially evil reputation for agrarian crime, and as being heavily amerced[13] by the grand jury. A very slight acquaintance with them excites amazement that cess, rent, or anything else can be extracted from the utterly wretched cabins looking on the broad Atlantic. A large number of these are built on the slope of a lofty peninsula rising to 1,172 feet from the sea-level, and marked on the maps as Rinvyle Mountain. It is better known to the natives as Lettermore Hill, and forms part of the Rinvyle estate, one of the encumbered properties alluded to in my last letter. The hill-folk, who appear, on the best evidence procurable, to have had hard measure dealt to them by the Mr Graham who bought part of the old Lynch property, declaim against the "new man," as others ascribe every evil to the middleman; but others again hold that the old proprietors, who remain on the land, fighting against encumbrances, are the "hardest of all," and that the whips of cupidity cannot compare with the scorpions of poverty. Be this as it may, the present holder of Rinvyle is by no means personally unpopular, and has helped the district lately in getting subscriptions and a Government grant for building a pier, extremely useful both as a protection to fisher-folk, and as providing labour for the still poorer people. It is also only fair to state that much of the local congestion of inhabitants at Rinvyle is due to the kelp-manufacture. The kelp-trade was at one time very prosperous, and employed a large number of people in collecting, drying, and burning seaweed. At that period it was the object of proprietors on the seaboard to attract population to their domains, on account of the royalty levied on kelp, which exceeded by far the rent asked for a little holding. While some proprietors were wiping off the map great villages, containing hundreds of families, like that of Aughadrinagh, near Castlebar, the holders of the sea-coast encouraged people to settle on their estates. No reasonable person can blame them for doing so. The proprietor was poor, and saw that a large accession to his means might be secured by attracting kelp-burners. He made a good thing of it. The people paid about £3 or a little more a year for their cottage and little, very little, paddock, not bigger than a garden; about 11s. a year for the "right to gather seaweed," and one-third of the proceeds of the kelp they made as "royalty" to the landlord. It should be added that the owners of Rinvyle were not themselves dealers in kelp, like some middlemen along the coast, and that their "people," - save

---

[13] 'fined', [Clachan ed.].

the mark! - could sell to whom they pleased, but the lords of the seashore took their third of the proceeds. Within comparatively recent times kelp has been worth £6 and £7 per ton. Putting the "royalty" at £2 per ton, and the production of each family at a couple of tons per annum, we arrive at the position that the landlord drew, in rent and royalty, about half his tenants' summer earnings. The tenants obtained about £8 clear per family for the summer's laborious work in collecting, drying, and burning seaweed. The rest of their living was made either out of a conacre potato patch, for which they were charged a tremendous rent, or eked out by the excursion of one member of the family to England for the reaping season. It was not a prosperous life, except in comparison with that which has succeeded it. For the last few years kelp has been almost thrown out of the market, and such small prices are obtainable that it is not worth while to collect it. But the population originally attracted by kelp remains to starve on the rocks of Rinvyle.

Lettermore Hill, rising directly from the sea level, is a magnificent object glittering in the sun. It is "backed" rather like a whale than a weasel, and includes some good rough mountain pasture, as well as green fields near its base. As one approaches it a ring of villages is seen delightfully situated, high for the most part above the sea and the green fields, and lying back against the huge mountain. It is natural to suppose that here resides a race of marine mountaineers seeking their living on the deep while their flocks and herds pasture on the hill. But no supposition could be wider of the actual fact. Neither the fields beneath nor the mountain above belong in any way to the villages which form a belt of pain and sorrow half-way up its side, drooping at Derryinver to the sea. One of these villages, Coshleen, surely as wretched a place as any in the world, is unapproachable by a wheeled vehicle. The pasture land in front is walled off, and, together with the mountain behind, down almost to the roof of the cabins, is reserved to the use of a great grazier living far away. Below, near the sea, stands Rinvyle Castle - whence the name Coshleen, the village by the castle - the ruined stronghold of the O'Flahertys who ruled this country long ago, either better or worse than the Blakes, who have held it for some generations, and under whose care it has become a reproach to the empire. There is a little arable land farther down Lettermore Hill, which, being also called Rinvyle Mountain, might well receive the third name of Mount Misery. This bit of arable land is let to the surrounding tenants on the conacre principle - that is, the holders are not even yearly tenants, but have the land let to them for the crop, the season while their potatoes or oats are on the ground. By letting this conacre land in little patches, a high rent is secured, which the tenants have no option but to promise to pay. Apparently it is these wretched people who, maddened by the sight of a stranger's flocks and herds pasturing above and below them, have risen at times and driven his animals into the sea. All the notice he has taken of the matter is to make the county pay his loss, and leave the county to get the amount out of the offending townlands if it can. He is not to be scared, for he lives far away, and apparently his herds are not much afraid either - at present, that is. How any compensation money is to be got from the hundreds of miserable people who inhabit Coshleen and Derryinver I cannot conceive. They have, it is true, potatoes to eat just now, and may have enough till February; but their pale cheeks, high cheek-bones, and hollow eyes tell a sorry tale, not of sudden want but of a long course of insufficient food, varied by occasional fever. With the full breath of the Atlantic blowing upon them, they look as sickly as if they had just come out of a slum in St. Giles's. There is something strangely appalling in the pallid looks of people who live mainly in the open air, and the finest air in the world. Doubtless they tell a good story without, as I have already said, any very severe adherence to truth; but there can be no falsehood in their gaunt, famished faces, no fabrication in their own rags and the nakedness of their children. I doubt me Mr Ruskin would designate the condition of Mount Misery, otherwise Lettermore Hill, as "altogether devilish."

The cabins of Connemara have been so frequently described that there is no necessity for telling the English public that in the villages I have named anything approaching the character of a bed is very rare. A heap of rags flung on some dirty straw, or the four posts of what was once a bedstead filled in with straw, with a blanket spread over it, form the sleeping-place. Everybody knows that one compartment serves in these seaside hovels for the entire family, including the pig (if any), ducks, chickens, or geese. Few people hereabouts own an ass, much less a horse or a cow, and boats are few in proportion to the population. Such a cabin as I have rather indicated than described is occupied by the wife of one John Connolly, of Derryinver. When I called the husband was away at some work over the hill, and the two elder boys with him, the wife and seven younger children remaining at home. I had hardly put my foot inside the cabin when a "bonniva," or very little pig, quietly made up to me and began to eat the upper-leather of my boot, doubtless because he could find nothing else to eat, poor little beast. Besides the "bonniva," who looked very thin, the property of the entire family consisted of a dozen fowls and ducks, some potatoes, a little stack of poor oats, not much taller than a man, and a still smaller stack of rough hay. An experienced hand in such matters, who accompanied me, valued the stacks at £2 15s. together. This was all they had at John Connolly's to face the winter withal, and I was curious to know what rent they paid for their little cabin and the field attached. An acre was quite as much as they appeared to have, and for this they were "set," as it is called here, at £3 per annum, and, in addition, were charged 2s. 6d. for the privilege of cutting turf, and 5s. 6d. for the seaweed. This toll for cutting seaweed is a regular impost in these parts, sometimes rising for "red weed" and "black weed" to

11s. The latter is used only for manuring the potato fields, the former being the proper kelp weed, and must be paid for whether it is used or not. As a matter of fact, Mrs Connolly's place assigned for cutting red-weed is the island of Innisbroon, some four or five miles out at sea, and as her husband has never been worth a boat she has paid her dues for nine years for nothing. The seaweed dues in fact have for several years past represented merely an increase of rental. It should not, however, be forgotten that when kelp was valuable the lords of the soil took their third part of it when it was burnt, in addition to the first tax for collecting the weed, a most laborious and tedious operation.

It may be asked, and with some appearance of reason, why, if people are hungry, they do not eat what is nearest to hand. That one owning a dozen fowls and ducks and a stack of oats, be the same never so small, should be hungry, seems at a superficial glance ridiculous. But the fact is that this is just the flood time of harvest, the oats are stacked and the potatoes stored, but there is a long winter to face; and, what is more depressing to hear, these people who rear fowls would as soon think of eating one as of flying. They do not even eat the eggs, but sell them to an "eggler," and invest the money in Indian corn meal, a stone of which goes much farther than a dozen or a dozen and a half of eggs. Those, and they are greatly in the majority, who have no cow are obliged to buy milk for their children, and find it difficult and costly to get enough for them.

In equally poor case with the cottiers is the woman who keeps the village shop at Derryinver. Those who know the village shops of England and the mingled odour of flour, bacon, cheese, and plenty which pervades them, would shudder at Mrs Stanton's store at Derryinver. It is a shop almost without a window; in fact, a cabin like those occupied by her customers. The shopkeeper's stock is very low just now. She could do a roaring trade on credit, but unfortunately her own is exhausted. Like the little traders during English and Welsh strikes, her sympathies are all with her customers, but she can get no credit for herself. She has a matter of £40 standing out; she owes £21; she has sold her cow and calf to keep up her credit at Clifden, and she is doing no business. When I looked in on her she was engaged in combing the hair of one of her fair-skinned children, an operation not common in these parts, where the back hair of even grown women in such centres of commercial activity as Clifden has a curious knack of coming down. It is part of the tumble-downishness of the neglected West. At some remote period things must have been new, but barring Casson's Hotel, at Letterfrack, there is nothing in good order between Mr Mitchell-Henry's well-managed estate at Kylemore and Galway. At Clifden and all through the surrounding country things appear to be decaying or decayed. The doors will not shut, and the windows cannot be opened; the bells have no handles, and if they had would not ring; the wall-paper and the carpets, the houses, the land and the people seem to be all very much the worse for wear. The dirt and slovenliness are unspeakable. I tried to write on the table of the general room of a well-known inn, or so-called hotel, the other day, and my arm actually stuck to the table, so adhesive was the all-pervading filth. The white flannel cloaks and deep red petticoats of Connemara women are picturesque enough on market-day in Clifden, but, like Eastern cities, they should be seen from afar. I have a shrewd suspicion that the blight has gone beyond the potato, and it is not very difficult to see how it strode onward. The little towns of the West depend entirely upon the surrounding country for their subsistence, and, when the peasantry are poor, gradually undergo commercial atrophy. Just at this moment they are in a livelier condition than usual, somewhat because the comparatively well-to-do among the peasants have taken advantage in many places of the popular cry to pay no rent, and have, therefore, for the moment a little ready money. But there is no escaping the saddening influence of a general aspect of dirt and decay.

It is a significant feature of the present agitation in Ireland that all parties are nearly agreed so far as the Connaught peasant cultivator is concerned. That anything approaching agreement on any part of the complex Irish problem should be arrived at is so remarkable that I am inclined to hearken to the popular voice. Whatever may be done for the benefit of other parts of the country, something must, it is thought, be attempted for the counties of Mayo and Galway. So far as I have been able to arrive at facts and opinions, it is not altogether a question of rent. A general remission of rent in these two counties would merely have the effect of enriching those farmers who are already "snug," but would leave the peasant cultivators exactly as they are at present. It is quite true that in some of the most wretched places I have seen the rent is extravagantly high; but while exclaiming against attempted extortion, I cannot shut my eyes to the fact that for the last two years the attempt has been in the main abortive. Everybody is not so deep in his landlord's books as the irreconcilable Thomas Browne, of Cloontakilla; but a vast number of poor tenants owe one and a half and two years' rent. I speak of those whose holdings are "set" from £3 to £8 per annum. The rent has not impoverished them this year at any rate; they have had a fair harvest, their beast or few sheep have fetched good prices, and yet they are miserably poor. It is quite true that two very bad years preceded the good one, but allowing for all this there is no room for hope that under their present conditions of existence they will ever be better off than they are now - when they are practically living rent free.

Letting for the moment bygones be bygones between landlord and tenant, what is to occur in the future? Hunger is an evil counsellor, and there would apparently always be hunger and consequent discontent among the little cultivators of Connaught, even if the land were given to them outright. The fact is that, despite the assertions of demagogues, the holdings on which the people now live cannot support them, and, in fact, never have supported them. It is, as I remarked in one of my previous letters, the harvest money from England and the labourers' wages brought from Scotland which have kept body and soul together after a poor fashion. The annual migration of reapers and labourers has been a matter not of enterprise, but of necessity; for on the summer savings, varying from £10 to £15, the family entirely depend. It is, therefore, an absolute mistake to speak of the Mayo and Galway men as peasant cultivators living on the produce of the soil they cultivate. It cannot be done. I have talked to scores of these people, and have invariably found that a decent cabin with properly clad inhabitants depended upon something beyond the food produced on the spot. Either the father went to England for the harvest, or the boys were working in a shipyard on the Clyde, or the girls were in America and sent home money. On the seashore, among the wretched people who send their children out on the coast to pick shell-fish worth fourpence per stone, I found here and there a household such as I have described really depending on money earned far away. I have thought it well to put the case somewhat strongly because it is sheer absurdity to expect that a living for a family can be extracted from five Irish acres of land in Connaught. In very good years, and when credit is abundant, not so unusual an occurrence as might be supposed, it is just possible for the peasant to struggle on; but he can never be said to live. His land is exhausted by the old Mayo rotation of "potatoes, oats, burn," and he has no manure but guano and seaweed.

It is like inhaling fresh air to turn aside from poorly nourished people and land to look, from the window of Casson's hotel at Letterfrack, on two bright green oases rising amid a brown desert of bog. Turnips and mangolds are growing in great forty-acre squares. Dark-ribbed fields of similar size show where the potatoes have been dug, and men are dotted here and there busily engaged with work of various kinds. The green oases at the mouth of the magnificent pass of Kylemore are the work of Mr Mitchell-Henry, M.P. for the county of Galway. When Mr Henry first went salmon-fishing in the river Dowris, which flows from Kylemore Lake into the sea at Ballynakill Harbour, Kylemore was a mountain pass and nothing more. Now it not only boasts a castle, but is the centre of extraordinary activity, the first fruits of which are seen in the villages of Currywongoan and Greenmount already alluded to as forming conspicuous objects in a landscape of strange grandeur. Mr Henry, who was an eminent surgeon before he became a great landowner, has gone about the work of reclamation with scientific knowledge as well as vigorous will, and now has a great area in the various stages of conversion from bog into productive land. When he began to reclaim land at Kylemore the neighbouring gentry smiled good-humouredly, plunged their hands into their (mostly empty) pockets, and wished him joy of his bargain. Now the Kylemore improvements are the wonder of

Connemara. The long unknown mangold is seen to flourish on spots which once nourished about a snipe to an acre. Root crops are very largely grown, and it is to these that the climate and reclaimed bog of Connemara are more particularly favourable; but there is abundance of grain at Currywongoan, at Greenmount, and at the home-farm at Dowris. Neighbouring proprietors are thinking the matter over, and are wondering whether an Irish landlord ought, like an English one, to do something to employ and encourage his poor tenants, and help on with improvements those inclined to help themselves. Even the tenants themselves on the Kylemore Estate are beginning to wake up under the care of a resident landlord inclined to set them in the way of improving their condition. With the run of the mountain in addition to holdings varying from twelve to forty and fifty acres in extent, Mr Mitchell Henry's people are learning by example, are breaking up land, and every year increasing the area under the plough. It would thus seem that the Connemara peasant is not unteachable, if only some patience be shown and fair breathing space allotted to him.

Mr Mitchell Henry's idea of reclamation was purely scientific at first, and has only by degrees been developed into a large enterprise. He was struck by the fact that the bog lies directly on the limestone, as coal, ironstone, and limestone lie in parts of Staffordshire, only awaiting the hand of man to turn them to practical account. Draining and liming are all that bog-land requires to yield immediate crops. The main difficulty is of course to get rid of the water, which keeps down the temperature of the land until it produces nothing but the humblest kind of vegetation. All the steps of the reclaiming process may be seen at Kylemore. The first thing to be done is to cut a big deep drain right through the bog to the gravel between it and the limestone. Then the secondary drains are also cut down to the gravel, and are supplemented by "sheep" or surface drains about twenty inches deep and twenty inches wide at top, narrowing to six inches at the bottom. This process may be called "tapping the bog," which begins to shrink visibly. The puffy rounded surface gradually sinks as the water runs off, and the earth gains in solidity. When this process is sufficiently advanced the drains are cleared and deepened, and a wedge-shaped sod, too wide to reach the bottom, is rammed in so as to leave below it a permanent tubular covered drain, which is thus made without tiles or other costly material. Then the surface is dressed with lime, which, as the people say, "boils the bog" instead of burning it in the old-fashioned Irish manner. On such newly broken-up ground I saw numerous potato ridges, the large area of turnips and mangolds already spoken of, grasses and rape for sheep-feed. The celery grown on the reclaimed bog is superb, even finer than that grown on Chat Moss, which gave Manchester its reputation for celery-growing.

It is not pretended that all the bogs in Ireland are susceptible of similar treatment, nor is it by any means necessary that they should be. For there is plenty of bog-land less than four feet in depth, and this alone is worth draining and liming at present. According to Mr Mitchell Henry's calculation he can drain and lime the land, take a first crop off it, and then afford to let it at fifteen shillings per acre. This is thirteen shillings more than it is worth now, and would return interest for the necessary outlay at five per cent. per annum. It is well known that Mr Mitchell Henry has pursued his work at Kylemore in the spirit of a pioneer, and that he looks to the employment of the poor Connemara folk on reclamations as the loophole of escape from their present miserable condition. But, while anxious for the people, he is not unjust to the landlords who, whatever their wish may be, are too poor to attempt any extensive improvement of their estates. With the exception of Mr Berridge and Lord Sligo, nobody has much money in these parts besides Mr Henry, whose example is followed slowly, because proprietors lack the means to undertake anything on a grand scale. His impression is, that to effect any good the matter must be made Imperial. The suggestion is, that suitable tracts of the best waste lands should be acquired by the Government; that the work of reclamation should be carried on by labourers who would be paid weekly wages and lodged in huts close to their work; and that when the land had been properly fertilised it should be divided into farms of forty acres and the men who have worked at reclaiming it settled upon it with their families, and instructors appointed to teach them farming. It is no part of the scheme that the land should be given to the people. On the contrary, a rent should be charged them, calculated upon the basis of a percentage on the original outlay in the purchase of the estate and of the amount paid in wages, together with a small sum to pay off the capital in the course of a term of years. The occupant would thus in time become a freeholder, and as much interested in maintaining the law as any other proprietor. Meanwhile he would, like the Donegal folk mentioned by Mr Tuke, live on hopefully under the rule, for the time being, of the Kingdom, as landlord.

I am far from inclined to detract in any way from the merit of Mr Mitchell Henry's project for Imperial reclamation any more than from his scheme for draining and for improving the internal navigation of Ireland. Although born in Lancashire he is a thorough-bred Irishman, and naturally hopeful of his country. But, although I am most painfully impressed by the fearful degradation into which a part of the Western people has fallen, I cannot on that account shut my eyes to their failings any more than to their poverty. Mr Henry's scheme, if it deferred actual proprietorship in fee simple till the next generation, would I hope prove of incalculable benefit to Mayo and Galway, especially if his excellent idea of appointing agricultural instructors were carried out faithfully. But I fear from what I have actually seen and heard from the most trustworthy informants of all classes, that the forty-acre farmer of this generation would require a firm hand to guide him. This is no insolent Saxon assumption of superiority, but is said, after due consideration, sadly and seriously. The poor people of the West have been brought very low, so low that even their very virtues have become perverted into faults. They are affectionate to their kith and kin; but this amiable quality leads to their huddling together in a curiously gregarious way, and in some cases has been made the means of extorting money from them. It is this tendency to live together and thus divide and subdivide whatever little property they may have, which will require to be most strenuously guarded against.

It is of no use assigning to a man forty acres of land to get a living out of, if he immediately sublets some of it to a less fortunate friend, or takes all his remotest relations into partnership. It requires no prophet's eye to discern that the instant the tenant's son got married he would bring his wife home to his father's roof, and that if the energies of the united family did not suffice to cultivate the whole of the forty acres, part would be let at "conacre," that is, for the period of one harvest, to a man with or without a holding of his own. The tendency to bring several families together in one cabin is almost irresistible, and has, as mentioned above, not been wisely and firmly met by proprietors, but taken a mean advantage of to wring money out of tenants.

Subdivision of holdings has in many cases been, not sternly forbidden on pain of eviction, but made the occasion of inflicting a fine. This shabby and extortionate kind of protest against subdivision has long obtained on certain estates. If one may believe evidence given on oath in a court of justice, as reported in a local newspaper, there was within the last twenty years on at least one estate a custom of exacting a fine from tenants who married without leave. Probably this originated in some clumsy attempt to prevent the subdivision of holdings and the accumulation of population in certain places - in itself a laudable and necessary precaution. Whatever shape any attempt to settle the unfortunate peasants on fresh holdings may take, the tendency to subdivide and sublet must be sternly resisted - and prevented. A thousand excuses will be made for taking partners, for subletting on the "conacre" and other systems. "Sure I was sick, your honour, and the farrum was gettin' desthroyed;" or, "I was too poor to buy seed for the whole of it, and let some at conacre to Thady O'Flaherty, that's a good man, your honour, as any in Galway!" or "Wad ye have me tur-r-r-n my own childther out like geese on the mountain?" are a few of the replies which would, I am assured by a native, be made to any inquiry or reproof concerning the subletting of land or the accumulation of people. But if any attempt be made to help the West, nothing of the kind must be listened to. The young bees must depart from the parent hive and begin life on their own account. This may appear the harsh judgment of a half-informed traveller. It is, on the contrary, the mere reflection of native opinion.

VI - THE RELIEF OF MR BOYCOTT

BALLINROBE, CO. MAYO, Wednesday, Nov. 10th

Finding that despite all the influence brought to bear upon it the Boycott Brigade was actually going to invade Lough Mask, I came from Galway to-day by the route preferred by Mr Boycott himself, just before I met him and Mrs Boycott herding sheep more than a fortnight ago. The steam packet Lady Eglinton conveyed an oddly assorted freight. Among the passengers were Mrs Burke, the wife of Lord Ardilaun's agent, two commercial travellers, the representative of the Daily News, and thirty-two of the Royal Irish Constabulary, who had been summoned from Galway to the scene of action. From every side soldiers and constabulary - soldiers in everything but name - converge upon Ballinrobe and Claremorris, townlets, which, if one could quite believe their artless inhabitants, are Arcadian in their simplicity, prosperous to every degree short of the payment of rent, and absolutely safe as to life and property.

When the good ship Lady Eglinton had puffed and scraped her way through the tortuous shallows of Lough Corrib to Cong, she was received by a large meeting of the country folk assembled on the pier. Fortunately I had secured a car from Ballinrobe to await my arrival, and the driver, a perfect "gem of the sea," received me with high good humour. "To Ballinrobe, your honour?" he said, and drove off like a true son of Nimshi[14]. As soon as he was fairly on the way, I said that I should like to drive to Ballinrobe by Lough Mask House. "It's not on our way, your honour," was the first and civil objection. I then observed that I wished to go that way in order to call on Mr Boycott. "Sure it's a different way altogether, your honour," was the answer. "A long way round, your honour." Then I said, after the brutal Saxon fashion, "Go that way, nevertheless." No answer, but the speed of the car relaxed until two other cars came up. Then a particularly wild Irish conversation was kept up among the drivers, and I observed a pleasant commercial gentleman who was bound for the village, as distinguished from the landing-place of Cong, laughing consumedly as his car branched off and left me to pursue my way in the twilight. Then my car-driver, evidently backed by a brother car-driver, put his case plainly. He had been engaged to drive a gentleman from Cong to Ballinrobe, and would do what he had engaged to do cheerfully, but he had not engaged himself to go to Lough Mask House. It was not, as a notorious claimant said, "in the contract." I hinted that a mile or two out of the way, even Irish miles, could not matter; that at complete sundown there would be a moon; that increased pay would be given. Not the slightest effect was produced.

---

[14] Character in the Hebrew Bible [Clachan ed.].

My driver would go to Ballinrobe and nowhere else. He had not engaged to go to Lough Mask House, and he would not go. I confess that for an instant I asked myself should I threaten my man and make him take me to Lough Mask whether he liked it or not; but an instant's reflection convinced me that any such attempt would be worse than futile. The horse would go lame or fall down within a quarter of a mile, and I should never arrive anywhere. So I tried coaxing, much against the grain, but it was of no use. To Lough Mask House the car-driver would not go. He would drive me to Galway or to Newport, "bedad," but "divil a fut" would he stir towards the accursed spot. He was good enough to say that he would not interfere with me. If I liked to walk, I was welcome to do it. Now a walk of seven Irish miles at sundown in a steady rain, over a line of road watched at every turn by disaffected peasants, was not attractive; so I made a last appeal to my car-driver's personal courage - Was he afraid? "Begorra, he was not afraid of anything, but would my honour want to set the whole country against him?" This is what it all came to. He durst not for his life drive anybody to Mr Boycott's with or without escort. He was compelled to form part of the strike.

Here in Ballinrobe we are in a state of siege. About 600 soldiers came in last night, who, together with the resident garrison, make a rough total of 750 military. Claremorris, I hear, is also strongly occupied to-night. In Ballinrobe are now stationed, under Colonel Bedingfeld, R.A., commanding the district, two squadrons of the 19th Hussars, or 123 sabres, commanded by Major Coghill. The Royal Dragoons, under the command of Captain Tomkinson, number sixty sabres, and with the Hussars will probably perform the main work of convoy tomorrow. The Royal Engineers are also represented, and 400 men of the 84th Regiment from the Curragh, under Lieut. Colonel Wilson, have reinforced the resident detachment of the 76th Regiment, commanded by Captain Talbot. Moreover, there are nearly two hundred Royal Irish Constabulary in the town, and the sub-inspector, Mr McArdle, has his work cut out for to-morrow. A great part of the troops are now under canvas, and last night were in even worse condition.

As one trudges across the slushy road over Ballinrobe Fair Green, the illuminated tents light up the foreground pleasantly, while the moon tinges the tree-tops and the river Robe with silver. All is beautiful enough were it not for the persistent rattle of the sabre and the jingle of the spur. So far as can be ascertained at present the Ulster contingent will consist of no more than fifty men, who will probably arrive by train at Claremorris about three o'clock to-morrow afternoon. Early in the forenoon a hundred infantry and sixty sabres of the Royal Dragoons will occupy Lough Mask House and the surrounding fields, and about four hundred infantry, a strong detachment of police, and the two squadrons of the 19th Hussars will receive the harvesters at Claremorris and escort them to   Lough Mask House.

It has been suggested that if sufficient cars can be requisitioned the Boycott Brigade might be mounted upon them and sent through guarded by the cavalry alone. The pace at which this evolution could be performed is its greatest recommendation. Any encounter with the people of the country side, who are sure to assemble in large numbers, would be completely prevented, and, what is of greater importance, the reapers would reach their destination before sundown. The long distance from Claremorris would be certain to prolong a foot march into the night, when all kinds of complication might occur. At the moment of writing the streets are dotted with little knots of people, and the excitement concerning the morrow is intense.

BALLINROBE, CO. MAYO, Thursday, Nov. 11th

Hearing that the march of the Ulster men upon Lough Mask House would not commence till nearly nightfall, I drove over early this morning to Mr Boycott's in a private carriage, hired cars being, for the reasons stated yesterday, quite unattainable. "Did your honour wish to set the country on me?" is the only reply vouchsafed by car-drivers since one of their body was cruelly beaten, presumably for the unpardonable sin of driving a policeman to the house under taboo.

The drive through the warm soft morning air was much pleasanter than that of yesterday evening; nor did people start up in an uncomfortable way from behind the stone wall, as they did last night. At intervals the sun shone out on the reddened foliage, greatly changed in hue since my first visit to Lough Mask. The half-dozen persons I met appeared to be going about their daily work like good citizens; and a casual visitor might, if he could have persuaded anybody to drive him along the road to Lough Mask, have gone away convinced that the whole story of wrong and outrage was the work of a distempered brain. The isolated dwelling itself was by far the most gloomy object in the landscape - grey and prison-like as most of the Irish houses of its class.

Mr Boycott's habitation has thoroughly the look of a place in which crimes have been, or, as a native of these parts suggested, "ought to be committed." Two dark figures of the Royal Irish Constabulary occupy the front-door step, and others of the same keep watch and ward over stables and ground. Nearly three weeks of painful excitement had made but slight change in Mr Boycott's family. His wife and daughter live under circumstances which would drive many people mad, and the combative land-agent and farmer himself maintains a belligerent attitude, the grey head and slight spare figure bowed, but by no means in submission. On the contrary, never was Mr Boycott's attitude more defiant. It is only by skilful subterfuge that he can get a shirt washed for his outer, or a loaf of bread made for his inner man. The underground routes which existed a fortnight ago are closed. In fact "every earth is stopped," and the hunted man is driven to the open. Not a soul will sell him sixpence-worth of anything. He cannot even get a glass for his watch, for the watch-maker no more than anybody else dare serve him. Every feature of his extraordinary situation depicted in my first letter on "Disturbed Ireland" is exaggerated almost to distortion.

Last evening the following letter was handed to him by the tenants of Lord Erne: -

> "Kilmore. Nov. 10, 1880. C.C. Boycott, Esq. Sir, - In accordance with the decision made in Lord Erne's last letter to us, we want you to appoint a day to receive the rents. - THE TENANTS. A reply requested."

Mr Boycott's reply was that he was ready to receive the rents at ten o'clock this morning, an hour after which time he received the following notice: - "The tenants request an answer to the following before they pay you the rent: - 1st. Don't you wish you may get it? 2nd. When do you expect the Orangemen, and how are they to come? 3rd. When are you going to hook it? Let us know, so that we may see you off. 4th. Are you any way comfortable? Don't be uneasy in your mind: we'll take care of you. Down with the landlords and agents. God save Ireland." Such communications as this are agreeable and amusing enough when addressed to a distant friend, but are hardly so diverting when directed to one's self. It is also disquieting to hear people say, as one passes, "He will not hear the birds sing in spring."

Next to open and secret enemies, indiscreet friends are, perhaps, the most disagreeable of created beings. Unfortunate Mr Boycott, who wanted a score, at most, of Northern men to get in his crop, has been threatened with an invasion from Ulster. The opposition of the Government to such "Ulsterior" measures, as a Galway man called them to-day, has at least had the effect of moderating the rancour of the relief expedition. Only fifty, with baggage and implements, are announced as on the march, but even this number is a hideous infliction on Mr Boycott. He has nowhere to lodge them but in a barn, and has assuredly not the wherewithal to feed them, so that their help and sympathy are somewhat overwhelming. Three hundred men of the 76th Regiment have been sent over from Castlebar to Claremorris to keep order, with Captain Webster's squadron of the 19th Hussars to furnish escort to Hollymount, where a troop of the Royals, under Lieutenant Rutledge, and 200 men of the 84th Regiment meet them. To Lough Mask House itself a squadron of the 19th Hussars and 100 infantry have been despatched to occupy the ground inspected and selected this morning by Colonel Bedingfeld and Captain Tomkinson during my visit to Mr Boycott.

BALLINROBE, CO. MAYO, Friday Night, Nov. 12th.

The march of the Ulster contingent last evening commenced smoothly enough at Claremorris. The dismal little country station was lined with troops, and perhaps made a more brilliant show than at any other period during its existence. After the manner of this part of the country the train due at 2.41 arrived at 3.30 P.M., and it was almost twilight before the well-guarded procession commenced. Perhaps two thousand persons assembled at dreary Claremorris, but the small representation of the countryside made up for the paucity of its numbers by the loudness of its voice. The groans which announced the arrival of the train were repeated again and again as the sixty-three officers and men of the Ulster contingent made their way towards the cars engaged for them. At the cars, however, some difficulty occurred; for the drivers absolutely refused to carry anybody but police. They were not bound, they said, to carry Orangemen, and would not carry them. This difficulty occasioned some little hustling, but the upshot was that the Ulster men, a well-grown, powerful set of fellows, were compelled to walk all the way from Claremorris to the infantry barracks at Ballinrobe.

The march was inexpressibly dreary. When any sound was heard it was a yell, and these expressions of disapprobation were repeated at Hollymount, and with increased vigour at Ballinrobe, where the streets were full of people. The Boycott Brigade was last night kept strictly within barracks, not a soul being allowed to venture out of the gate.

The general aspect of everybody and everything in Ballinrobe this morning expressed fatigue. The Ulster contingent, who call themselves "workmen," were terribly knocked up by their walk of about thirteen miles from Claremorris, a fact which hardly speaks well for their thews and sinews, but in fairness it must be admitted that they were obliged to undertake their march after a long and fatiguing railway journey, at sundown, on a muddy road, and in alternate light and heavy rain. They were also poorly fed, for their carts and implements generally only came in here this afternoon, escorted by the Royal Dragoons, under Captain Tomkinson, during part of the distance, and for the remainder by a troop of the 19th Hussars; wherefore the Ulster "workmen" hardly appeared to advantage this morning until breakfast had been supplied them in the infantry barracks. Then they straightened their backs and stood squarely enough to make a very old soldier exclaim with delight, "Foine men, sorr, they'd be with me to dhrill 'um for a couple o' weeks."

Poorly fed as the Orangemen were, their case was not nearly so hard as that of the military. It is all very well to send "the fut and the dhragoons in squadhrons and plathoons" to the fore, but it is not clever to send them to Ballinrobe or elsewhere without tents, baggage, or food. That furious Ulster Tories, "spoiling for a fight," should leave everything but repeating rifles and revolving pistols behind when rushing to possible fray is quite conceivable;

but that the Control Department should always blunder when troops are moved rapidly is not quite so easy to understand.

By what appears almost persistent clumsiness the troops sent hither were allowed to arrive many hours before their tents, baggage, and provisions. Suddenly ordered to leave Dublin, two squadrons of the 19th Hussars, a not very huge or unmanageable army of a hundred and twenty men, came away without being allowed to bring rations with them. The effect of this blundering is that the Hussars have been pursued by their food and tents, and on the night of their arrival were utterly without any accommodation whatever. The cooking pots have only just arrived here. Why it should take three days to convey a cooking pot over the distance a man travels in less than ten hours it is difficult to imagine; but the fact is absolutely true, nevertheless. The officer commanding the unlucky Hussars has more cause to complain than any of his men, for, owing to an accident to his own charger on the railway platform, he was obliged to ride a fresh horse, which, startled by the crowd, yesterday reared suddenly, and fell backwards upon Major Coghill, who is now confined to his room. It is hoped that no bones are broken, but this is not yet accurately ascertained, so great is the swelling and inflammation.

The hour of starting was late, by reason of everybody being tired with the hard, dull, wet work of yesterday, unrelieved by the slightest approach to a breach of the peace. Fatigue and disappointment had done their work, and only a few of the more ardent and sanguine spirits looked cheerfully forward to the march to Lough Mask House. The Orangemen, however, had not lost all hope, and one stalwart fellow, who told me he was a steward, and not an agricultural labourer, rejoiced in carrying a perfect arsenal, including a double-barrelled gun of his own, a "repeater" of Mr Maxwell's, and several full-sized revolvers. This honest fellow confessed that digging potatoes and pulling mangolds were not his regular occupations, but that he had come "for the fun of the thing," and to show them there were still "loyal men left in Ireland." This is hardly the place in which to discuss the loyalty which goes on an amateur potato-digging excursion armed with Remington rifles and navy revolvers and escorted by an army of horse, foot, and police.

The quality of loyalty, like that of mercy, is not strained, but it has fallen upon Mayo unlike the "gentle dew from heaven." The people here are undoubtedly cowed by the overwhelming display of military force, but they vow revenge for the affront put upon the soil of the county by the Northern invaders. Against the soldiers no animosity is felt, but the hatred against the cause of their presence is bitter and profound. Mayo has its back up, and only waits for an opportunity of vengeance.

At eleven o'clock the march from the barracks to Lough Mask commenced. First came a strong detachment of constabulary, then a squadron of the 19th

Hussars, commanded by Captain Webster, and next two hundred men of the 84th and 76th Regiments, who completely surrounded and enclosed the so-called "workmen" and their leaders, Mr Somerset Maxwell, who contested Cavan at the last election in the Conservative interest, and Mr Goddard, a solicitor of Monaghan, who led the men of that county, with whom was the Mr Manning to whose letters in the Daily Express, a Dublin newspaper, the Orange movement is attributed in this part of the country. In the rear came the men and waggons of the Army Service Corps.

To the astonishment of most of those who formed part of the procession the number of persons assembled to witness it was almost ridiculously small, and popular indignation roared as gently as a sucking-dove. In their own opinion the most law-abiding of Her Majesty's subjects, the Ballinrobe folk indulged but very slightly in groaning or hissing, and when the little army got clear of the town its sole followers were a couple of cars, a market cart, and a private gig driven by a lady, the tag-rag and bobtail being made up of a dozen bare-legged girls, whose scoffs and jeers never went beyond the inquiry, "Wad ye dig auld Boycott's pitaties, thin?" There was no wit or humour racy of the soil, no flashes of bitter sarcasm, no pungent observations: everybody felt that the thing was going off like a damp firework, and that, barring the "Dead March" from Saul, it was very like a funeral. Still, those who ought to know declared that the absence of any demonstration was in itself a bad sign. Hardly any men were seen on the line of march, but it was said that scouts were on every hill, and that pains were being taken to identify the Orangemen. It was also heard on the best authority that Mr Ruttledge's herds had been threatened and ordered to quit his service by the mysterious agency which rules the rural mind of Mayo.

Silently, except for an occasional laugh or two from a colleen standing by the wayside, we kept the line of march towards Lough Mask. At the village, standing on two townlands, a few more spectators hove in sight, but at no point could more than a dozen be counted. As the sun now shone through the western sky it revealed a picturesque as well as interesting scene.

Like a huge red serpent with black head and tail, the convoy wound gradually up a slight hill, the scarlet thrown into relief by the long line of grey walls on either side, beyond which lay green fields and clumps of trees dyed with the myriad hues of autumn, the distance being filled in by the purple mountains beyond Lough Mask. Presently came the angle which marks the extremity of Captain Boycott's land. Taking the road to the right, we approached the house under ban, and around which a crowd of peasants had been expected. The only human beings in sight were the police guarding the entrance by the lodge, and those stationed near the hut on a slight eminence to the right. Here the surrounding trees contrasted vividly with the animated and highly coloured scenes beneath. Completely enclosed by foliage was an encampment of the most picturesque kind.

On the greenest of all possible fields in front of the tents the officers commanding the escort, the leaders of the Ulster Brigade, and the resident magistrates were received by Mr Boycott, who appeared in a dark shooting-dress and cap, and carried a double-barrelled gun in his hand. A little further on stood Mrs Boycott and her nephew and niece, the house itself seeming almost deserted. The workmen, like the troopers, formed in line, and appeared to be equally well armed.

Presently the arduous task of stowing the uninvited Northern contingent was undertaken. The troops, who had remained on the ground all night, and had been reduced to straits by the failure of the commissariat, had, after some reflection and the exercise of considerable patience, taken care of themselves as best they might. Sheep had been slain, and chickens and geese had lent savoury aid to the banquet of the warriors, who also, in the absence of other fuel, were constrained to make short work of Lord Erne's trees. But they had done their work cheerfully in the cold and wet, and had pitched tents for the Ulster men. When the belligerent "agriculturists" came to be told off into these tents an amusing difficulty, illustrative of the light handling necessary to the conduct of affairs in Ireland, interrupted the dullness which had hitherto oppressed all present.

Those "agriculturists" who hailed from Cavan insisted that they would foregather only with Cavan men, while the men of Monaghan were equally indisposed to give a Cavan man "as much space as a lark could stand on" in their tents. Moreover some jealousy was exhibited as to the situation and furniture of the tents assigned to the two wings of the army of relief. At last harmony was restored, and the edifying spectacle of Cavan and Monaghan fighting it out then and there, while Mayo looked on, was averted, greatly to the sorrow of a Mayo friend of mine, whose eyes sparkled and whose mouth watered at the delicious prospect.

It seems that Mr Boycott, fully aware of the feelings of Mayo folk after having Orangemen set on them, is about to leave the country, at least for a while, after his crop has been got in - probably a rational decision on his part. Meanwhile he is having a hard time of it between friends and foes. His enemies have spoiled a great part of his crop, and what they have left his defenders threaten to devour.

BALLINROBE, CO. MAYO, Nov. 13.

A wild night of wind and rain was borne with unflagging spirit by the unlucky troops condemned to the most uncongenial of tasks. The fair green of Ballinrobe is now a quagmire, and the men under canvas have had the roughest possible night of it. Only two tents were actually carried away, but the hurricane made all those in the others uncomfortable enough. For ordinary pedestrians, perhaps, the slush of this morning was better than the sticky mud of yesterday, in which it was impossible to move; but the autumnal charm of Ballinrobe was gone for this year.

In the cavalry encampment the leaves lay thick around the unfortunate horses exposed to the weather with miserably insufficient covering. There was a general air of wetness and wretchedness from the infantry to the cavalry barracks, and some misgivings were entertained as to the condition of the garrison of Lough Mask House. General opinion has set in decidedly against the Ulster contingent: horse and foot, and police, magistrates and floating population unite in wishing the Ulster Orangemen "five fathoms under the Rialto." In the language of those who dwell habitually on the banks of the river the wish is epigrammatically expressed, "May the Robe be their winding-sheet."

Originally imagined as a scheme to force the hand of the Government, the Ulster invasion has been so far successful. The great actual mischief has been already done. According to public opinion in Mayo, the Government had no more than the traditional three courses open to them - they could have let armed Ulster come in hundreds or thousands, an invading force, and civil war would have ensued; they could have allowed the small number of labourers really needed by Mr Boycott to arrive by threes and fours, at the risk of not getting alive to Lough Mask at all; and they could do as they have done. The probable effect of the movement, if any, will be to bring Mr Somerset-Maxwell to the fore at the next contest for the county of Cavan. It may be imagined that the picked men of Monaghan are not very pleased at playing second fiddle to an electioneering scheme. Concerning Cavan, the hope of a fight between the men of the two counties has by no means died away.

To do justice to the Ulster men, they displayed a great deal of earnestness at Lough Mask House this morning. In the midst of a hurricane a large number of them went bravely out to a potato field and worked with a conscience at getting out the national vegetables, which ran a risk of being completely spoiled by the rain. The potatoes, however, might, as Mr Boycott opined, have been spoiled if they had remained in the ground, and might as well be ruined in one way as the other.

The remainder of the Orangemen, when I saw them, were busy in the barn with a so-called "Tiny" threshing-machine, threshing Mr Boycott's oats with all the seriousness and solemn purpose befitting their task. Nothing could have been more dreary and wretched than the entire proceedings. Mr Boycott himself had discarded his martial array of yesterday, and appeared in a herdsman's overcoat of venerable age, and, as he grasped a crook instead of a double-barrelled gun, looked every inch a patriarch. He exhibits no profuse gratitude towards the officious persons who have come to help him, thinking probably that he would have been nearly as well without them. Thanks to his obstructive assistants, he is almost overwhelmed with sympathisers gifted by nature with tremendous appetites. Keen-eyed officers detect the mutton-bones which tell of unauthorised ovicide, and "clutches" of geese and chickens vanish as if by magic. There will be a fearful bill for somebody to pay when the whole business is over, whenever that may be.

From every quarter I hear acts of the so-called "staunchness" of the population. When Captain Tomkinson went over to Claremorris yesterday with dragoons to convey the carts and other impediments of the Ulster division, it happened that one of the cart-horses lost a shoe. Will it be believed that it was necessary to delude the only blacksmith who could be captured with a story that the animal belonged to the Army Service Corps? Simple and artless, the Claremorris blacksmith made the shoe: but before he could put it on he was "infawrrumd" that the beast he was working for was in an Ulster cart. Down fell the hammer, the nails, and the shoe. The blacksmith was immovable. Not a blow more would he strike for love or money; nor would any blacksmith for miles around this place. At last the shoe was got on to the horse's foot among the military and police; but not a soul belonging to this part of the country would drive a cart at any price.

All this appears to point to the conclusion that when Mr Boycott's potatoes, turnips, and mangolds are got in, and his oats are threshed out, when his sheep are either sold or devoured on the spot by his hungry defenders, he will accompany the Orangemen on their return march, at least to the nearest railway station. That neither he nor his auxiliaries would be safe for a single hour after the departure of the military is certain, and the expense of maintaining a huge garrison in Ballinrobe will therefore of necessity continue until the last potato is dug and the last turnip pulled.[15] If the weather were only moderately favourable, the work might be got through in a week or ten days; but if it rains as it has done to-day, it is quite impossible to say when it will be done. As I was looking at the men potato-digging the rain seemed to cut at one's face like a whip, and all through the afternoon Ballinrobe has been deluged. In this beautiful island everybody disregards ordinary rain, but the downpour of the last few days is quite extraordinary. The river is swollen to double its usual size, and the slushy misery endured by the military under canvas is quite beyond general camp experience. The soldiers have only one consolation - that the Orangemen are under canvas too.

GALWAY, Tuesday, Nov. 16th.

---

[15] This prediction was literally fulfilled, [original footnote].

"Thim that is snug, your honour, is slower in payin' than thim that is poor," said one of my informants a few days ago, just as I was setting out for the seat of war in county Mayo. The speaker was a Connemara man, and his remark was applied more particularly to his own region; but the state of affairs in the neighbouring county illustrates his opinion in the most vivid colours.

Ballinrobe is the centre of a by no means unprosperous part of Ireland. Pretty homesteads are frequent, and well-furnished stackyards refresh the eye wearied with looking upon want and desolation. Between Ballinrobe and Hollymount the country is agreeably fertile; toward Cong and Cloonbur, where Lord Mountmorres was shot, and in the direction of Headford, on the Galway road, there is plenty of evidence of prosperity. It is, however, precisely in the rich country lying east of Lough Mask that the greatest disinclination to pay rent prevails. Nowhere is the disaffected party more completely organized, and nowhere is it, rightly or wrongly, thought that some of the tenants could more easily pay up if they liked. As contrasted with the hovels of the northern part of Mayo and the west of county Galway, the houses at Ballinrobe are comfortable, and the people apparently naturally well off. Moreover, they have a better idea of what comfort is than the inhabitants of the seaboard. I cannot better show this than by describing the houses in which I passed part, at least, of the last two Sundays.

When I arrived at Ballinrobe on Wednesday last it was almost impossible to obtain quarters either for love or money. I had telegraphed beforehand to that most civil and obliging of hotel-keepers, Mr Valkenburgh, of Ballinrobe, to secure rooms for me and send a car to Cong. The car came, and the driver with whom I had the debate already recorded, but it had been impossible to obtain a room for me anywhere. Mr Valkenburgh's own house was crammed to the roof with closely laid strata of guests, from the American reporter under the roof to the cavalry officer in the front parlour. There was nothing for it but to be bedded out - a severe infliction in some parts of Ireland. The polite hotel-keeper finally bethought him that in the house of a widow, who had only four officers of Hussars staying with her, a stray corner could be found; and I was finally established in the widow's drawing-room or best parlour, in which a cot, only a foot too short for me, was placed.

The excellent woman, whose house was converted into military quarters, is by no means rich. Her late husband was in the office of a neighbouring landlord, and would appear to have been just getting on in the world when he died. He certainly lived in a house properly so called; not a house in the Irish meaning of the word, which includes a Connemara cabin. It is only one storey high. The ground floor is occupied by two parlours, a kitchen, and offices; the bedrooms being upstairs. There are curious signs of better times about the place. My bed was far too short, but by the side of it was an old-fashioned square pianoforte. There was no carpet on the floor, but the lamp was a very good one, and well trimmed. The fire was entirely of turf, but of enormous size, and on the mantelpiece were some excellent photographs. Hens clucked as they hopped on to the table, and a red-headed colleen was perpetually chasing a cat of almost equally ruddy hue, but everybody was mightily civil and kindly. The room was full of peat-smoke, but the eggs were undeniably fresh; so that there were compensations on every side. The widow, her step-daughter, and the colleen before mentioned did all the work. They made my bed, what there was of it, they tended the fire with unflagging zeal, they brought water in very limited quantity for the purposes of ablution, they dried my boots and clothes with almost motherly care and tenderness when I came in out of the pouring rain. In fact, nobody could have been kinder or more attentive, and when Major Coghill was laid up by his accident their sympathy was almost overwhelming. Yet I believe that we annoyed them and deranged the tenor of their lives by our matutinal habits. Perhaps they might have been strong enough to resist my desperate efforts to get a cup of tea at some time before nine o'clock in the morning, but the officers' servants were too strong for them. They came and knocked the house up betimes, and then the bustle of the day began.

Now, I have been assured by the Irish priests and people that whatever faults your Commissioner may have, prejudice against Ireland and the Irish is not one of them. But at the risk of being thought a censorious Saxon I must confess that I am quite at issue with Western Ireland on the question of early rising. It is impossible to get anybody out of bed in the morning except the Boots at an hotel, and then the chances are that no hot water is to be obtained.

A housemaid in one of the Mayo hotels on coming up to make a fire complained bitterly, not of the toil of coming up stairs, but of the early hour of ten, and do what I would I could get nothing done earlier. On another occasion I was told that people out West rose late because the "day is long enough for hwhat we have got to do." I retorted that they did not do it, but fear that my remark was put down to prejudice. It is not my function to indulge in sweeping assertions, but if I were asked why the Western people do not prosper I should be inclined to reply - Because they will not turn out early in the morning.

But they are pleasant people in Ballinrobe nevertheless. Our widow never complained of our unearthly hours any more than we did of the turf smoke which communicated a high flavour to all our habiliments. The widow, although not rich, is evidently "snug" in her circumstances. She has a farm or two, part of which is underlet of course. This is another peculiarity of Irish life very remarkable to the stranger. Everybody seems to do work by deputy. A proprietor of a landed estate, not worth a thousand pounds a year when interest is paid on the various mortgages, would never think of being his own agent - that is doing his own work on his own estate. Not at all. He employs an agent who, thinking him rather small fry, neglects him or hands him over to the bailiff, who again transfers him to his "headmen," so that three people are paid for looking on before anybody does anything. This practice also may be in part the cause of the decay of the wild West.

I have been so far particular in my remarks concerning the Ballinrobe widow, in order to compare the inland standard of comfort with that prevailing on the seacoast. Just before the Ulster invasion as it is called here, I was induced to go to Omey Island. It is a place of evil repute for poverty, but is as healthy as it ought to be, having the blue Atlantic for one lung and the brown hills of Connemara for the other. It is one of those interesting islands which become peninsulas at low tide, a charming natural feature making it a matter of tidal calculation whether one can drive on board of them or not. It is not as bad as Innishark, which requires a trained gymnast to effect a landing, for it only needs nimbleness of brain instead of that of limbs.

While that zealous and hard-working young minister of the gospel, Father Rhatigan, was saying mass, and visiting that part of his flock congregated at Claddaghduff Chapel, I made my way over the intermittent isthmus of dry, hard, fine sand. It was an agreeable change from the road, which for some distance had lain over a "shaved bog" - that is, a locality from which the peat had been cut away down to its rocky bed. For some distance nothing was visible but stones, on which the rain came plashing down like a cataract. But the aspect and situation of Omey Island are such as to suggest to the speculative mind another and better Scheveningen without anything between it and Labrador. The island is not, however, purely sandbank, as Scheveningen appears to be, for it has a nucleus of rock, the sand being a later accumulation, every year increasing in volume, after the manner observed in Donegal, or as stones are amassed at Dungeness. I had heard wild stories of Omey Island, of troglodytes, hungry dwellers in rocky seaside caves, and rabbit-people burrowing in the sand. As Maundeville observes, "Verilie I have not seen them," but I can quite understand how the story was spread.

Over against the inhabited part of the island is what is now a mere sandbank. It is now covered with sand, and not a soul dwells thereon. But there were people there once who clung to their stone cabins till the sand finally covered them; so that they might fairly be described as dwellers or burrowers therein. At last their cabins became sanded up, and the poor folk moved to their present situation. Now I have seen superb potatoes grown literally in the sand at Scheveningen, and was not surprised to hear that

Omey Island was once so famous for the national staff of life that few cared to grow anything else. But there are difficulties everywhere, and it is parlous work to break up ground at Omey. There is too much fresh air; for it blows so hard that people are afraid to disturb the thin covering of herbage which overspreads the best part of the island. "If ye break the shkin of 'um, your honour, the wind blows the sand away and leaves your pitaties bare. And, begorra, there are nights when the pitaties thimselves 'ud be blown away."

Statements like this must always be taken at a reduction, but, judging from my own experience, Omey is a "grand place for weather entirely." Half of the island is rented by a considerable farmer, for these parts. He pays a hundred pounds a year for his farm at Omey, and a hundred and fifty for another cattle farm up on the hills. When I said he "pays," I am not at all sure whether he has paid up this year or not, but he has flocks and herds, and of course is a responsible tenant. Yet he lives with his family in but a "bettermost" sort of cabin. His wife treated me most hospitably; in fact, she paid me too much honour, for she insisted that I should not sit round the fire with the countryfolk, but occupy the best parlour, a room large enough, but blackened with smoke, and unutterably depressing, despite the cabinet pianoforte opposite the fireplace. Musical instruments of torture appear to be considered a necessary mark of competence in Western Ireland, just as a big watch-chain is in certain parts of England. Not a soul on Omey Island could play the pianoforte, thank heaven; so it remained with its back against the wall, as mute evidence of solvency. There was no carpet on the floor, which was of a fine dirt-colour, and the chickens, ducks, and geese circulated freely about.

Here now was a man paying, or promising to pay, £250 a year in rent, and who yet seemed to have not the faintest idea of comfort. It should be recollected that my visit was paid on a Sunday, when his family would be seen at their best; but the girls were running about with bare feet and dirty faces, and the neighbouring gossips, also barefooted and dirty beyond all imagination, were hanging round the fire, talking amongst themselves about the stranger, and half mad with curiosity concerning him. The farmer lived, it is true, in a wild place; but sand is so clean a thing in itself that it is a mystery how his tribe of children got so abominably dirty.

The drive homeward past Streamstown was wet enough, but still interesting in many ways. In no part of Ireland has the curse of middlemen been felt more severely than in Connemara. The middleman is specially abhorrent to the people when he is one of themselves. He is "not a gentleman, sure," is a deadly reproach in this part of the country. Practically he is objectionable because, being one of the people, he is aware of their tricks and their ways, and suspects them as they hate and suspect him. What would be urbanity on the part of the real "masther" is in the middleman viewed as deceit. The sharp tone of command endurable in a superior is resented when employed by a person of low origin. And it would seem that middlemen are not as a race persons of agreeable character. All the old rags of feudalism which have hung about Connemara long after their annihilation elsewhere, have been saved wherever it was possible by the middleman.

I am not quite certain that any one of these has ever "hung out his flag for fish" after the manner of the old proprietors who, when they wanted fish for dinner, made their tenants obey their signal and put back, whatever might be the chance of the night's catch. This flag was, so "men seyn," hung out often by the Bodkins, the ancient owners of Omey Island, but how long it is since it was last done is hardly worthwhile to inquire. Far more interesting is the much talked of "survival" of feudalism in the shape of what is called "duty work." Something analogous to the corvee[16] existed, I believe, in Hungary till a comparatively recent period, when it was commuted for rent. Within the limits of the English Kingdom, however, stories about "duty work" clash oddly on the ear, and yet I am assured that in the lesser island of Turk such work has been insisted on and "processed" for within twelve or eighteen months. Vexatious processes are not undertaken just now for very obvious reasons.

"Duty work," so far as I can gather, is, or was - for no such work will be done again in Ireland - a modified, form of the corvee. Here and there it was enforced in various shapes. At Omey, in Aughrisbeg, at Fountainhill, and at the lesser isle of Turk, the conditions varied greatly. The general principle appears to have been that besides rent in money, fine on entry, and dues analogous to tithes on stock of pigs and poultry, a certain number of days in the year were the property of the landlord. The usual term was about a week in spring and a week at harvest-time. In some places five days only were exacted; in others three. In the case concerning which I am best instructed, five days in spring and five in harvest-time were demanded, together with any one day in the year on which the tenant might be wanted, at a wage of sixpence. If the tenant refuse "duty work" he may be sued in court - the damage incurred by his default being generally assessed at five pounds.

Now it does not require any very clear perception to discover that among agriculturists or fishermen "duty work" is an improper mode of levying tax. In spring and autumn, and especially in the latter, the tenant requires for getting in his own crop precisely the week that the landlord is entitled to claim. Yet he must leave his own to assist his landlord. On one of the little islands, let to a middleman, all the evil features of the corvee are brought into prominence. The island produces three kinds of sea-weed, the so-called "red weed," cut off the rocks and used for kelp; the "black weed" on the

---

[16] unpaid labour required of labourers or tenants by a landlord [Clachan ed.].

shore, used for manure for potato-fields - often the only manure to be got; and the drift, or mixed weed.

After spring tides there is a great mass of drift-weed on the rocks, half of which is on the territory reserved by the middleman, and the other on that half rented by the tenants. The latter must give their master his day's work first to get in his weed, and take the chance of seeing their own washed away during the night.

From Ballynakill - where the ribs rising in the green grass-land, like waves in an emerald sea, tell of extinct cultivation, of depopulated villages, and an "exterminated" people - to the supremely wretched islands of Bofin and Turk, the record is fearfully consistent. A people first neglected, and then crushed by evictions, has sunk quite below the level of civilization.

VII - MR RICHARD STACPOOLE

ENNIS, CO. CLARE, Nov. 21st

At the seat of war by Lough Mask, I was informed that it would be sheer waste of time to go to Clare; that all was peaceful in the county which Daniel O'Connell formerly represented in Parliament; that at Ennis, under the shadow of the Liberator's statue, rebel commotion was unknown. All was quiet. It was true that people did not pay their rent, but that was all. I should waste my time, and so forth. But no sooner had I set foot in Ennis than I found that the jacquerie[17] which broke out in Mayo and Galway had reached county Clare, and that at least one gentleman living close to the principal town is at war with his tenants and the country side.

The condition of affairs at Edenvale is in many respects even more curious than that at Lough Mask House. There is none of the pomp and circumstance of open war. There is not a soldier or a policeman on the premises. All is calm and pastoral. From a lodge so neat and trim that it is a pleasure to look upon it, a well-kept road winds through a well-wooded and beautiful park, in the centre of which, on the brink of a lake, stands a large and handsome country house. All is ship-shape, from the gravel on the path to the knocker on the door, which is promptly opened, without grating of bolt or rattle of chain, by a clean, well-dressed, civil servitor.

All such signs of peace, order, and plenty are very noteworthy after one has been four or five weeks in Mayo and Galway, and convey a first impression that law, order, and civilization generally are to the fore in county Clare. The large and handsome drawing-room strengthens the conviction that here at least life and property are secure. It is true that several double-barrelled guns are on the hall-table; but country gentlemen in Ireland go out shooting as they do elsewhere. Several large dogs, too, are running about outside the house; but as Mr Richard Stacpoole is a celebrated sportsman, there is nothing wonderful in that.

Mr Stacpoole, whose appearance and manner are as frank as his welcome is hearty, is by no means reticent as to the matters in debate between him and the tenants holding from him and other members of his family for whom he acts as agent. To the question whether he goes in fear of his life, he replies, "Not at all; I take care of that," and out of the pocket of his lounging jacket he takes a revolver of very large bore. It is a curious picture, this drawing-room at Edenvale. On his own hearth-rug, in his own house, with a silky white Maltese lapdog and a beautiful terrier nestling at his feet, stands no English or Scotch interloper, agent, middleman, or "land-grabber," but the

---

[17] A peasant revolt, named after a revolt in medieval France [Clachan ed.].

representative of one of the oldest, most honourable, and, I may add, till recently most honoured families in the county, with his hand on the pistol which is never out of his reach by day or night. There was once no more popular man in Clare. His steeplechasers win glory for Ireland at Liverpool, whether they return a profit to their owner or not. He keeps up, with slight assistance from members of the Hunt, a pack of harriers, and hunts them himself. His cousin, the late Captain Stacpoole, of Ballyalla, was the well-known "silent member" who for twenty years represented Ennis in Parliament. Finally, he is spending at least £3,000 a year in household expenses alone; but he never leaves his revolver; and he is in the right, for not two hours ago a local leader declared to me with pale face and flaming eyes that he would "gladly go to the gallows for 'um."

But the local leader does not, or at least has not yet shot at Mr Stacpoole because he "can't get at 'um" - a phrase which requires some explanation. I had, with an eye becoming practised in such matters, scanned the house and its approaches as I drove up to the door, and had discussed with the friend who introduced me to its master the chances of "stalking" that gentleman on his own ground. Trees and brushwood grew more closely to the house than a military engineer would have permitted, and I hazarded the opinion that it would be easy to "do him over," as it is called. But on talking to Mr Stacpoole I quickly discover that the real reason why he is now alive is that ninety-nine out of a hundred of his enemies are as afraid of him as the Glenveagh folk up in Donegal are of Mr J.G. Adair. Brave and resolute to a fault, he has openly declared his dislike for what is called "protection." "But," he observes, quietly and simply, "I always carry my large-bore revolver, and I never walk alone, even across the path to look down at the lake. Whenever I go out, and wherever I go, I have a trustworthy man with me carrying a double-barrelled gun. His orders are distinct. If anybody fires at me he is not to look at me, but let me lie, and kill the man who fired the shot. And I am not sure that if he saw an armed man near me in a suspicious attitude that he wouldn't shoot first. I most certainly will myself. If I catch any of them armed and lurking about here near my house, I will kill them, and they know it."

There was no appearance of emotion in the speaker, whose collection of threatening letters is large and curious. His position was clearly defined. There was no longer any law in Clare. It was everybody for himself, and he would take care of himself in his own way. Mr Stacpoole's situation is certainly extraordinary. He is not an "exterminator," but perhaps he is a "tyrant," for everybody is considered one who tries to exact obedience from any created being in the west of Ireland. He has incurred the ill-will of the popular party, mainly through his debate with one Welsh, or Walsh, a small farmer.

So far as it is possible to understand the matter, this Welsh and two other persons held a farm of about fifty acres among them as co-tenants, paying each one-third of the rent. Whether Welsh had reclaimed bog and increased his store is not clear, but it is certain that when the lease fell in he had about half of the farm and the other two tenants the other half between them.

Moreover, the land was not "striped" in blocks, but remained in awkward patches, so that each man was obliged to cross the other's land, and perpetual squabbling occurred. So when the question of a new lease arose, Mr Stacpoole sent a surveyor to divide the holding into three equal shares as justly and conveniently as might be with reference to the tenants' houses. This was done, the land was re-valued at 12s. 6d. per acre, the tenants preferring to hold it without a lease. Thus two were pleased and one displeased by the new arrangement, and the displeased one, Welsh, or Walsh, was finally evicted a short while since, and his house pulled down. Only the other day a mob assembled, rebuilt Welsh's house, and reinstated his wife and family, who occupy it at this moment. Welsh himself is not with them for the reason that Mr Stacpoole has an attachment out against him. However, the family remains, and no process-server would show his face at the rebuilt house for fifty pounds. Mr Stacpoole could, of course, go and turn the people out as trespassers, but does not think it worth while until he joins issue with all the recalcitrant tenants under his control. Some forty of these will neither pay up nor surrender their holdings, and Mr Stacpoole declares that he will get Dublin writs against the whole of them, and that if they do not yield he will evict them all and compel the authorities to support him. There is no concealment about all this, and it is quite certain that if Mr Adair's action in the Derryveagh matter is imitated it will only be by aid of the military. The landlord declares he will "have his own," and the tenants talk ominously of the "short days and long nights" between this and spring.

Meanwhile they carry on the war after their fashion. Only a few days ago they levelled the walls of a holding which had not been administered to please them by Mr Vesey Fitzgerald. The week before last when Mr Stacpoole's harriers met there was a crowd assembled of men on foot and on horseback, and the huntsman was ordered by the fugleman[18] of the mob to go home. Luckily Mr Stacpoole himself was at Liverpool, winning races with Turco, or something serious might have happened. As it was, Mr Healey and Mr Studdert, well-known cross-country riders, and very popular here, being present, as well as one lady, the sport of hare-hunting was allowed to go on; but this week, although ordered to go out with his hounds, the huntsman thought it wiser to stay at home, and a meeting of the Hunt has been called to consider what shall be done.

---

[18] A person who heads a group, esp. political. Originally a soldier who served as a guide, [Clachan ed.].

The people can and will prevent Mr Stacpoole from hunting unless members of the Hunt think it worth while to turn out with carbines and revolvers, with the possible result of bringing on a civil war. Probably the harriers will be taken over by a Committee of the Hunt to whom the present owner offers them, as well as the use of his kennels. Should his harriers be effectually prevented from hunting he will have no farther reason for remaining in the country, and will probably shut up his house, dismiss his servants, and leave Ireland; but this he will not do until he has "had his own."

VIII - PATRIOTS

ENNIS, CO. CLARE, Nov. 22nd.

Ennis, on deliberate inspection, proves to be by far the most interesting western town I have yet visited. To paraphrase a familiar saying, its politics and its liquor are as strong as they are abundant. Ennis is famous for its electioneering fights, for its three bridges, for its public square "forenint[19]" O'Connell's statue, said to have held thirty thousand people on a space which would not contain a fifth of that number, for its numerous banks, for its fine salmon river, the Fergus, for its police barrack, once the mansion of the Crowe family, and for its long since closed Turkish bath, the ruined proprietor whereof is now in the lunatic asylum on the road to Ballyalla. Ennis is also proud of its County Club, of its handsome drapery stores, of its brand-new waterworks, of its hundred and odd whisky-shops, and of its patriots. Of the latter by far the most eminent is a certain man named in newspaper reports M.G. Considine, Esq., but better known to his fellow-citizens as "Dirty Mick." Mr Considine is a fine specimen of the good old crusted Irish patriot. He has pursued patriotism ever since the day of Daniel O'Connell, and it redounds greatly to his honour that he is now as poor as when he started in that profession.

This Milesian Diogenes is in many respects the most remarkable man in county Clare, after, if not before, The O'Gorman Mahon himself. He is also the dirtiest. But the grime on Mr Considine has a romantic origin. It is the fakir's robe of filth. When he was only a budding patriot the great Liberator once kissed him. Mr Considine determined that the cheek sanctified by the embrace of O'Connell should never again be profaned by water, that the kiss should never be washed off. Without speculating as to the degree of cleanliness previously favoured by Mr Considine, it must be conceded that it is very difficult to wash day by day, or week by week, as the case may be, round a certain spot on one cheek which, moreover, would soon get out of harmony with the remainder of the countenance. It is easier, "wiser, better far," to bring the whole face into harmony with the sacred sunny side of it.

This has been done; and the result is a picture worthy of Murillo or Zurbaran. From the grimy but handsome well-cut face gleam a pair of bright, marvellously bright blue eyes, and the voice which bids welcome to the stranger is curiously sweet and sonorous. Mr Considine is quite the best speaker here, and his summons will always bring an audience to Ennis. One enthusiast said to me, "Whin he dies, may the heaven be his bed, and his statue should be beside O'Connell's in Ennis." Now this model patriot, whom every one must perforce respect for his perfect honesty and

---

[19] Opposite, [Clachan ed.].

disinterestedness, keeps a wretched little shop in a trumpery cabin. His stock-in-trade consists of a few newspapers, his pantry holds but potatoes. Yet he is a great power in Ennis, and the candidate for that borough who neglected him would fare badly. I am not insinuating that any charge of venality can attach to him. Quite the contrary. He is admitted to be a perfectly disinterested citizen by those most opposed to him socially and politically. He is not only one of those who have kept the sacred fire of agitation burning since the days of O'Connell, but he is the possessor of relics of '98. He owns and dons upon occasion the Vinegar Hill uniform, and has '98 flags by him to air on great days. By dint of sheer honesty and truthfulness this poor grimy old man has become actually one of the chiefs of county Clare.

Another patriot came under my notice in a queer kind of way. I had gone to look at the reclamation works on the Fergus river, and there encountered a scene odd and peculiar beyond previous experience. Shortly before me, had arrived Mr Charles George Mahon, the nephew of The O'Gorman Mahon, and a Mr Crowe. These two gentlemen being neighbours of Mr Drinkwater, had looked in to see his works, and in a friendly way were chatting to one of his foremen, bringing work to a standstill, but conducting themselves with the easy affability common to the lesser proprietors of county Clare. All was going smoothly when, like his predecessors, disregarding the warning that no person could be admitted except on business, a strange personage put in an appearance. Neither Cruikshank, Daumier, nor Dore ever conceived a more grotesque figure than that which entered the Clare Reclamation works.

Imagine a singularly small rough-coated donkey stunted by too early and too hard work, and on its back a cripple - *a cul-de-jatte*[20] - carrying his crutches with him, laid across the withers of the unfortunate animal he bestrode. Imagine also a face, very cleanly washed, and of that Semitic outline and expression by no means uncommon in Connaught, dark flashing eyes, an aquiline nose, and a wide expressive mouth. Dismounted from his steed and placed up against the wall, the decently dressed and well-spoken man, propped up on his crutches, would have been thought rather an object of charitable interest than of distrust, if not of fear.

This poor and apparently helpless man is a popular speaker and lecturer - one who does not deliver his harangues in high places, but rides on his donkey from village to village, spreading the doctrines now acceptable to the rural population. By the upper classes he is abhorred as a specially obnoxious and pestilent person. He, on the other hand, considers himself oppressed. He was a National Schoolmaster, but got into a scrape about a threatening letter, which, it is fair to state, was not completely brought home

---

[20] *cul-de-jatte* – (Fr) a legless cripple, someone with both legs amputated, [Clachan ed.].

to him. However, he lost his place. In the hope that he might be reinstated he passed a science and art examination, but he fared no better, and then found that the trade of a popular agitator was the most congenial one he could pursue. He is also an itinerant scribe, writing letters for people who cannot write, making aggrieved people aware of the full extent of their grievance, and assisting them to send furious letters to the smaller local newspapers, concerning which I hesitate to express any opinion, lest the readers of the Daily News should think they had stumbled upon the Commination Service.

The bright-eyed, flexible-mouthed *cul-de-jatte* was firmly planted against a stone wall, when his eye caught the figures of the two gentlemen talking to Mr Drinkwater's quarrymen. Immediately the eye before-mentioned was aflame, and in sonorous tones the owner "war-r-r-ned" the foremen and workmen from holding any converse with Mr Charles George Mahon, whom he addressed personally as "a rack-renting landlord," and otherwise held up to scorn and derision. Perched on his crutches, the cripple defied him, and poured out a torrent of eloquence on "the fiery dthragon of hunger" and other direful creatures, including landlords, which would have set at defiance Canon Dwyer's "exploded shaft of Greek philosophy." The scene afforded, at least to many there present, as much amusement as astonishment. That a nephew of a county member should be publicly attacked before a large number of people and be compelled to hear them "war-r-r-ned" not to buy an egg or a pat of butter from his tenants would be incredible anywhere else than in Ireland at this moment. But people are growing accustomed to strange things in these parts.

The Clare Harriers Hunt Club met on Saturday, when Mr Richard Stacpoole formally made the offer of the hounds, got together by himself at great expense, to the members of any Hunt Committee that might be found. The offer was declined. Mr Stacpoole then declared his resolution to sell off the pack. He cannot keep them at Edenvale, for his "dog-feeder" has been "warned" not to give bite or sup to the animals for his life. So the hounds go to England to be sold, and the eviction - of landlords - goes merrily on. Such things may appear impossible. But it is precisely The Impossible which occurs every day in Ireland.

IX - ON THE FERGUS

ENNIS, CO. CLARE, Friday, Nov. 26th.

It is noteworthy that the only two persons who are doing much reclamation work in the West of Ireland are Manchester men. Mr Mitchell Henry has awakened Connemara, and Mr Drinkwater has performed a similar operation upon county Clare Nothing in connection with the Kylemore and Fergus Reclamation works, which have brought to and distributed a large sum of money in their respective districts, is more remarkable than the apathy of the surrounding proprietors in one case and their hostility in the other. Mr Mitchell Henry could afford to wait, and his patience has been attended with success; but Mr Drinkwater was compelled to encounter, not mere passive indifference, but active acquisitiveness. For a time stretching beyond the memory of man the reclamation of what is called the Clare "slob" has been talked about. This talking stage is not unfamiliar in the recent history of Ireland.

Everything has been talked about, and some few things have been done after a fashion. There remains in Galway a very comfortable and well-managed hotel at the railway station, which was originally built with a view to the American traffic scheme since become notorious; but the Galway people still believe that their ships were wrecked by a combination of Liverpool merchants interested in destroying them. The Harbour of Foynes, on the Shannon, was once talked about, but never grew into a seaport; while the fishing-piers, as they are called, lie dotted around the coast in places to which nobody ever goes and from which nobody ever comes. But it was seen long ago that something could be done with the Fergus "slob" if anybody could be found to do anything. Companies were formed and concessions were obtained, but nothing was done, although several square miles of magnificent alluvial deposit sixteen feet in depth were to be had for the asking.

In 1843 The O'Gorman Mahon himself, as a county member, talked about the grand lands to be reclaimed from the Fergus, and the county talked about it; but nothing was done. This is the pleasant way of the West. All take an interest in any possible or impossible enterprise; but when it comes to finding some money and doing something, the scheme is relegated to the limbo of things undone.

The principal riparian[21] proprietors were Lords Inchiquin, Leconfield, and Conyngham, mostly absentees. Lord Conyngham was naturally indifferent, for his estate in Clare was to be sold in Dublin on Tuesday, and his interest

---

[21] The interface between land and a river or stream, [Clachan ed.].

in the county thus had ceased. Lord Leconfield is also an absentee, without even an address in the county. Perhaps, as the three noblemen mentioned own between them 85,226 acres in county Clare alone, without counting their other possessions, they thought that at any rate there was land enough, such as it is, in the county. Judging by the Government valuation the land held by them is not of the best quality, for it is set down at £38,188, and probably is not let at very much more than that sum; but at the most moderate estimate they draw, or rather drew, more than £40,000 a year from county Clare. When they were invited to share in reclaiming the rich mud-banks of the Fergus, and thus add 10,000 acres of virgin soil to the rateable value of the county, they declined with perfect unanimity. They did more than this. When Mr Drinkwater had bought out the concessionees of 1860 and 1873 - who had not struck a single stroke of work - and was endeavouring to get the necessary Bills through Parliament, he found himself confronted by the seignorial and other vested rights of these great landowners, who appeared determined, not only to do nothing themselves, but to prevent anybody else from doing anything - unless he paid handsomely for their permission.

I do not cite this as an act of special iniquity. Their action was only part of the general system of taking as much out of Ireland as possible and putting nothing into it. A claim of £20,000 and 5 per cent. of the land reclaimed for manorial rights over a mud-bank could hardly be overlooked by the Crown; and it is, I believe, not quite settled how this large sum of money and valuable land is to be divided, if at all. The landowners base their claim on various grants and charters and the Crown opposes them on public grounds, while the Court of Chancery takes care of the money. Contending against "landlordism" and other difficulties Mr Drinkwater pushed vigorously on, almost, as it has turned out, a little too vigorously for his own interest. The English public is aware that the Government has at various times encouraged Irish landlords to improve their property by offering to lend, at different rates of interest, two-thirds of the money to be spent, always with the proviso that the Government engineer approves of the plan and sees the work well and duly performed. Under the old Act of William IV, passed in 1835, the rate of interest was fixed at 5 per cent. Under this statute Mr Drinkwater applied for £45,000 and thanks to his ill-timed energy in urging his application, obtained his loan at 5 per cent., just before the Act of 1879 was brought in for affording somewhat similar help at 1 per cent.

Mr Drinkwater has thus the satisfaction of knowing that his neighbour, Lord Inchiquin, who has commenced improvements on his own account, has obtained £8,000 at 1 per cent., while he pays 5 upon the large sum employed on the Clare Slob Reclamation; a state of things greatly enjoyed here as turning the laugh against "the Saxon."

Being sceptical about the "slob," I went to see it. When I started the moon was shining so brightly that it would have been impossible to miss a landlord at forty yards. The sky was as blue and clear as that of Como or Lugano; but the wind which swept over Ballyala's sapphire lake was of a "nipping and an eager" quality, not commonly encountered in Italy. The ground was as hard as steel and as slippery as glass, and the first half-mile convinced us that the best thing to be done was to get off the car, catch hold of the mare's head, and try to hold her on her legs while struggling to keep on our own. It was three miles to the nearest blacksmith's, but there was nothing for it but to walk to Ennis as well as might be along the slippery road.

This mode of progression was very slow, and it was nearly half-past eight when we reached that centre of political and alcoholic existence. Leaving the mare to be "sharpened" we strolled through the town in contemplative mood. Not a shop was open. Not a blind was drawn. Not a soul was stirring excepting the blacksmith, who had been knocked up comparatively early by the market folk. There was ample time and space to inspect the fierce but sleepy-headed town. In the main street I observed six grog-shops, side-by-side, actually shoulder-to-shoulder, cheek-by-jowl. Another street appeared to be all grog-shops but for the ominous exception of an undertaker. About nine o'clock a few people came out of chapel, and shortly afterwards the butchers' shops gave signs of life, one opening on each side of the main street, and blinking like a bloodshot eye upon the slumbering groceries and groggeries, drapery stores, and general drowsiness. Ennis was evidently sleeping off the previous day's whisky, and preparing to renew the battle with "John Jamieson."

Presently the mare came round to the door of the principal hotel. The people there were just stirring, and visions of brooms and unkempt back-hair were frequent. At last we were on the road to Clare Castle, which might, in the high-flown language of the West, be fitly described as the "seaport" of Ennis. The river Fergus flows through Ennis, but it is broader and deeper at Clare Castle, a village of ordinary Connaught hovels. There is, however, a quay here, a relic of "relief-work" in famine time, and affording "convenience" for vessels of considerable size. Below the bridge and alongside the quay lies a large steam-tug, and lower down the stream is moored a similar vessel. A large number of rafts are being laden with stone to be presently towed down to the reclamation works. As we steam down the Fergus towards its junction with the Shannon at "The Beeves" rock, the stream spreads out to a great width, enclosing several islands, green as emeralds, of which Smith's Island and Islandavanna are, perhaps, the principal.

There is, however, a marked difference between the area of the Fergus at high and low water. What at one time is an inland sea, is at the other a vast lake of mud rich in the constituents of fertility. As we reach this point of the river a mist arises compelling reduced speed, and as we pass by the upper station of the Slob Works a low range of corrugated iron shedding shines out suddenly through a break in the vapour, and, as the sun again pierces through, a long, low, dark line is seen stretching from the shore into the water like the extremity of some huge saurian of the Silurian period reposing on his native slime and ooze. But the lengthy monster lying in a vast curve is not at peace, for on the jagged ridge of his mighty back a puffing, snorting, smoking plague perpetually runs up and down. The apparent plague, however, is really increasing the size of the saurian. Every day hundreds of tons of stone are carried over his back-ridge and tipped into the water at the end of him, while scores of raftloads are flung into the water on the line staked and flagged out by the officials of the Government. Within a few weeks the growth of the saurian will not cease by day or night, until, as in the case of his kindred ophidian[22], his two extremities are brought together. For Mr Drinkwater has contracted with the British Electric Lighting Company to supply him with the electric light. The motive power is all ready, and no sooner is the apparatus fixed than county Clare will be astonished by the sight of work going on perpetually till it is completed, and amazement will reach its highest pitch. The people, gentle and simple, already confess themselves astonished at what can and has been done, and those who at first laughed are now seeking how they may best imitate.

As the tail of the saurian may be said to stretch into the water high above Islandavanna, so may his head be said to project from that pretty patch of verdure. Islandavanna is already a peninsula being connected with the mainland by a massive stone causeway, traversed every half-hour by a locomotive, hauling a train of trucks laden with stone, which, passing over the end of the island, runs out into the water to the "tip end," as it is called.

So the work is carried on, like modern railway tunnelling, from both ends simultaneously, and when head and tail of the saurian meet the first 1,500 acres will be reclaimed. The "slob" will be easy to drain, and it is tolerably certain that within twelve months the first instalment will be ready for cropping. It is a sight to make a Dutchman's mouth water - a "polder" of surpassing excellence, but it is viewed in a different light by enthusiastic wild duck shooters, who, like the owner of a grouse moor, look upon drainage and reclamation as the visible work of the devil. I do not think they need be alarmed for some time to come, for, without exaggeration, I have seen so many duck on the Fergus and the lower Shannon that I hesitate to speak of figures and incur the fate of Messer Marco Polo, who, when he spoke of the vast population of China, was nick-named by his incredulous countrymen "Marco Millione." But when I say that I have seen scores of flights a quarter

---

[22] relating to, or resembling snakes, [Clachan ed.].

of a mile long, that I have seen reaches of water so full of ducks and other water fowl that they looked like floating islands, I only give a faint idea of the quantity I have beheld between Islandavanna and the abortive ocean steam-packet port of Foynes.

Islandavanna is one of three stations of the reclamation works, and is occupied by about a third of the four hundred and fifty men now at work. In the summer seven hundred were employed, but the present season is not so favourable for getting stone and pushing on operations.

The electric light, however, will, it is hoped, help matters greatly, and redress the balance of the "long nights and short days." By the way, I saw at Islandavanna, or rather at the other end of the causeway which connects it with the mainland, a man who once employed that expression in the menacing manner I have previously alluded to, with the effect of causing the foreman of the works to seek occupation in another and far distant land. Owing to some disagreement the foreman had dismissed or suspended this man, who had already been tried for murder and acquitted. Hereat he took his gun to go snipe-shooting as he said, walked about lanes and generally hovered about the place in such threatening fashion that it was thought well to persuade the foreman to go away. At the present moment Mr Drinkwater and his friend Mr Johnstone, the civil engineer from whose plans the work is carried out, are on the best terms with the workpeople; but the process by which comfortable relations have been brought about has been gradual. It is not pretended that when labour is required, and there is money to pay for it, any prejudice is felt against the Saxon as an employer. Far from it. A downright, straightforward Saxon, even if he be a Protestant, is looked upon by the Irish working folk with far less suspicion than one of their own class, and there is little fear of their combining against him, for they are far more likely to quarrel amongst themselves.

It is hardly possible to convey more than the faintest idea of the rancour evolved by the jealousy of the Clare men against the Limerick men, of the hatred of both against a Galway man, and of the aversion of all three counties for Mayo and Donegal people. The citizens of the petty republics of Greece and Italy never abhorred each other more fervently. Now on large works with sub-contractors, gangers, artizans, and labourers, by piece and by day, it is no easy matter to keep matters going smoothly. It is needless to say that skilled artizans, such as engine-men and the like, are not picked up in county Clare; but no especial spite is felt against them. They are Englishmen, and that is sufficient; but if a gang of Clare men be dismissed and one of Limerick men taken on, there are signs of trouble in the air. Justice must be done to county Clare. Are the children of the soil to want bread while strangers eat it? For a Limerick man to the poor untravelled folk of Clare Castle, of Kilrush, and of Kilbaha is a stranger. Yet the small peasant cultivators on an islet near Islandavanna flatly refused to work at the "slob." Smoking a pipe and looking at a cow and calf grazing was a more congenial occupation, so they preferred staying at home. The slob work was too hard entirely. Now, this may appear incredible to those who have only seen the awakened Irishmen who do a vast quantity of the hardest and roughest kind of work in Great Britain and in the United States. In the latter country it is a matter of notoriety, supported in my own case by the evidence of my eyesight, that almost all the hard manual labour is performed by Irishmen and negroes. But downright steady hard work is just what the Western Irishman is not accustomed to at home. He will work nobly for a spurt, but when the spurt is over he loves to loiter and do as he likes.

It is no easy matter to found such a centre of industry as the works on the Fergus, but it is to be sincerely hoped that many such attempts will be made despite of discouragement. Experience has shown that the neglected and, in many localities, degraded West is abundantly capable of improvement. Mr Drinkwater determined to take the only way possible in these parts, that is, to feed and lodge his little army of workpeople, to establish a club for them, to give them a reading-room, to get porter for them at wholesale price - in short, to afford them every inducement to prefer the new settlements on the Fergus to the wretched huts and groggeries of Clare Castle and the surrounding villages. He insists, moreover, that every man shall have his half-pound of meat, either beef, mutton, or bacon, every day but Friday.

There is no pretence of philanthropy in all this. It is done on the ground that it is foolish to pay a man liberal wages, if he have to walk several miles to work and home again, and be allowed to live on a scant supply of potatoes and bread, washed down with too much of the whisky of the country. An ill-fed man can no more work well than an ill-fed horse, and inasmuch as the sooner the work is done the less interest will be paid on the Government loan, it is obviously important to get the work done as soon as possible. Hence high wages, on the condition that a certain proportion shall be spent on food and lodging, in a range of labourers' houses admirably built of iron lined with wood, perfectly warmed and lighted, and kept wonderfully clean. There are a store-house and a refectory, a cooking department and dormitories, perfectly ventilated and swept and garnished every day. Tea, beer, and other beverages except whisky can be obtained, and there is an abundant supply of books and newspapers. Every facility and encouragement is given to the priests to visit their people. In short, the colony on the Fergus Reclamation Works is one of the most extraordinary sights in the West of Ireland. As the entire work will hardly be completed under five or six years, the influence of such a community of people doing their work steadily and thoroughly ought to be very valuable.

Such works, as well as the reclamation of mountain and bog suggested and tried by Mr Mitchell Henry for the benefit of peasant cultivators, are absolutely required to quicken the industry of the languishing West. The poor people here require to be taught many things; notably to obey orders, to mind their own business, to hold their tongues, and to wash themselves; but it is impossible to expect four such virtues as obedience, industry, silence, and cleanliness to be acquired all at once by people who have been neglected for centuries. But there can be no radical defect in them, for they work hard enough in America, and under strict taskmasters too, for a Yankee farmer is like a Yankee skipper, inclined to pay good wages, but to insist on the money being earned. So far as discipline is concerned there is no better soldier or soldier-servant than a Western Irishman, none more patient under difficulty and privation, none so full of cheerfulness and resource. Probably the conditions of life are more favourable elsewhere, as they may easily be. Here in county Clare there seems to a perhaps too-hasty observer a complete want of social homogeneity. What lamps of refinement and intellectual culture burn here burn for each other only, and serve but to intensify the darkness around.

In no part of Ireland that I have seen are class distinctions more sharply defined. The landholding gentry are with but two or three exceptions Protestants, and, with the exception of Lord Inchiquin, are of English, Scotch, or Dutch descent, as such names as Vandeleur, Crowe, Stacpoole, and Burton indicate. I am not aware of the landed possessions of The O'Gorman Mahon, but I have already stated that his nephew holds only a moderate estate, let by the way at about three times the Government valuation - but not, I must add, necessarily, rack-rented, for Griffiths is, for reasons fully explained by a score of writers beside myself, a deceptive guide in grazing counties. The gentry of the county, however, are nearly all Protestant, and it is curious to note on Sunday at Ennis how the masters and their families go to one church and their servants to another. I am not insinuating that there is any sectarian squabbling. There is not, for the simple reason that the two classes of gentry and tradesfolk are too far apart to come into collision. On one side of a broad line stand the lords of the soil, of foreign descent, of Protestant religion, of exclusive social caste; on the other stand the people, the shop-keepers, the greater farmers and the peasants, all of whom are Irish Roman Catholics, and bound to each other by the ties of common religion, common descent, and often of actual kinship. There is, excepting perhaps a dozen professional men, no middle-class at all, through which the cultivation of the superior strata could permeate to the lower.

Probably no more difficult social condition ever presented itself. To show how completely the members of what ought to be a middle-class, I mean the large tenant-farmers, are identified with the peasant class, I may add that many of them, working with a capital of many thousands of pounds, are subscribers to the Land League, and that many are not paying their rent. Lord Inchiquin enjoys a good reputation as a landlord; but his tenants refuse to pay more than Griffith's valuation, and I hear that other great landlords in the county are not much more fortunate. What is most singular of all is that the middlemen, who are subletting and subdividing their holdings at tremendous rack-rents, are among the most prominent in refusing to pay the chief landlord. They see a great immediate advantage to themselves in the present movement, for they give but short credit to their tenants, while they enjoy the full benefit of a "hanging gale," or owing always half a year's rent, according to the custom of this county.

ENNIS, COUNTY CLARE, November 28th

The first news which greeted me on Friday night was, that, at a meeting of magistrates on Wednesday morning, Mr Richard Stacpoole had been persuaded to accept police protection, and that two men living at Ballygoree, near Ballyalla, had been taken out of their houses on Thursday night and severely taken to task for having committed the atrocity of paying their rent. The poor fellows urged, in extenuation, that they had the money, that they owed it, and that their holdings were not "set" at an extravagant price. All this availed them nothing. They were compelled to kneel down in the midst of the muddy road, in the dead of the night, and to solemnly swear never to behave so wickedly again, after which six guns were fired in a volley over their heads, and they were allowed to regain their houses.

The event which had drawn me back to Ennis was a meeting of the magistrates of Clare, specially called to consider the state of the county. A large attendance was looked for, and Saturday being market day in Ennis, two more things were certain - the first, that the town would be full of people, and the second, that the people would be full of whisky. A great crowd assembled to greet the magistrates on their arrival, but, owing to the meeting taking place two hours before the published time, a grand opportunity of hooting the more unpopular justices of the peace was lost, and the "makings of a shindy" evaporated in some sporadic groaning. There was a very large attendance of magistrates. Lord Inchiquin, the Lord-Lieutenant of the county, was present, as well as Mr Burton, of Carnelly; Mr T. Crowe, of Dromore; Colonel Macdonell; Mr Hall, of Cluny, who has outlived sundry attempts at assassination; Mr Dawson, of Bunratty; Mr Hewett; and thirty-eight other magistrates. The formal business of the day was got through without speechifying, and after some little consultation the following resolutions were adopted: -

First Resolution - That the state of lawlessness and intimidation at present existing in this county is such that the law is utterly unable to cope with it, and urgently demands the attention of her Majesty's Government.

Second Resolution - That the landowners, having hitherto shown the greatest forbearance, will doubtless now be compelled to take legal proceedings to enforce the payment of rent, in order to meet their own pressing obligations, and as this can only be done at the imminent risk of life we consider that the general peace of the county will very shortly be seriously endangered.

Third Resolution - That with a view to the maintenance of law and order we respectfully call on her Majesty's Government immediately to summon Parliament, in order to obtain such extraordinary powers as shall enable them to deal effectively with a conspiracy unprecedented in character, which aims at the total disorganization of society.

It is quite possible that these resolutions may produce some astonishment in England, especially now that it is well known that nothing beyond a special emergency will induce the Government to adopt coercive measures. But things said and done in the West of Ireland are apt to be somewhat after date. Still the resolutions of the Clare magistrates have their value as giving a tolerably clear idea of what may be designated the landlord mind. Minute subdivisions set aside, there are at least four ways of looking at the subject of the day in this part of Ireland. There is the view of a great landlord who, because he helped his people with food during the potato famine and with money to emigrate with afterwards, and has spent a little money here and there out of a huge income, thinks he has amply discharged his duty to his tenants. It is true that he began by charging them 4 and 5 per cent, respectively on building and drainage improvements, a tolerably round percentage; but it is fair to admit that for several years past he has not charged more than 2½ per cent, for such improvements as he has made. The great landlords of this county are less attacked than others by popular orators, mainly because their rents are not exorbitantly high in the first place. The land is let on lease for terms as long sometimes as sixty-four years, and is sometimes underlet at greatly increased prices to the ultimate tenants, whose precarious condition brings the "head" landlord into undeserved odium. The great landholders and their agents maintain that to quote Griffiths[23] against a landlord who has spent money in improvements since that valuation was made, and let his farms so low that other people can relet them at a profit, is a manifest absurdity.

Another practical view of the landlord mind is that it is foolish to go on borrowing money under the Act of 1879 during the present uncertain condition of tenure and impossibility of getting in rents. Hence the Scariff drainage works, for which £34,000 was to be borrowed by the owners of the

---

[23] Griffith's Valuation was an evaluation of property values used controversially by tenants against landlords to seek lower rents, [Clachan ed.].

property affected by the scheme, have been suddenly abandoned, and will not be carried any further, at least during the present winter. One consequence of this decision will be to throw a large number of people out of employ, who must either leave Clare or ask for relief.

The first order of the landlord mind, however, is, to do it justice, not affected very seriously by the present crisis. The great landholders of Clare and Limerick are not in a heavily mortgaged or downright insolvent condition. Like the wealthy manufacturer during a strike, they do not care either to employ or to threaten harsh measures against their tenants. There is time enough for the present agitation to subside, as others have subsided, and if the Government should wish to acquire their land and disestablish "landlordism," as Mr Parnell suggests, so much the better, especially since it has become manifest by the example of the Marquis of Conyngham's estate that purchasers, other than tenants, are hardly to be found for Irish property. And - as the agent of a great absentee landholder observed to me - of what avail would it be to proceed to ulterior measures against the tenants? Granted that all the weary delays of the local courts were got rid of by a Dublin writ, what would be the consequence? The tenant would, unless he chose to spend his own ready money to defend his case in Dublin, be swiftly ejected - that is, if sufficient police were requisitioned to make any attempt at resistance absurd. The landlord would get his own after a fashion; but unless he chose to keep a force of police on his farms the dispossessed tenants would be reinstated and their houses rebuilt by the mob; and nothing would be got in the shape of rent. As no person in the possession of his senses would take any farm from which a tenant had been evicted, the landlord would have only one course to pursue. He must farm his land himself, and then he would be "isolated" or "Boycotted." Nobody would work for him; nobody would buy anything from his farms.

Everybody in Ennis knows the case of Littleton, whose farm is now under "taboo," and whose oats no man dare buy, and the similar case of a draper who had sold some material to a man working on the "Boycotted" farm, and was compelled to take it back. "There is nothing now," added another informant, "but to touch your hat to tenants, for they have left off doing so to you. And it is folly to talk of reprisals, or of persevering in hunting and going armed to the meet. Suppose an affray occurred and I shot a tenant, I should be most assuredly identified, tried, convicted, and severely punished, if not hanged. But if a tenant shot me it would be difficult to identify him, more difficult to arrest him, and downright impossible to convict him. Since Lord O'Hagan's Jury Act it is quite impossible to get convictions against the lower orders - witness the memorable instance of Mr Creagh, when the assassin's gun burst and blew his finger off. The prisoner and his finger were both in court, there was no manner of doubt, and yet the jury acquitted him."

Thus far the greater landowner or his agents. The tone is one of patient, if not amused, endurance, mingled, of course, with profound contempt for the personnel of the Land League. But the smaller and resident landlord is of much more inflammable stuff. A strike against rent-paying signifies to him an end of all supplies. Whether he have two thousand or five thousand a year in land - for I omit the little "squireen" class as of no importance on either side of the question - he has almost certainly settlements and probably mortgages on his estate. Now, mortgagees in Dublin or London are not at all ready to take into account the difficulty of collecting rents in Connaught, and insist on being paid.

Even their rancour, however, has moderated slightly just of late, for they are as afraid to foreclose on unsaleable property as the mortgagor is of losing his claim on it for ever. But the settlements must be paid, and as no rents are coming in, dowagers are obdurate, and the landlord lives well up to his means, times are hard just now in county Clare.

It is not exactly "tyranny" which inclines the lesser landlord to get the rent out of his tenant, but his own need, which drives him to extreme measures. In bitterness of spirit he bewails his dulness in not following the example of some of his peers in getting rid of their tenantry and farming their land themselves, like Colonel Barnard in King's County. He also envies the lot of Mr "Tom" Crowe, of Dromore, who, without acquiring the name of an "exterminator" or a "tyrant," has succeeded in shaking off the load of teeming population and the abomination of "duty work" by degrees, and has now a magnificent farm of his own which might bear the inspection of Mr Clare Read himself, and of all Norfolk to boot. Mr Crowe, too, has not gone through the ordeal of being shot at like Colonel Barnard, and if not specially loved by the people, has no kind of quarrel with them. Mr Burton, of Carnelly, who owns 9,669 acres in Clare, has been fortunate in getting some rent, mainly in consequence of his tact in driving round one day to collect it himself and taking his tenants by surprise. But Mr Burton is an exception, both in tact and fortune, to the majority of landlords of the second rank. Colonel Vandeleur has been very unfortunate, like all landholders encumbered with what would be called small farmers in England. The few really large farmers in Clare, as a rule, have paid up either openly or privately, and in sentiment are quite with the landlord class. The lesser landlords are talking of nothing but Dublin writs, and declare that the so-called peace of the county is only unbroken because no attempt is made to execute the law.

The farmers are of course peaceful enough so long as they are permitted to send a rich harvest to market, to pocket the proceeds, and to pay no rent. "But," said a small landholder to me, "is this law and order? Because I know it is hopeless at this moment to recover my rent, and therefore abstain from proceedings, does it follow that the peace would not be broken were I to put the law into operation?" I am sorry for this gentleman, for I know that he is what is called in commerce a "weak holder," or one who can afford neither to conduct his business with a firm hand nor to throw it aside till better times. He must go on, for he has mortgages and settlements on his estates; and, admitted that his tenants would go away to-morrow without any trouble, he could not spare what they owe him, and assuredly would not find new tenants for his farms. He of course is for the immediate suspension of the Habeas Corpus Act, and declares that to be the most merciful solution of the immediate difficulty. To him the "Three F's[24]" appear altogether diabolical, and he proposes the substitution of "Three D's" - Disarmament, Disfranchisement, and a Dictator, the more military the better.

From the medium and smaller farmers, who with the whisky dealers and the majority of the other tradespeople form the opposite camp, I hear that no measure that the Government can pass before the present Parliament will be acceptable to what is called the Irish people. It is now averred that the extension of the borough franchise to counties must be carried before a Parliament adequate to deal with the Irish question is formed. This appears a strong demand, and one likely to protract the present distracted state of the country. But I hear, on the best authority, that the Land League and the associated farmers can wait. They are in no hurry. England can take her own time and they will wait patiently, meanwhile of course paying no rent, nor any other debts which may prove inconvenient.

Having passed their resolutions, the magistrates drive off quietly enough - but by daylight. Within the last three weeks the County Club sittings have been earlier than usual, the members thinking it at least as well to get home before dark. The valedictory wish expressed here just now is of itself ominous. It is not "Good-bye" or "Good-night," but "Safe home."

---

[24] Demands first issued by the Tenant Right League and taken up by the Land League - Fair rent, free sale, fixity of tenure, [Clachan ed.].

X - PALLAS AND THE PALLADIANS

LIMERICK.

In a previous letter I hinted that the well-to-do farmers of the West were not a whit more prompt in paying their rent than the starveling peasants of Mayo and Connemara, who, at the best, are barely able to keep body and soul together. Trusting far more to what I see than to what I hear, I become aware that in these troubled districts of Ireland, it is precisely the most favoured spots which are the most mutinous. Ballina, the most prosperous town in Mayo, is a stronghold of the anti-landlord party; and the Ballinrobe, Claremorris, and Cong country, full of good land and comparatively large farmers, is the district which has isolated Mr Boycott, whose turnips and potatoes will probably cost the country and the county at least a guinea a piece. In no part of Mayo or Galway is the Land League more perfectly organised than in Clare, yet the farmers in that county are confessedly well off. There are some of course towards the sea, in the direction of Loop Head, who are poorly off, but the great majority are by no means in evil case. Ocular demonstration of this fact is supplied by the numerous farmhouses of the better class with which the country is studded. These are not merely large cabins, but houses, some of which are whitewashed. The haggards are full of corn-stacks, the rich pastures are full of kine. There is every visible evidence of material prosperity. It is true that when one has driven up the private road, be the same a mere "boreen" or a "shplendid avenue," the bell is found to be broken, the knocker wrenched off, the blinds hauled up awry, and the servants hard to be got at; but the householder is prosperous nevertheless. His larder is well supplied with poultry and wild fowl, his cellar contains "lashings," not only of "Parliament and pot," or "John Jamieson" and illicit "potheen," but of port and sherry, claret and champagne. His daughters are at the costly training schools of the *Sacre Coeur*, his lads are studying law in Dublin. Yet this man is a subscriber to the Land League either by sympathy or, as is quite as probable, by terror.

Farmers of not quite such large acreage live in almost equally luxurious style. Their houses, that is the "show" rooms, are solidly if tastelessly furnished. Their horses and jaunting cars carry them to chapel; they live in the midst of rude plenty. If further demonstration be needed, I will point to the groceries and wine stores of Ennis. There are at least three of these almost on the scale of Fortnum and Mason's or Hedges and Butler's. Now Ennis is what an American traveller might be tempted to call a "one-horse" town of some six or seven thousand inhabitants, yet its grocery and drapery stores would hardly be beaten in York or Chester. Every imaginable eatable or drinkable can be obtained always for ready money, and very often on credit, and I am informed that all articles of feminine adornment, including cosmetics, are also to be had. Passing still farther from the domain of things seen to that of things heard of, I am assured on the best authority that for years past the banks have not held so much money on deposit as at the present moment. Yet nobody pays his rent. The form of offering Griffith's valuation is gone through, albeit it is known that that calculation is absolutely untrustworthy so far as a pasture county like Clare is concerned.

My remarks concerning county Clare will apply, almost with greater force, to county Limerick. The city is of course a very different place from Ennis; but it is impossible to avoid noticing from the window at which I sit writing the crowds of purchasers streaming in and out of Cannock and Co.'s store, from late in the morning till early in the evening. I use the last words advisedly, for the people of the West seem to have accepted Charles Lamb's humorous quibble in good faith. If they begin work later than any other civilized people, they assuredly leave off earlier. But until evening sets in there is a torrent of customers pouring in over the way, and wooing the eye from the contemplation of the Shannon at the Thomond Bridge. Of the groggeries of Limerick and of the poison vended in them, I will forbear to discourse, for my business just now is with the country rather than with the town.

Having heard much of the outrages at Pallas on the Tipperary border, I determined to drive over and visit the scene of action. For this country the journey was a short one; fifteen or sixteen miles out and in on an outside car is thought a mere trifle in Limerick. The trip occupied the entire day nevertheless. As we drove out of Limerick past the great pig-slaughtering and curing houses, we soon became aware that an immense convergence of the farming interest on Limerick was taking place. Car-load after car-load of well-dressed people passed us, and then came horsemen riding in couples or by half-dozens. For the most part the cavaliers were very well mounted, and also well and warmly dressed in the fashion of the day. Neither Connemara nor Claddagh cloaks were seen in the cars, nor were the blue or grey frieze swallow-tailed coats of Mayo and Galway seen on the powerful horses pounding along townward through the heavy road. All was sleek, prosperous, and quite modern, and was as refreshing to look upon after the frieze and flannel aforesaid as the green hills of Limerick and Clare after the brown mountains of Joyce's country. I naturally asked the meaning of such an important meeting of well-to-do folk. It was a funeral. An old lady was to be buried, and the whole country-side for twenty miles around had turned out to do honour to the deceased, and to enjoy a holiday on the principle that "a wake is better than a wedding." Not one in a hundred of those who rode by had paid his rent, nor was he prepared to pay more than Griffith's valuation, although he might have a deposit note for one, two, or more thousands of pounds in his cash-box.

Pushing along this lively road we entered a famous part of Ireland, the Golden Vale, so called from its great fertility. Great part of the land here is composed of alluvial bottoms, a large area of which was drained by the Mullkear Cut, through the exertions of Mr William Bredin, of Castlegard, a charming old fortress overgrown with creepers, and standing like a sentry over the more modern part of the dwelling. As we neared Pallas I was reminded that I was on classic ground, and that Old and New Pallas and Pallas Green formed the scene of the never-to-be-forgotten feud of the "Three and Four Year Olds," the tradition whereof hath a rich and racy savour. Readers of the Daily News will hardly need to be reminded that this historic vendetta commenced with a dispute concerning the age of a bull, one disputant maintaining that the animal was four, while the other insisted he was but three years old. The matter was settled, or was rather put on the footing of a "mighty pretty quarrel," by a desperate fight, wherein one of the combatants was either slain or grievously maimed, whereupon his cause was taken up by his family and friends, and a feud inaugurated which lasted many years, and led to the death of a considerable number of persons, besides continual "diversion" in the way of faction fights. Pallas is in the midst of the Golden Vale, a deliciously pastoral country, admirably fitted on such a glorious spring-like morning as that of yesterday for the sports of shepherds and shepherdesses as Watteau and Lancret loved to limn. But the first object which catches the eye in Pallas is not a bower of ribbons and roses, but a stiff-looking police barrack. Close at hand is the railway station, another unlovely edifice, and lounging about in groups are seventy or eighty of the gloomiest and most sullen-looking people I have seen in this country. The very little cheerfulness there is in Connaught is quite absent from Munster, or at least the Tipperary border of county Limerick. I learn that the occasion of this general loafing is a "rent-gathering," or rather an attempt to gather rent, and that Mr Sanders, the agent for the Erasmus Smith School Trusts, is sitting, but not in receipt of custom. There has been the usual talk of Griffith's valuation and the usual result of not a shilling being paid; the present fear on the part of landlords of fixity of tenure being established being so great that nobody will accept payment according to Griffith lest his receipt should be taken as permanently settling the value of his land for ever. No money passes, as a matter of course, and the tenants mutter among themselves, "nor ever will." One neck-or-nothing friend of the people assures me that Griffith and rent and the rest of it is all "botheration," and that Pallas folk are going to "have their own" again, as was once said of a Stuart king, who did not get it nevertheless. I am not assuming that the opinion of a farmer anxious to get rid of his principal debt is that of all Munster; I merely give his observation for what it is worth, and as a sign that the hope of concession is gradually enlarging demand.

Driving in the direction of Castlegard, I pass the signs of an eviction which took place at least a fortnight ago. The outgone tenant's bedsteads and wash-hand-stands are piled up against the wall as if crying to Heaven for vengeance against the oppressor. The display strikes me as entirely theatrical, for it is well known that vengeance is not left to Heaven by Pallas people, but confided to Snider bullets[25]. The bailiff's left in charge of the house have been attacked, and yesterday an iron hut for lodging four policemen on the disputed property was brought to Pallas station. It went no further, however, for neither horse nor cart could be got to convey any fragment of the accursed fabric to the spot required. It is expected that the district will, after this display of "tyranny" on the part of the police, "strike" against them and refuse to supply them with food or forage. Pursuing the road past Castlegard I meet another crowd of tenants and learn that they also have been to a rent gathering, and have been offered acceptance of Griffith's valuation if the balance between that and the rent be considered as a "reduction" without prejudice to further arrangements, and without fixing a standard of value. This proposition remains under consideration, and is favourably viewed by the tenants. It seems, however, that everybody is afraid, or pretends to be afraid, to act without the sanction of the Land League. I am vastly inclined to think that in many parts of the country farmers pretend to be more scared than they really are, but around Castlegard they have evidently some cause for alarm. I called upon a farmer who has committed the unpardonable crime of failing to be, as Ouida[26] would say, "true to his order." He has been so lost to all the sentiments of manhood and of patriotism as to pay his rent. No sooner was it known that he was guilty of this dastardly deed than he was spoken of as a marked man, and three nights ago a Snider bullet was fired through his front door into the hall of his newly-built house. I saw the hole made by the bullet through the door, and also the mark where it tore out a piece of the balusters before striking the ceiling.

The farmer in question is one of those extraordinary persons who only exist in Ireland. He is a sturdy, pleasant-looking man of forty, and has made his way despite what would appear intolerable difficulties. He has farmed for some considerable time about thirty-three acres of good land, and must have worked hard, for during that time he has had a large family to maintain. His father died but a short time since, and reduced the number by one, but he now supports his mother and his aged aunt and uncle, as well as his wife and himself and six children. With all these mouths to feed he has built him, well and solidly, a thoroughly good house, with extensive outbuildings and other improvements, obviously worth many hundreds of pounds. It might be thought the people of Pallas and Castlegard would have been proud of him; but he has paid his rent, and is marked for "taboo," if for nothing worse.

---

[25] The Snider-Enfield rifle [Clachan ed.].
[26] Pseudonym of the English novelist Maria Louise Ramé, [Clachan ed.].

Trudging across some fine pastures, and jumping sundry ditches, we regain the main road and our car, and proceed on that instrument of torture back to Pallas. Here we find the "threes" and the "fours," not at issue with each other, but united like brothers against the common enemy. Fearful howls arise from the railway bridge and the railway station, both covered with Palladians, male and female. A thoroughly good Irish yell of execration acts differently on different persons. The blood of those unaccustomed to it is apt to turn cold at the savage sound; but, with a little practice, "the ear becomes more Irish and less nice," and a good howl acts as a stimulant on the spirits of many landlords and agents. All the screeching at Pallas is brought about by the departure of Mr Sanders, who, escorted by the police till he is safely off, rentless, but undismayed, slips away in the train, leaving the "Threes" and "Fours" to talk the matter over, not unaided by the presence, in the spirit, of all-powerful "John Jamieson."

TIPPERARY, Tuesday Night.

Another proof has been given that it takes more people to do less in Ireland than in any other country in the world. The attitude of the combined "Three and Four Year Olds" was yesterday so threatening that the authorities decided that the police-hut at Pallas could only be erected in the teeth of the Palladians by dint of an overwhelming display of force. There is no doubt of the wisdom of this policy. A small force, insufficient to overawe the country side, only provokes the resistance it is unable to overcome, but a strong detachment of redcoats thoroughly cows the adventurous spirits of the most mutinous localities. What threatened at one moment to become a civil war in Mayo was put down without the loss of a drop of blood by an imposing military force, and the lesson so well illustrated at Ballinrobe is hardly likely to be lost in other rebellious districts. Yesterday, the affair at Pallas came to such a pitch that extraordinary measures were resolved upon.

A bailiff had been shot because he, in the execution of his duty, occupied the dwelling of an evicted farmer, one Burke; hence it was decided that a police-hut should be built on the ground lately occupied by Burke, but, as readers of the Daily News are aware, the Palladians actually struck against the police, and proceeded to "Boycott" those "myrmidons" after the most approved manner. Not only did Pallas refuse to aid in conveying the materials for a police-hut to a short distance from the railway station, but prevented the police from doing their work themselves. Yesterday, the whole border-folk of county Limerick and county Tipperary turned up at Pallas, and the conduct of the crowd was such as to lead persons by no means of an alarmist character to expect an ugly morrow. The authorities had determined that a police-hut should be erected on the spot chosen, and the populace had equally made up their minds that although "the makings" of a hut had been brought to Pallas railway station, they should remain there, and never be allowed to defile the land of Burke's farm. The police, despite their barrack, which looks strong enough to bear a siege, were obviously unable to quell the people, and it would hardly have been politic to let the latter enjoy a victory; consequently it was determined to employ the military to convoy the police-hut, or rather its *disjecta membra*[27], from the railway to its proposed site.

It was pitch dark at five o'clock this morning, the hour for parade at the fine new barracks at Tipperary. The air, too, was keen, and the detachment of the gallant 48th Regiment ordered for service at Pallas paraded in no very affectionate spirit towards the Palladians. The ill-humour of the 48th is easily accounted for. After twelve years' service abroad no regiment would be cheered by the announcement that instead of Portsmouth its destination was Queenstown, en route for Tipperary. Such, however, has been the fate of the unlucky 48th, from whom the mob of Pallas, or any other centre of mutiny, could expect but little mercy. Tempers, however, brightened at sunrise, and by the time the hundred men under the command of Captain Cartwright and Lieutenants Fraser and Maycock arrived at the Tipperary station every one was in a good-humoured, contemptuous frame of mind. Everybody knew that there was no chance of a row, and that the very presence of all the Queen's horses and all the Queen's men would make it certain that a blank would be drawn. The whole military plan of campaign had been well imagined. While the 48th came on from Tipperary the 9th came on also by rail from Limerick, together with a half battery of the Royal Artillery. It must not, however, be supposed that cannon was deemed necessary to quell the ardent spirits of Pallas. The guns were left at Limerick, and only the waggons brought as a means of conveyance for the makings of the hut. But the Limerick contingent was imposing nevertheless. It consisted of 105 men of the 9th Regiment, of a squadron of Hussars, who went by road, and of the artillery before-mentioned, who came, like the infantry, by rail. So well was the movement timed by Colonel Humphreys, R.A., in command, that the trains from Tipperary and Limerick met almost exactly at New Pallas station a little before nine o'clock this morning, just as the busbies of the Hussars appeared upon the bridge. Pallas was evidently taken by surprise, for any movement on a western Irish town before nine in the morning may be taken as a night attack. The people of the border of county Limerick and county Tipperary are quite ready to "muster in their thousands" at a convenient hour, but they are sure to be taken at a disadvantage before nine o'clock. The Palladians rubbed their eyes to find the classic battle-ground of the "Three Year Olds" and "Four Year Olds" occupied by the matutinal redcoats, and horse, foot, and artillery already in possession. As Pallas woke up about a hundred and fifty or a couple of

---

[27] scattered remains, [Clachan ed.].

hundred roughs made up "the name of a crowd," but those in command were informed that this poor show of resistance was really a feint, and that no sooner would the materials for the hateful hut be put in motion than a rush would be made by the people collected "in thousands" behind the village, either upon the railway station or upon the convoy in motion. I had no opportunity of getting round behind the village to review the supposed thousands who were to make the ugly rush and overwhelm the redcoats, but I have a strong impression that the Palladian army might have been dubbed the "Mrs Harris" brigade. With the respected Mrs Prigg, I disbelieve in its existence absolutely. Two arguments will destroy it. On the one hand, it is incredible that thousands of persons were out of their beds at ten minutes to nine A.M.; on the other, if they had sat up all night in the hope of a fight with the police they would most certainly have anticipated that diversion by a preliminary "shindy" among themselves, and have broken up in disorder.

But when horse, foot, artillery, and police converge on a disaffected spot, it is hardly the province of their commander to disbelieve in the existence of an enemy. Colonel Humphreys accordingly made the wisest use of his forces. He had at his disposal 200 infantry, a squadron of cavalry, a demi-battery of artillery, and 70 armed constables - in all about 350 men. His first care was to secure his base, the railway station, and this point *d'appui* was strongly garrisoned by the 48th Regiment. Then the road between the station and Burke's farm was strongly patrolled - so strongly as to keep up an unbroken line of communication between the farm and the railroad. When this was established, the procession, bearing the materials of the hut, set forth. First went the armed police, then an escort of Hussars, and then the Artillery waggons, carrying the pieces of the hut, guarded by the soldiers of the 9th Regiment. It is hardly necessary to add that no attempt at rushing or crowding the station was made by the populace. Father Ryan, the parish priest, behaved in the most praiseworthy manner, and exhorted the people to be quiet; but my own impression is that they were already completely cowed by the sudden appearance of the military from two quarters at once. By no means wanting in keenness of perception, they knew that, if ordered to do so, the soldiers will fire "at" them, and not vaguely, after the manner of the police. So the whole affair passed off quietly, and after trebling the ordinary police garrison of Pallas, the military returned to their respective quarters.

A beginning has been made of building the hut, and at the moment of writing (9 P.M.) all is quiet at Old and New Pallas, as well as at Pallas Green. Whether the blood of the "Threes" and "Fours" will endure the sight of the detested hut gradually rising on the farm of the sainted Burke remains to be seen; but it is doubtful whether the "Boys" will attempt a *coup de main*. Should such an attempt be made, the police would be compelled to make a desperate resistance, and serious consequences would certainly ensue. There is a curious contrast between the state of the "Three and Four Year Olds" yesterday and to-day - between the bragging of the one and the cowed look of the other. There is also something of amusement, were not the entire question all too serious, in the sudden and contemptuous withdrawal of the troops to-day, after having shown the Palladians that, however they felt about the hut, it should be built, and law and order maintained "maugre[28] their teeth."

[28] in spite of, [Clachan ed.].

XI - GOMBEEN

CORK, December 2nd.

Among the many spectres which haunt the sadly-vexed West and South of Ireland, there is one far more grim and real than the *spectre vert* who is either buried for ever and aye, or has undergone gradual transformation since '98 into Repeal of the Union, Young Ireland, Fenianism, Nationalism, and finally perhaps into Anti-Landlordism; albeit this latter avatar of an ancient and familiar spirit is by no means imbued with the poetic attributes of the original spectre. During my stay in Ennis and Limerick I succeeded in holding somewhat protracted conversations with three landed proprietors, three of the largest land-agents in Ireland, two bank managers, an influential lawyer, three leaders of the people, and one probable assassin. Through the discourse of all of these - varied and contradictory as much of it necessarily was - I could see distinctly one ugly shadow, as of an old man filthy of aspect, hungry of eye, and greedy of claw, sitting in the rear of a gloomy store looking over papers by the light of a miserable tallow dip. From the papers the figure turned to a heap as of bank-notes, and there was in the air the chink of money. For the name of this grisly and terribly real spectre is gombeen; which, in the Irish tongue, signifies usury.

To Thackeray's truthful remark that there is never so poor an Irishman that he has not a still poorer countryman as a hanger-on, it may be added that when an Irishman is not a borrower he is almost certain to be a lender - the advice of Polonius being abhorrent to the spirit of a free-and-easy, happy-go-lucky people. When a man in these parts gets or keeps out of debt himself, he is mostly engaged in encouraging others to get into it. Often he has little or nothing himself, but acts after the Irish fashion as deputy gombeen man for the pleasure of the thing, and also for a commission well and duly paid. This determination towards borrowing and lending is not confined to any particular class, but is characteristic of all. As the peer, who would never have put his hand into his own pocket to pay for improving his property, suddenly awakes to the value of drainage when the Government offers a million and a half at one per cent., so did the gombeen man, who would never have dreamed of lending more than a pound at a time to a peasant, extend his credit four or five fold when the Land Act of 1870 gave him the first instalment of proprietary right in the land he occupied. The instalment was a very small one, but it was at once discounted by the gombeen man, whose rate of interest enabled him to run extraordinary risks. As the poor pay dearly for everything, so do they pay an extravagant interest for money. There was once a fashionable West-end usurer, who, pretending to know nothing about arithmetic, met his clients on the subject of percentage with "I don't understand figures, but my terms are a shilling per pound every month. It is easy to reckon up without going into sums on

102

slates." This poor innocent was charging just 60 per cent., but his terms were lavishly liberal as compared with those of the gombeen man. Instead of a shilling per month the latter charges a shilling a week for every sovereign advanced, and then "Begorra, it's only the name of a sovereign," which being interpreted signifies that an advance of one pound, less charges, only amounts to 18s. 10d., and that upon this sum a shilling interest must be well and duly paid weekly. Any failure entails a fine, and a failure to pay off the original sovereign borrowed within six months is very heavily fined indeed. I am told that the gombeen man actually puts on cent. per cent. for this failure of redemption; but, on my principle of believing only a percentage of all I hear, and of taking a liberal discount off all I see, I doubt this enormity. Concerning the shilling interest per week on a pound there is, however, unhappily no room for doubt, and for small unsecured loans 260 per cent. per annum is still the ruling figure.

This enormous rate of interest, however, is now only exacted on the very smallest loans, for the old-fashioned gombeen man has lost his customers for larger sums. In old times he was the only means of obtaining such little sums as five and ten pounds on personal security; but since 1870 the banks have entered into competition with him, have undersold him, and, in fact, "run him out of the market," except for sums under four or five pounds. The unfortunates who are short of a sovereign or two must look up their old friend in the back shop smelling of bacon, tallow, pepper, tea, and whisky, just as their social superiors seek the intrepid sixty per cent. man of St. James's, whose snuggery is perfumed by the best Havannahs that other people's money can buy. But when the soul of Mike rises to the sublime conception of a loan of five pounds he dismisses the old-fashioned usurer, and hies him to one of the branch banks which abound in every petty townlet in Western and Southern Ireland. When I say "abound" I mean to be taken literally. What would be thought in England, I wonder, of four banks in a town like Ennis, or of two in pettifogging places like Kilrush or Ennistymon - mere hamlets of some two thousand inhabitants? Yet these three places have eight branch banking establishments among them. It must not, however, be supposed that Mike gets his paltry four or five pounds on his promissory note without further security. Nothing of the kind. Mike must go through as much artful financiering to raise his five pounds as the Hon. Algernon Deuceace[29] to raise his "monkey." His bill must be well backed by his friends, Thady and Tim. Now, Thady's name on the back of a five-pound bill is not good for much. He is but a peasant, like Mike, not a farmer, properly so called, and even as two blacks will not make a white, so will the joint credit of Mike and Thady not rise to the height of five one-pound notes. But they have a potent ally in Tim, who married Thady's wife's

---

[29] a character in novel by William Makepeace Thackeray, [Clachan ed.].

cousin. Tim is a prudent man, has worked hard at his farm, and, as a rule, has a matter of twenty or thirty pounds on deposit note at the bank, receiving for the same interest at the rate of one per cent. per annum. His name at the back of a five-pound bill is therefore a tower of strength, and, in fact, floats the entire speculation. In commercial phrase, he "stands to be shot at" while his own deposit money, on which he receives one per cent., supplies the funds for the bank to lend Mike and Thady, at ten or twenty per cent., for there is no pretence made of doing very small bills at anything approaching ordinary rates. In fact, the peasant cultivator, having acquired under the Land Acts now in force a species of proprietory interest in the soil, has a sort of credit which, backed by a friendly and innocent depositor, can be made an engine for raising ready money in a small way. This help from the banks is so far good that it has relieved the decent peasant from his ancient bloodsucker, the gombeen man. Admitting that with charges and fine for renewal and so forth the loan ultimately costs Mike fifteen or twenty per cent, he is vastly better off than he was under the old system. He gets money to buy pigs to fatten for sale, or manure for his bit of arable land, and if the rate appears high, it is wondrously merciful as compared with that to which he was formerly accustomed.

But there is an awkward side even to the business which enables the principal Irish banks to pay large dividends. So long as care is taken that Mike and Thady do not overdo the accommodation bill system, perhaps no very great harm is done in extending the advantage of moderate credit to the humblest cultivator; but when competition is sharp in a petty townlet between two rival banks, the tendency towards a mischievous extension of credit is almost irresistible, and bank managers are at last driven to look sharply after their clients on market days, lest the ready money which is their due should be deflected to other purposes. The provision man, who has supplied bacon and other necessaries, is on the alert to secure something on account; and if, as is most probable, he has been giving credit somewhat recklessly, he is pinched for money, despite the high rate of profit he has been charging to cover his risk. For some time past the game of credit has been going on gaily; but since the commencement of the present agitation both banks and gombeen men have distinctly narrowed their operations, and the landlord is now the almost universal creditor. The harvest-money has either gone to pay advances or to settle accounts with tradesfolk, so that an awkward future is in preparation for all but the prosperous tenants, of whom there is no lack in counties Clare and Limerick. Whatever the details of the forthcoming Land Act may be when it has passed the ordeal of both Houses of Parliament, the work of passing it will take time, and at least another half-year's rent will accrue before it takes the shape of law. Now, with all the talk of Griffith's valuation, there has been, except in a few cases, no hint of paying that sum "without prejudice" into court or into any bank whatsoever; and the cash held by both farmers and peasants runs, in the opinion of many well qualified to judge, sore risk of diminution before any comprehensive measure can pass through Parliament. Even the well-to-do farmers will be called upon to expend their balance in hand in many ways which they will find difficult to resist. Not only the provision merchants, but the drapers and milliners of Limerick, Ennis, and Galway, will hold out allurements to those in possession of ready money. To put the case briefly, there is great danger that, without any intentional dishonesty on their part, the cultivators, great and small, of Western and South-Western Ireland will hardly be in as good a position for the discharge of their liabilities six months or a year hence as they are at present. The three "F's" will hardly wipe off existing debt, and the result of a division of the population into two sharply defined classes of debtors and creditors is viewed by many thoughtful people with considerable apprehension.

XII - THE RETAINER

CORK, December 4th

In describing the character of the Western and Southern Irishman nothing would be more unfair than to leave out of the estimate his curious faithfulness to some persons, and the tenderness with which he cherishes the traditions of the past. In no country in the world is the superstition concerning the "good old times" more fervently believed in than in Western and Southern Ireland. And in the opinion of the mass of the people the good old times extended down to a recent date. One is asked to believe that before the period of the potato famine Ireland was the abode of plenty if not of peace, and that landlords and tenants blundered on together on the most amicable terms. It is hardly necessary to state that the golden age of Ireland, like the golden age of every other country, never had any real existence. It is like the good old-fashioned servant who from the time of Terence to our own has always lived in the imaginary past, but never in the real present. The belief in a recent golden age is, however, so prevalent in Ireland that I have thought it worth while to investigate the grounds on which it is based and the means by which it has been kept fresh and green.

The first fact which strikes the observer is that since the potato famine the West and South have been going through a period of transition still in progress. Under the authority of the Encumbered Estates Court a vast area of land has changed hands, and the new proprietors have only in rare cases succeeded in securing the affection of their tenants and neighbours, who sit "crooning" over the fire, extolling the virtues of the "ould masther" and comparing him with the new one, very much to the disadvantage of the latter. It is not remarkable that such comparisons should be instituted. The people have very little to do, and do that in a slovenly, slip-shod way, and they have therefore plenty of leisure for gossip. As they are ignorant of everything beyond their own county, it is only natural that the new proprietor or lessee should be discussed at great length, and all his acts and deeds be fully commented upon. And it is not remarkable that the judgment should be adverse to the new man. He is generally North Irish, Scotch, or English. The two former are hated at once, at a venture; but the "domineering Saxon" is given a chance, and with a little tact and good temper can secure, if not affection, at least toleration.

But it is not easy to get the good word of the people, even when one is neither a "tyrant" oneself nor the lessee of an "exterminator;" for the ways of the most just and generous of the new men do not suit those of the natives like the system, or rather want of system, of the old chiefs. Even when a demesne only is leased by a "foreigner," and all risk of quarrelling with tenants is thus avoided, it is hard work to achieve popularity. As I drove up the avenue of a dwelling thus inhabited, I asked the driver what he and the country-side thought of the new tenant of the old house. "A good man, your honour," was the cold answer; followed by an enthusiastic, "Och, but it was the ould masther that was the good man! Sorra the bite or sup any one wanted while he was to the fore!" Now, the "ould masther" was, I understand, a worthy gentleman, of good old county family, who lived in the midst of his tenantry for several months every year, and "kept up his old mansion at a bountiful old rate," like a fine old "Celticised Norman," as he was. Like the descendants of the early settlers described by Mr Froude, he and his had retained their popularity by concessions to Celtic habits, not in religion or personal conduct be it understood, but in letting things go on easily, in a happy-go-lucky way, without any superstitions concerning the profuse employment of soap and water by their dependents. Probably no lady of the house had for many generations entered the kitchen, which apparently served as a focus for the country folk. The stone floor was a stranger to hearthstone and to water, except such as might be spilt upon it; and was either slippery or sticky here and there, according to the nature of the most recent deposits. The table and dressers were in such a condition when taken over by the "domineering Saxon" that washing was abandoned as hopeless, and scraping and planing were perforce resorted to. But overhead, firmly fixed in the beams of the ceiling, hung many a goodly flitch of bacon, many a plump, well-fed ham. Under the shadow of this appetising display might be found at any time during the day about a score of persons who had no business there whatever, but found it "mighty convanient" to look in about meal times for the bite and sup my car-driver so regretfully alluded to, and to sit round the fire smoking a pipe and talking for hours afterwards.

It was in the larder attached to this fine old kitchen that I met a glorious specimen of the fine Old Irish Retainer, faithful to the memory of the "ould masther," who had left him an annuity of eight shillings per week, and not unmindful of the virtues of the new one, who keeps him on the establishment as an interesting "survival," and lodges, feeds, and clothes him, in order that he may not be obliged to divert any portion of his income from its natural course towards Mary Molony's shebeen, to the purchase of the prosaic necessaries of life. The Retainer, who was enjoying the occupation of turning some hams and bacon in salt, and inspecting the condition of some pigs' heads in highly spiced pickle, was a singularly good-looking man, with, well - I will not say "clean" - cut features and a generally healthy look, speaking wonders for the vigour of constitution which had successfully withstood sixty odd winters and an incalculable quantity of the poisonous new whisky of the country. He was interested in the subject of obtaining sundry rounds of salt beef for Christmastide, holding that roast beef is but a vain thing, good enough for Saxons, no doubt, but not to be compared with corned beef or bacon and cabbage. The Retainer spoke kindly of his new master, but at the mention of the old one at once kindled to fever heat. "Thim was times, your honour. Niver a week but we killed two sheep, or a month that we didn't kill a baste. And pigs, your honour. If we didn't kill a pig every day, as your honour says, we killed a matther of four score every sayson. And there was lashings and lavings of mate for every one. And the ould masther said, says he, 'As long as it's there,' says he, 'all are welcome to a bite and a sup at my house. As long as it's there,' says he. And he was the good man, your honour."

This was it. The present tenant's Celticised predecessor, whose glory still fills the land, lived the life of an African chief. When ox, sheep, or pig was slain, the choice morsels of the animal were perhaps reserved for the chieftain's table, and the remainder of the carcase was distributed among the tribe assembled in that part of the kraal called the kitchen. Odds and ends of food were always on hand; and if there was not much to eat at home there was always something to be had at the chieftain's tent. Outside of the kitchen door was the stable yard, knee deep in the accumulated filth of years, and the garden was a wilderness. "But, your honour," said the Retainer, "it was the foine gentleman he was, and it tuk three waggons to carry away the empty champagne bottles when the new masther came, and long life to him and to your honour; and I wish your honour safe home and welcome back."

Thus far the Retainer, who is fairly well cared for, and ought to be satisfied whether he is or not; but it is otherwise with the surrounding public. As the old order changes and gives place to the new, the poorer tenants have seen one privilege depart from them after the other. To the new occupant, however much inclined he may be to deal liberally, nay, generously with the country folk, it appears preposterous that a score or more of loafers should assist his servants in "eating up his mutton." The new comer is prepared to deal handsomely with the people, who with all their faults have endearing qualities almost impossible to resist; but the fact is that he does not understand the situation till it is too late. A good Scotch or English housewife going into her kitchen and finding it so inexpressibly dirty that her feet are literally rooted to the ground, is apt to express a very decided opinion, despite the presence of a dozen or more of gossips smoking their pipes round the fire; but her remarks are hardly likely to be taken in good part, and she is classed as a "domineering" person forthwith. And a general misunderstanding can only be averted by timely concessions and the prompt dismissal of English servants who neither can nor will live with their Irish peers. And yet it cannot be fairly said that anybody is to blame. The "foreigner" cannot endure to be kept in bed till late in the morning, and hence easily acquires the reputation of a "tyrant." And the small tenants feel the loss of the African system, under which they never actually went short of a meal. As the right of mountain pasture and of cutting turf have vanished on some estates, so has the privilege of living at free quarters disappeared on others, to be replaced by no compensating advantage. This is one of the features of a period of transition during which, without ill-will on either side, the gulf between rich and poor is becoming perceptibly wider.

Inasmuch as I am just now contradicted by peers in the columns of the Daily News itself, and attacked - I must add, in very courteous as well as brilliant style - by a leader writer of the Irish Times, and held up to public opprobrium at Sunday meetings, I thought it well to submit the foregoing to a friend, born and bred in Ireland, before committing it to print. Where, except so far as the retainer is concerned, I was obliged to depend so much on hearsay evidence, I thought it just possible that I might have selected an extreme case instead of a fair type of what I have ventured to call the African system. I am quite reassured. My friend, who is an accomplished and experienced Irishman, tainted only by a very few years' residence in England, assures me that I have considerably understated the wild, wasteful profusion, slothfulness, and dirt of the old-fashioned chieftain's kitchen. He assures me that families are now abroad in the world without an acre of land or a halfpenny beyond their earnings, who, within his recollection, have been "ruined by their kitchen," - literally eaten up by hungry retainers and tenants. He mentioned one family in particular, whose income sank from £12,000 to nothing a year under the ancient system which united almost every possible defect. The tenants were not, it is true, charged a heavy rent in money, because civilisation had not advanced quite so far as the commutation of all dues into cash; but "duty work" was as strictly exacted on the lord's farm as it is now on some estates when coal is to be drawn, and "duty" tribute in kind was levied as well. Thus the tenant was obliged not only to cultivate the "ould masther's" land, but to give him at Christmas tide a "duty" pig and "duty" geese and fowls according to a fixed percentage. My friend, whose position places his assertion above all doubt, assures me that in old leases it is quite common to find a sum of money specified as the equivalent of a "duty" hog; and other tribute of similar kind. The "ould masther," whose bailiffs looked sharply after "duty" of all descriptions, himself dispensed the indiscriminate hospitality already described, and "masther" and man floundered in the slough of debt and poverty together, making light of occasional hardship. All this feudal fellowship has gone with the old chieftains, whom the people profess to admire, and compare regretfully with the new men who expect to pay and be paid. But I am reminded that I have omitted to mention an important factor in the older polity of Ireland. The opposite ends of the social chain were brought together by that time-honoured ensign and instrument of authority, one end of which was in the master's hand and the other in the man's ribs or across his shoulders. It was "the shtick" which kept things together so far as they were kept so at all. The descendants of the masters say little or nothing about the good old custom of their forefathers in "laying about them with their rattan;" but the Retainer has not forgotten the ungentle practice which stimulated him to exertion in his youth. To hear the Retainer one would believe that the great smoother of difficulties, stimulant to exertion, and pacificator of quarrels was the "shtick." The idea of one of the tribe "processing" his chief for assault was never dreamt of in the good old times; for the recalcitrant one would have been "hunted out" of the county by the indignant population. To the Retainer the old time has hardly passed away, for it is not long since he actually recommended a "domineering Saxon" on the occasion of a domestic disturbance to "take the shtick to 'um, your honour. Sure the ould masther always did. And when he had murthered 'um they was as saft as silk." It is curious that the wand of the enchanter during the Golden Age of "Ould Ireland" should prove to have been the all-persuasive, all-powerful "shtick."

XIII - CROPPED

GORTATLEA, CO. KERRY, Monday, Dec. 6th

Having heard agrarian outrages reported one day and denied or explained away the next, I thought it worthwhile to ascertain the exact truth concerning the case of Laurence Griffin, of Kilfalliny, Co. Kerry. It had been reported at Cork that Griffin had been taken out of his bed in his own house, that his ears had been slit, and that he had been otherwise maltreated by a band of ruffians, on the night of Monday last. Then it was roundly asserted that he had never been attacked at all, and that he was a malingerer who had slit his own ears, or persuaded his wife to slit them for him, with an eye to the excitement of sympathy and charity; that winter was coming on; and that, after all, the ear is not a very sensitive part of the human form. To ascertain the exact truth there seemed to be only one method - to see for oneself. Having seen the man, and assisted at the application of a fresh dressing to his wounded ear, not ears, I must confess myself incapable of entertaining any doubt as to his veracity. His mutilated ear is not slit, nor is he "ear-marked" like a beast, by a notch being cut in that organ. The upper and exterior convolution of his left ear is cut clean off, so that its outline, instead off being rounded at the top, is straight. The wound is of course still fresh and sore, but is already showing signs of healing. The poor man has evidently been not only barbarously mutilated, but nearly frightened to death. With his pale face and half-grown beard, and his head bound up, he is a pitiable object. Obviously he was nearly as much afraid of me as of his midnight assailants, and was far too much bewildered by the harsh tone of "the Saxon" to tell a smooth and coherent story. Bit by bit, amid many interruptions, he told his pitiful narrative, only one part of which I consider doubtful. He denied that, either by their clothes or any other sign, he could identify any one of the men who attacked him. I am obliged to believe that, despite their blackened faces, he could have done so, were he not in fear of his life. The hand of his enemies is still heavy upon him, for his wife cannot get milk from the neighbours for her children. They are either afraid, or say that they are, to give or sell to Laurence Griffin, his wife, or his children. He is thrown out of employment, and may, so far as the anti-landlord party are concerned, starve. The causes which led to the outrage on this poor man afford such a curious picture of the present state of county Kerry as to be worth narrating.

A man named Sullivan occupied a farm at Kilfalliny, on the little river Main, a spot almost equidistant from each of the three railway stations of Farranfore, Gortatlea, and Castleisland. When Sullivan died several years ago, the farm, for which he paid about £190 a year rent, was divided between his three sons, the man who obtained the middle or best section being "set" to pay £5 more than either of the others, as having the best farm. The brothers on the outside sections have prospered. One has saved some hundreds of pounds; the other has given good, substantial portions to his three daughters. No objection was made to the manner in which the land was subdivided by the agent, Mr Hussey, of the firm of Hussey and Townsend, of Cork, Tralee, and other places. The Sullivan who inherited the "good will," as it is called here, of the "Benjamin's mess" has not succeeded in life so well as his brothers. At the October sessions of 1878 an ejectment order was obtained against him for one and a half year's rent, equal to £100 10s. In January, 1879, possession was taken, and the farmer formally ejected, but immediately reinstated as "caretaker," a convenient practice, when it is borne in mind that in Ireland an ejected tenant has six months allowed him for "redemption," during which the landlord can only let the farm subject to the risk of the late tenant paying up his rent, less whatever has been taken off the farm in the meanwhile. Sullivan then was re-established in his farm as "caretaker," and there he remained with the consent of the agent until last spring, when he was summoned to depart. To this request he has declined to pay the slightest attention. When he is summoned for trespass and sent to gaol the Land Leaguers pay his fine and restore him to his family, who still keep houses on the farm as before. As the case at present stands he is indebted to his landlord (deduction being made for sums received for grazing and for about £100 worth of hay still stacked on the farm) in the sum of £100 The agent, anxious to settle the matter, persuaded the landlord to offer him a receipt for this, and a bonus of £100 in cash, if he would go away, but this he, or the Land League for him, declines to do.

It was obviously necessary at the end of the hay harvest to appoint a caretaker to see that the crop was not "lifted," after the manner of that of the irreconcilable Tom Browne, of Cloontakilla, county Mayo. Hence, Laurence Griffin, a labouring man, with an acre patch of land to his house, was given the job of looking after the hay, and occasionally summoning Sullivan for trespass. It must be understood that Sullivan's family have never been disturbed, and that Griffin lives, not like a man in possession of their holding, but in his own little house hard by with his own family. The supervision exercised was, therefore, of the mildest character, but the summoning for trespass was accounted a dire offence by the popular leaders. Hence Griffin was first "noticed" to give up the occupation assigned to him by his employer, Mr Hussey, who had given him his house and potato patch. The poor fellow was sadly exercised in his mind, but he kept on with his duty until a second notice was affixed to his door. Then he lost heart, and a fortnight ago gave up his dangerous occupation.

On the Saturday following, however, he happened to go into Tralee, and the exponents of the popular will made up their minds that he had not given up his employment as he was "noticed" to do, that he was still persevering in the nefarious career of a caretaker, and that he had actually dared to go in the light of day to Tralee to receive the wage of his iniquity. If not actually guilty of this enormity, he had at least a guilty look, and it was determined to punish him, and make him a warning to other evildoers.

According to the man's account, given in a disjointed manner under severe cross-questioning, he had gone to bed on Monday last, when somebody tapped at his door and called to him to open. Thinking the visit was from the police, who occasionally looked in upon him, he got up, and huddling on some clothes as he went, made for the door. As he was on the point of opening it, a voice called out to him to "make haste," for the speaker was "starved with the cold;" then he knew the voice was not that of the policeman, and he would fain have closed the just opening door, but a gun was thrust through the opening, the door was pushed open, and a dozen men with blackened faces and armed to the teeth burst into the room.

The ringleader then proceeded to go through some form akin to a trial, and asked his companions what should be done with Laurence Griffin, who had disregarded the notices served on him, and persevered in his villanous calling. It was suggested that death alone would meet the case. "Shoot 'um, says they," said Griffin to me. At this his wife sprang out of bed shrieking, and his children collected round him. Almost out of his wits with terror, the poor fellow declared that he had obeyed the notice, that he had relinquished his office, and that he was out of work, and full of trouble in consequence.

After some little consultation the chiefs of the Blackfaces consented to swear Griffin as to the truth of his statement, and while guns were held to his breast and to each side of his head, he swore solemnly that he had obeyed the notice, that he was no longer watching Sullivan's farm, and that he would never offend in such wise again.

When an end was made of swearing him, poor Griffin, more dead than alive, was marched out alone between his guards into the road, where he found himself among a score more of men, all with blackened faces. Then, so far as I could understand Griffin, the leader of the men outside displayed some dissatisfaction at the way in which things had passed off, and expressed his determination that the unhappy caretaker should not go scot free.

"What did we come out for to-night?" growled the chief; "did we come out for nothing?" Muffled groans followed this appeal, and encouraged the spokesman to add, "Shall we go back as we came, boys?" the answer to which was a decided negative. Then the unlucky man, Griffin, saw something glitter in the chief's hand, and while he was kept steady by gun barrels pressing against each side of his head, he felt a sharp pain in his left ear, and the blood running down his neck.

As to what followed he was very incoherent; but it seems that the Blackfaces departed, leaving him with his wife and children nearly frightened to death, and with the top of his ear cut clean off.

I may add, as an indication of the state of Kerry, that a gentleman invited to meet me last night postponed the meeting till daylight, on the ground that night air is not good for landlords. Not a single person directly or indirectly connected with land ventures out unarmed even in broad daylight. It is needless to say that no money would hire a man to watch Sullivan's farm.

XIV - IN KERRY

The character of the principal estates in counties Cork and Kerry appears to be like that of their bacon and beef - streaky. There are to be seen some admirable specimens of skilful and liberal management, as well as instances of almost insane blundering on the part of both landlord and tenant. From Blarney to the Blaskets, the distance is not that of a couple of counties, but the gap between Kylemore and Rinvyle - between civilization and savagery. It would be thought that worse degradation than that on Innisturk and Innisbofin would be difficult to find; but in poverty, misery, and lawlessness the population of those inclement isles is far outdone by the five-and-twenty families now in the position of squatters on the Great Blasket. This is an island some three miles and three-quarters long, lying off the peninsula of Corkaguiny beyond Dunmore Head, on the northern side of Dingle Bay, as Bray Head and the island of Valentia lie on its southern side. Of old the Greater Blasket, which has some good pasturage upon it, was let to a few tenants who made a sort of living on this wild spot. They fed their sheep, they grew potatoes, caught great store of porpoises, which they converted into bacon, and thus kept body and soul together in a rough way. But whatever of rude plenty once existed on Great Blasket has vanished before its increasing population. The island is now asked to maintain some hundred and forty persons, and refuses to respond to the demand.

The tenants can hardly complain of much interference of late years, either from Lord Cork, the head landlord, or from Mr Hussey, who till just recently leased the island from him; for they have paid no rent for four or five, nor county cess for seven, years. They have never paid any poor-rate, and yet hunger after "relief meal." They are simply attempting the impossible - to live on a place which might perhaps support a score of people, but will not support six times that number.

Blarney, for other reasons than its groves and "the stone there, that whoever kisses he never misses to grow eloquent," is one of the most interesting places in the south of Ireland. It is not only the centre of a rich agricultural country and the abode of an improving landlord, Sir George St. John Colthurst, of Ardrum, but the seat of an important manufacture of woollens, a rare and curious industry in Munster. The Blarney mills make a great "turn over" of tweed, and employ five hundred and fifty men, women, and girls. I had an excellent opportunity of seeing the factory hands, for I went to Blarney on pay-day, and was greatly struck by the difference between their appearance and that of the people engaged in agriculture alone. The number and appearance of the women employed is a good answer to those pessimists who maintain that the curse of the poorer Irish is the filthiness, laziness, and general slatternliness of the women. In dress and general bearing the girls of Blarney would compare favourably with those of many English manufacturing towns; and, inasmuch as Blarney Mills are successful, their work must be well done. One reason of course of the comfortable look of the Blarney folk is that all the family work. Perhaps the husband works at agriculture, and the wife and daughter at the mill. All work, and hence a good income, as at Blackburn and other cotton towns, instead of the starvation which attends a useless woman who, with her string of helpless children, hangs like a millstone round her husband's neck. There are no "useless mouths" at Blarney, where everybody helps to maintain the family roof-tree, and to prove that the Irish of the south, like those of Connemara, are susceptible of being taught, if only pains be taken with them. It must be admitted that Blarney Mills are in the second generation, having been founded by Mr Mahony, the father of the late "Father Prout" and of the present proprietor. The houses of the workpeople at Blarney are neat and trim, white and clean, and a repose to the eyes of beholders, sick of slouching thatch and bulging mud walls.

Perhaps, however, the spot of all others in which the sharpest contrast occurs between the old life of Ireland and that brought about by "improving" landlords and tenants is the hamlet of Millstreet, situate on the line of railway between this place and Mallow, once a kind of Irish Tunbridge Wells, and famous for the "Rakes of Mallow," whose virtues are immortalised in verse[30]. When Mallow was the farthest south-western outpost of civilization it is possible that the "rakes" who converged upon that pretty spot from the surrounding country "ranted," "roared," and "drank" to the extent that the poet has credited them withal. But they are gone now, these rakes, and Mallow appears to get on very well without them.

It is remarkable for its pretty villas, and for a comfortable hotel, kept by a self-made man, who has risen from the ranks into prosperity by sheer industry and foresight. Millstreet is a very different kind of place from Mallow. The latter has the beautiful Blackwater river to give it beauty; but Millstreet is chiefly remarkable as the locale of the mill which gives it a name; as the habitation of the Rev. Canon Griffin, a Roman Catholic of high culture, who, unlike some of the priesthood, abjures the Land League and all its works; and as the spot on which "Ould Ireland" and New Ireland meet face to face.

The hamlet is mainly divided between two proprietors. That part known as the McCarthy O'Leary property is mainly composed of filthy hovels of the

---

[30] A traditional Irish song: "Beauing, belling, dancing, drinking,\Breaking windows, cursing, sinking \Every raking, never thinking, \Live the Rakes of Mallow."

worst Irish type - is, in fact, rather a gigantic piggery than a dwelling-place for human beings. The houses are not so small as the mountain cabins of Mayo or the seaside dens of Connemara, but they are small enough, crowded with inhabitants, and filthy beyond the belief of those who know not the western half of Ireland. It is hardly possible, nor would it be worth while, to inquire into the causes which have made one half of Millstreet an opprobrium and the other half a model hamlet. I simply record what I see - filth and swinishness on the left hand, order, neatness, and cleanliness on the right.

The white houses, the trim streets of the townlet, are on the Wallace property, which is at present, and will be for some little time to come, in the hands of the Court of Chancery. Skilfully administered for several years past, the Wallace property is very well known in these parts for the success with which its management has been attended. One of the principal tenants of this thriving estate is Mr Jeremiah Hegarty, whose peculiar position towards his landlords affords a curious instance of the working of the present land laws of Ireland. To begin with Mr Hegarty holds about eight hundred acres as a tenant farmer, without a lease or any guarantee against his being turned off by his landlords at any time, except the natural goodwill and joint interest of landlord and tenant. He has of course the Act of 1870 in his favour, but inasmuch as his "improvements" have extended over a long term of years, it is almost certain that if a series of deaths should bring the property into needy or unscrupulous hands Mr Hegarty might be removed from his farm, or rather farms, at great loss to himself, despite the compensation that would be awarded him, and on which the landlord would assuredly make a great profit. It may be thought hardly likely that any landlord would be mad enough to disestablish a tenant of eight hundred acres of land who pays his rent with commendable punctuality; but as such things, and things even more foolish, have been done during the present year, it is not agreeable to think of the risks run by an improving tenant in county Cork, and an improving tenant Mr Hegarty assuredly is.

It is a curious illustration of that difference between English and Irish farming which makes the agrarian question so difficult for Englishmen to understand, that Mr Hegarty, who may be accepted as a type of the Irish farmer, possessed by advanced ideas, conducts his operations successfully and profitably by almost exactly reversing the proportions of tillage and pasture existing on Mr Clare Read's famous farm at Honingham Thorpe. On the particular farm of Mr Read's here referred to, the quantity of pasture is about one eighth or ninth of the whole. On Mr Hegarty's farms, for he has more than one to make up his total of eight hundred acres, there is exactly one-ninth under tillage to eight-ninths of pasture.

This will not at first strike the English eye as any great thing in the way of reclamation; but it must be recollected that in this part of Ireland it is no small matter to obtain good pasture. One of the first sights the eye becomes accustomed to is the long bent or sedge, shooting rankly up among the sweeter grass, and telling surely of land overcharged with water. There is no escape from the fact that Ireland as a country is cursed with defective natural drainage. The fall of the greater rivers is so slight that they meander hither and thither in "S's," as they say here, and only require a little surplus on the average rainfall to overflow the more valuable land. And it is astonishing how quickly good land left untilled reverts to its primeval condition, or, in the expressive language of the country, "goes back to bog." This has been shown in many cases.

There is, for instance, a not small portion of Lord Inchiquin's and Lord Kenmare's land, which has been allowed by the tenants to gradually go back to sedge, if not to bog, for the want of keeping drains clear and putting on lime. A curious instance of the effect of not liming the land is supplied on one of the fields newly reclaimed by Mr Hegarty. Owing either to the supply of lime running short, for the moment, or to the carelessness of his men, a patch of recently drained land was left without lime which was liberally bestowed on the rest of the field. The forgotten patch can be seen from afar by the tufts of sedge sprouting from it.

Mr Hegarty's eight hundred acres are, saving one or two little lots, divided between the Millstreet farm and the mountain farm of Lackadota, for the goodwill whereof the incoming paid the outgoing tenants £560 before he began the work of thorough reclamation. His success on this hill-side has been remarkable. This season he has taken out potatoes from eight acres at the rate of £20 per acre, and the triumph of his method has been equally great in other crops - to wit, oats, mangolds, and turnips.

It is needless to remind agricultural readers that the artificial feeding of cattle is still in its infancy in the west and south-west of Ireland. The various kinds of cake - oil, cotton, and nut - and cattle "spices," made up of fenugreek seed and other condiments, are, if not unknown, quite unused by all but a few gentlemen farmers, of whom I shall in another letter have more to say. The old-fashioned notion was to rear cattle, turn them loose on the mountain, and sell them to be finished in the Meaths or elsewhere. On the Millstreet farm, however, root-crops are largely used for feeding, and the beasts are kept more under cover than is common here. All this means, of course, large outlay, and the farmer has expended not less than six thousand pounds in building, and in draining and liming four hundred acres of the eight hundred he occupies. He was, like Canon Griffin, one of the first to recognise the necessity for changing the potato seed, and imported "champions" before other people thought of it, and while they were growing potatoes not much bigger than marbles, and hardly fit to feed pigs upon, he was getting crops of fine tubers. In draining the portion of his farm near the river, he has found himself obliged to employ stone drains, the attempts previously made with tile drains having failed signally; and it may be added that his attempts, now shown to be successful, to drain the flat land near the river Oughbane were derided by neighbouring agriculturists, who could not see that if the land do not slope sufficiently towards the natural drainage the artificial drains may be made to do so. His farm-buildings, machinery for threshing, &c., are an agreeable sight. In building, concrete has been largely used, especially in the cow-houses and feeding stalls, and the general effect of this large farm in county Cork is that of a well-managed business, every detail of which is familiar to its head.

It can hardly be thought extraordinary that farmers like Mr Hegarty, even on a smaller scale, are anxious for a good, sound Land Bill. They, with all good feeling toward their present landlords, cannot avoid recognising that as the law stands the work of their lives may be taken from them by any accident of succession. Despite the Land Bill of 1870, they are harassed by a sense of insecurity. Monetary payment for the work of their best years would not compensate them for the loss of the holdings, the value of which has been created by their own intelligent work. In England farmers of this type would assuredly have a lease, and their Irish brethren hold that schemes for the gradual acquirement of land by tenants should be accompanied by the "Three F's," and extended over fifty instead of thirty-five years. The latter plan would, they think, be of little use to the present tenant, as it would practically raise his rent too far, and thus prevent him from doing his best by the land. Great force is given to these opinions by evidence in my possession, that, although a great deal of land has been reclaimed within the last fifty years, a large proportion is running barren for want of means on the farmers' part to cultivate it properly.

The panic among all classes connected with "landlordism" is on the increase. All who can conveniently leave county Kerry are doing so. If I go for a drive with one of those proscribed by the grogshop-keepers of Castleisland the muzzle of a double-barrelled carbine peeps ominously from the "well" of the car. Meanwhile all enterprise and development of the country is arrested. The North Kerry Railway, connecting this town with Limerick, will, I believe, be opened next week, "despite of foes," but other undertakings are for the moment paralysed. This is the more to be regretted, as Tralee is a rising place. After a desperate struggle against the inertness of Western Ireland on the subject of pure water, the uncongenial element has been introduced so skilfully and with so much fall that a jet can be thrown over any house in Tralee. The last new idea is a railway to Fenit Without, six miles down the bay. Up to the present time vessels have been brought to Tralee by a ship canal, but it is now sought to construct a railway running on to a pier, the elbow of which should be formed by Great Camphire Island. The cost of the railway will be £45,000, of which £30,000 is guaranteed by the county, and a large part of the balance taken up by the town. The pier is a far more serious business, depending on the Board of Works; but all attention is diverted from this and other important subjects by the terrorism which has, only just recently, extended to the county of Kerry.

The eviction - of landlords and landagents - is going on bravely. Mr Hussey, Lord Kenmare's agent, left Kerry a short time ago, and the Lord Chamberlain himself left Killarney House yesterday morning, not in a paroxysm of indignant "landlordism," but "more in sorrow than in anger." Lord Kenmare, who is a downright resident Irish landlord, *s'il en fust oncques,* confessedly leaves Ireland with great regret, and bade his people "Good-bye, for a long time" with no feigned grief. But he finds the country uninhabitable, while indignation meetings are held almost at his gates, and the very labourers whom he has done so much to employ make common cause with the farmers against him in paying no rent. The improvements going on here for some time past are stopped, and about £200 a week of wages lost to the neighbourhood. The causes which led to Lord Kenmare's departure have but recently sprung into existence. The jacquerie only reached Kerry the other day, and already the county is revolutionised. Thanks to The O'Donoghue and other Land Leaguers, Kerry is now in as unsettled a condition as Mayo, Galway, Clare, and Limerick. The flame was long in reaching this remote region; but when it came it fell among inflammable stuff, as will be gathered from the almost ridiculous circumstance of farmers and labourers combining together against a supposed common enemy. Farmers who a fortnight ago talked scornfully of those who "held the harvest" have, to my certain knowledge, subscribed to the Land League within the last few days, and I am informed that those who have hitherto held out will be members before another week is gone. It is true that additional allurements are held out to them. The three "F's" no longer satisfy the more advanced spirits who emulate Mr Parnell's magnificent vagueness, and declare it quite impossible that any measure likely to pass the Houses of Parliament as at present constituted will satisfy the people of Ireland. Meanwhile terrorism is upheld as a legitimate weapon of reform. If it were possible to be surprised at anything taking place in Ireland at the present moment, I should have been surprised at a farmer to whom I was talking a couple of days ago, and who farms between two and three hundred acres under an "improving" landlord. The farmer, who was evidently a local luminary on the land question, is only a recent convert to Land League principles; but he was nevertheless prepared to defend the cowardly kind of general strike against an individual, known as "Boycotting." He also talked a great deal about fair rents and the compulsion that farmers are under to pay anything that their landlords choose to ask. Yet this very man was, not long since, offered the profitable farm he now occupies in the place of smaller and less convenient holdings. Asked by his landlord what he thought he ought to pay, he offered two and a half times Griffith's valuation, and on the landlord asking him three times that rate, agreed with him to "split the difference," and was, or appeared to be, satisfied. But at that moment he had not been made conscious of his wrongs, and of his down-trodden, serf-like condition. He is fully aware of them now, and, in plain English, is prepared to make the best of the present opportunity.

As the possible peasant proprietor of the future is a personage much discussed among landlords and others just how, I thought it well to consult the farmer as well as the legal and proprietorial minds on this important subject. I was at once struck by the "so far and no farther" tone, so to speak, of the larger farmers. According to many of those I consulted, no greater disaster could occur to Ireland than the creation of peasant proprietors. I will endeavour to give, as nearly as possible, the exact words of farmers whose ideas concerning the claims of their own class are of the most advanced I have heard.

The instant I asked a question concerning the peasant-proprietor problem and the future of the "poor devil" cottiers, whose sufferings have made an excellent stalking-horse for the farmers, properly so-called, I was met with a well-formulated objection to any scheme of peasant proprietorship. The cottier *pauvre diable*[31] appears, I apprehend, to the farmers as a labourer, and they therefore look with anything but favour upon a scheme for raising the poor peasants above the necessity of working for them, by giving the poor a real stake in the country. The farmers hold that, unless some stringent regulations against subdividing or subletting be adopted and firmly enforced, the creation of peasant proprietors on an extensive scale will be the greatest misfortune that ever befell Ireland; as in the course of time it will create a nation of beggars, which cannot be maintained on the land. The farmer mind fails to perceive how any Act of Parliament can prevent an owner or peasant proprietor from selling his entire interest in his holding. This, they argue, will lead to the creation of a race of landlords who will bring more misery and ruin upon the country than anything that the present generation is acquainted with; as necessarily the class of landlords thus formed will be more exacting and severe upon their tenants than the present large territorial proprietors.

Thus far the farmer, who so far as the evils of subdivision or subletting are concerned is at one with the great landed proprietor, who, thanks to the recklessness of his predecessors, sees his efforts to improve his property paralysed, and his own personal honour and reputation endangered by the acts of the leaseholders or fee-farm, renters over whom he has no power whatever. Many large holdings are leased to middlemen who have sublet them at extravagant rents, but cannot be dispossessed. This is the system which now exists, yet the great landholders I have consulted describe it as the result which will be brought about by giving the fee-simple of holdings

---

[31] poor devil [Clachan ed.].

to cottier tenants. "And," I am asked on all sides, "is fixity of tenure to signify the fixture of little tenants in their present holdings, on which they cannot possibly lead a reasonably human existence? Is it intended to stereotype disaster, to perpetuate the blundering of the past? Or is it intended to give them at great expense to the country, larger holdings on partially reclaimed waste lands on the system commended by Mr Mitchell Henry, and perhaps applicable to Connemara, if not to other places? And is it intended that when Mike, and Thady, and Tim are settled on their new clearings they are to do as they like on them, to subdivide, to sublet, to conacre, to settle their numerous children and their children's children on the original forty-acre farm? And are they, after they have taken possession of it, partly reclaimed and brought under plough, to be allowed to cultivate it or not cultivate it as they like - to let it all go back first to pasture then to sedge, and finally to bog?"

Mainly with a view to elicit further expression of opinion, I hinted to the last and most accomplished person who put these queries to me, that it would be absurd to give the cottier absolute control over his land, and that he should have a conditional lease from the Government, the four cardinal conditions being - that he should not subdivide; that he should not sublet; that he should not take in a partner; that he should cultivate some portion of the land according to a prescribed system. I saw the fine Irish "oi" of my friend gleam with triumph. "A second Daniel," he almost shouted; "a second Daniel come from England. But are you aware, my friend, that you have evolved from your own unaided consciousness one of 'Lord Leitrim's leases' - the leases, which cost him his life? Bating the fines which he injudiciously levied you have exactly the programme for enforcing which he was shot, as you would probably be if you attempted anything of the kind. It is not at the signing of the leases that any difficulty would arise, but in carrying their letter and spirit into effect."

In view of the conflicting opinions held by able residents in the western and south-western counties, I thought it well to inspect a few estates, great and small, and to record such visible and otherwise well ascertained facts as might bear on the questions now at issue. My first visit in Kerry was to Clashatlea on the hill-side, opposite the station of Gortatlea on the railway line to Tralee. This townland is the property of Mr Arthur Blennerhasset, of Ballyseedy, and it has fallen into an awful condition through no fault of its present proprietor.

Years ago the land was let for electioneering purposes, akin to the creation of faggot votes, and a vast number of small holders became fixed upon land from which it is impossible to evict them. The approach to the small holdings lies along a cross road now in the course of construction from the lower road to the mountain road into Tralee. The cross road is in its present wet and unfinished condition a sore trial to man and beast; but it has a history nevertheless. Years ago it was a matter of complaint by the cottiers of Clashatlea that to obtain turf they were obliged to make a great detour involving the climbing of a severe hill. An attempt was made to lay a road on the lines now in progress; but it never grew into more than "the name of a road." So the little peasant cultivators whose land abutted on the abortive road gradually absorbed it into their possessions, each peasant taking his section in turn; a system exactly like that followed in bygone days by English landholders, and now attempted by the riparian proprietors of the Thames Valley. So far these poor people imitated the method of their social superiors; but they were not so fortunate as some of these in retaining their plunder. The new road was decreed, and Mike, and Thady, and Tim were obliged to withdraw within their ancient limits. Along the new road we went, bumping and jolting, at the imminent risk of the guns and revolvers in the car going off, until we reached the upper road by the glen. In parts the wretched houses were separated by a perceptible distance; but here and there they had been built side by side to accommodate the increasing population on the holdings.

How minute the subdivision has been may be gathered from the fact that 335 English acres, whereof some 250 are good for anything in their present condition, are divided among 40 tenant families, whose numbers may be safely put down at 200 souls. The land is therefore divided at the rate of one and a quarter English acres per head, and when it is mentioned that the most important tenant pays a rent of £17 10s., it will be seen that some of the holdings are ridiculously small. Many range from £4 to £5 per annum and are absolutely incapable of providing food for a family. It has been found impossible to reduce the number of tenants to any sensible degree without incurring the hatred of the country side, and the old and infirm whose children are dead or have emigrated, still cling to the miserable cabins in which their lives have been passed.

On the opposite side of Tralee I witnessed a spectacle of a widely different character. A smart drive from Tralee northwards through a blinding rain landed me at Ardfert, the village in the centre of Mr W. Crosbie's wonderfully improved estate. Going about his work quietly and unostentatiously, the proprietor has, in the course of forty-two years, completely altered the conditions of existence on his land. When it came into his possession in 1838, it was, as many Irish estates are now, suffering from local congestion of population. Mr Crosbie's father had inherited from the Earl of Glendore, who had given leases under the old penal laws. At the time only Protestants were allowed to hold leases, and in consequence of the small number of Protestants compared with the demand for lessees, the leases were obtained upon very advantageous terms - a long period, a low rent, and few conditions. The result was that the penal law, like other clumsy devices of the kind, defeated itself; for there was nothing to prevent the lessee from subletting the land. This had been done to an enormous extent when Mr Crosbie came into possession, and the lowland part of the estate was greatly over-populated. The upper part was greatly under-populated, and in the words of the proprietor, nothing could be worse than the way in which the tenants held the land. "No one knew from year to year which farm he had to till, and they used to divide every field and divide the crops every year." Mr Crosbie was not deterred by the difficulty of the task before him, and undertook the redistribution of his tenantry, on the anti-rundale system, and by degrees succeeded in planting the surplus population of the lowlands upon the higher ground. Moreover he anticipated the ideas of Mr Mitchell Henry and Canon Griffin by putting his tenants under the direct control of a skilled agriculturist, under his own supervision. Having thus redistributed his people on the land and taught them the elements of agricultural science, he commenced the work of building them suitable houses and farm buildings.

Mr Crosbie's estate in Kerry is of 9,913 acres valued by Government at £4,638, with a present rent roll of £8,500, thanks to the expenditure of £40,000 since 1839. As one approaches Ardfert the cabin common in Kerry vanishes to make room for houses well and substantially built of concrete, with whale-back roofs also of concrete. The merit of originally introducing concrete as a building material into this part of Ireland belongs, I believe, to Mr Mahony, of Dromore, who has employed it largely on his own estate; but Mr Crosbie was, at least, one of the first to perceive the advantage of using it. With Portland cement and the sand and pebbles of the adjacent sea-shore he has made a concrete village, and given his farmers houses of a kind previously unknown in his neighbourhood. Concrete has several advantages keenly appreciated in Kerry. It is dry - an immense advantage in a humid climate, and floors, ceilings, partition walls, and roofs, are all made of it, as well as the external walls. It also requires very little skilled work, and can be built up by ordinary labourers under proper supervision. Another great advantage is that it can be moulded to any shape and thickness, and is therefore most useful for barns, cowhouses, and feeding stalls.

The houses and farm buildings I have seen certainly seem perfect, and have, I am informed, been constructed at about the same price as corrugated iron. Those fond of tracing the genius of a nation in its constructive faculty will probably be amused at finding that the latest work of structural genius in Kerry is a development of that mud-hut order of architecture which has existed here from pre-historic times. But concrete well employed is a very different thing from the dirt-pie or mud-hut idea at the other end of the evolutionary chain.

Mr Chute, of Chute Hall, is also an improver and architectural reformer, his efforts being directed towards the abolition of thatch in favour of slate, an idea which has proved more fortunate in his case than in that of the great-grandfather of the present Lord Kenmare. The great estates of the Lord Chamberlain have curiously enough been equally damaged by the care and carelessness of his ancestors. His great-grandfather was disgusted at the condition of the town of Killarney, and offered any tenant who would build a decent house with a slate roof a perpetual lease of the land it stood upon and the adjoining garden for a nominal rent of four shillings and fourpence per annum, without other important conditions. The result has been that Killarney can boast of as filthy lanes as any in London or Liverpool. The ordinary process, the same as that which formed the hideous slums between Drury-lane and Great Wild-street, now happily demolished, has gone on in Killarney. Tenants under no restrictions gradually converted their gardens into lanes of hovels, and made money thereby, and the result is a concentration in Killarney of filth which would be better distributed on the side of a mountain, and which is under the nose of a landlord who is powerless to apply a remedy.

Not long ago Lord Kenmare sought to establish what is called here a Temperance Hall, for the purpose of giving lecturers and entertainers a chance of amusing the people; but the proprietor of the ground, after a prolonged negotiation, declined to surrender his property. Killarney is in the hands of the dwellers therein, and a very poor place it is.

Conversely Lord Kenmare's property suffers severely from the recklessness of the ancestor who flourished in the "comet year," famous for hock. That spirited nobleman, averse to the nuisance of dealing directly with tenants, leased a large portion of his property to middlemen in 1811 for forty-one years or three lives; that is to say, for a minimum of forty-one years with expansion to three lives. The effect of this fatal policy of giving away all power of supervision and management has been made manifest in the past, and is yet visible on those portions of the estate the three-life leases of which have not yet fallen in. The gross rental of Lord Kenmare's estates in Kerry, Cork, and Limerick, amounting altogether to 118,606 acres, is £37,713, against Griffith's valuation of £34,473, but the distribution of this sum is very unequal, especially since the rents of the yearly tenants were raised in 1876, in some cases to the by no means unfair extent of 50 per cent. above the poor-rate valuation.

The 3,300 tenants on Lord Kenmare's property have been mainly put upon the land by middlemen who made a great profit out of their three-life leases. The lands of Mastergechy, Knockacrea, and Knockacappul are all let at an immense reduction on Griffith's valuation, but to middlemen, who realise from 200 to 300 per cent. on their investment. Despite these drawbacks,

Lord Kenmare is an "improving" landlord, and has laid out in the last ten months some £7,000 on his property. The pretty tile-roof cottages outside of Killarney are a reproach to the town itself, over which Lord Kenmare, after the manner of many other Irish landlords, has no kind of control.

VALENTIA, CO. KERRY, Dec. 12th.

In a previous letter I alluded to the length of time it had taken the Land League agitation to make itself felt in Kerry, and to the swiftness with which, when once ignited, the far south-west of Ireland blazed into open disaffection. The causes of this slowness to light up, immediately followed by a fierce and sudden flame, are by no means obscure. Kerry has always been the last place to follow a popular movement, and the last to relinquish it.

As the French Revolution and its effects on Ireland were not heard of in Kerry till long after the establishment of the Empire, so was Ross Castle, on the lower lake at Killarney, the last stronghold subdued by Ludlow; and so also was Kerry the last stronghold of Fenianism. Moribund in the other parts of Ireland until Nationalists and Land Leaguers were united, by the prosecution of Mr Parnell, Fenianism still lingered and lingers on in Kerry. In the pot-houses of Tralee, Castle Island, and Cahirciveen the embers of Fenianism have smouldered since the outbreak of 1867. Slow to learn, Kerry has been slow to forget, and when once the emissaries of the Land League arrived here they found ready to their hand the cadre at least of a formidable organisation, and the reign of terrorism at once commenced.

Up to the present moment I have not heard of houses being blown up by dynamite after the fashion in Bantry, but the farmers who have already not paid their rents decline to do so, or pay in full secretly, while openly subscribing to the Land League and denouncing the mean-spirited serfs who would pay a farthing above Griffith's valuation.

There is no mistaking the strength of the movement which has at last reached this remote island, between which and America, as a native said to me yesterday, "There is not as much as the grass of a goat." This saying refers to the popular method of measurement, which is not by acres, but by the grass of so many cows, according to the richness of the pasture. Up to a month ago there was no talk of the Land League on Valentia Island. The tenants had for the most part paid their May rents, and the situation therefore afforded little scope for agitation; but the subtle spirit which spread instantaneously from Tralee to Cahirciveen quickly traversed the ferry, and now the Valentians are as keen on the subject of their grievances as anybody else in the western half of Ireland. At Cahirciveen anti-landlordism is as vigorous at this moment as at Tralee, or even at Ennis itself, albeit violent personal outrages have not been perpetrated in the immediate neighbourhood.

A resolute and influential leader of the people declared to me yesterday that the spirit now aroused would never be quelled but by a full and generous recognition of the claims of the cultivators. He averred that the people are not only awakened to their wrongs and determined to have them redressed, but that they possess the power of enforcing their will. I hinted that savage threats and deeds of violence might produce temporary anarchy, but that the end of all would be the crushing of the League with a strong hand. The answer was not argument, but defiance. It was impossible, the speaker asserted, to crush the combination now existing in Kerry. It could not be crushed, for the simple reason that it did not transgress the law. This was startling news, and I at once asked what was to be said of the dynamite affair at Bantry, the ear-cutting business near Castle Island, and the shooting of a bailiff in Tyrone? Only one of those things, I was instantly reminded, had occurred in Kerry, and I was moreover instructed that personal violence was preached against by the Land League priests, and opposed by all lay leaders. The crimes alluded to were the accidents of a great upheaval of the people, who could attain their objects perfectly well without violence.

To the objection that without occasional violence the terrorism now existing would lose all its strength, that threats never carried out would become ridiculous, that when violence ceased, tenants as well as landlords would set the Land League law aside and, do as they pleased, it was replied that the great agrarian movement had passed through the period of terrorism as nations pass through the early stage of baronial rights, especially that of private war. The present condition of the anti-landlord party was not that of a revolt, but of a strike, which whether it was wise and according to the laws of political economy or not, was clearly lawful. There was no constitutional right in any one man to compel another to work for him, and a strike was therefore clearly permissible. It was nonsense to cry out against combination. It was the only possible method of the weak making good their case against the strong, and the landlords might combine, and welcome, if they thought it would do them any good. Nobody wanted to shoot them any more, for they were "Quite, quite down." The present strike was of an unprecedented character. Strikes of workpeople were sometimes met and defeated by combinations of masters, because the masters held the property and plant, and the men had nothing but their heads and hands, and perhaps a little money in savings banks. So the masters lasted the longest and won, except when their number included a large proportion of needy, speculative manufacturers, who durst not stop their mills, and thus became the indirect and unwilling allies of the artisan. But where the masters were few and wealthy, the artisans had no chance against them.

It was far otherwise with the Irish farmers and cottiers, who not only "held the harvest," or rather its monetary result, but held the land and were "not going to give it up." The people, the speaker opined, had really won the battle already, and it was for them to exercise the power they had suddenly become aware of wisely and mercifully. There was no further need for violence or threats of violence, but what was called the law should not be carried out until the claims of the Irish people were fully admitted by the English Government.

How then was this gigantic strike to be carried on without violence or threatening life or limb? Quite easily was the reply - by extending the process of "Boycotting." This is, it seems, the great constitutional weapon on which neither horse, foot, nor artillery can be brought to bear. Those who will not join the Jacquerie, and aid and abet those Irish analogues of Jacques Bonhomme, Mike and Thady and Tim, in their resistance to "landlordism" shall be "Boycotted;" and all those who refuse to join in "Boycotting" an offender shall be treated in the same way.

Already the stoutest hearted are yielding on every side to the dread of being "Boycotted," a doom which signifies simply that the victim must surrender or leave the country. It means that nobody will buy or sell with any member of the family which is declared "taboo;" that the farmer may drive his cattle and pigs to market, but will not find a purchaser; that he may reap his grain and pull his potatoes, but that not a soul in the country will buy them for fear of being "Boycotted" himself. It means that the baker will refuse him bread, and the butcher meat; that no draper who knows his wife by sight will sell her as much as a ribbon; that not a creature will buy her butter and eggs, chickens and turkeys, geese and ducks; that she will be unable to buy any article of food or luxury for her children, and that they will be "sent to Coventry" at school.

There is not an atom of exaggeration in anything here stated. It is not a fancy picture, but as genuine as that of Mr Boycott himself; and there is no doubt that the taste for "Boycotting" is spreading rapidly, as my informant, who is heartily in favour of it, declares it is "clean within any law that could be made, let alone carried out." It is impossible to compel any community to have dealings with a person whom they dislike, and the anti-landlord party are determined to carry their point without, as appears on the notices served on farmers, "hurting one hair of their heads." "Isolation" has, in fact, been added to the number of the arts which soften manners and forbid them to be savage. It is the sprig of shillelagh in a velvet sheath.

XV - THE "BOYCOTTING" OF MR BENCE JONES

CORK, Friday, Dec. 17th

The present condition of Mr W. Bence Jones, of Lisselan, whom I called upon to-day, illustrates most vividly the advance made in the art of "Boycotting" since its invention. Early attempts in any artistic direction are apt to be crude, and when "Boycotting" was first practised at Lough Mask it put on the guise of a general strike of the country side against an individual, but its effect was purely local. Since that time great progress has been made in shaping and finishing what one of my informants defined as "a strictly constitutional weapon." At this moment the arm of the skilful "Boycotter" is long. It can stop the sale of the original victim's potatoes in a northern town; it can keep Mr Stacpoole from getting rid of his horses in Limerick; and can actually prevent Mr Bence Jones from sending his cattle from Cork to England. The latter gentleman is isolated on his estate at Lisselan, a place near Ballinascarthy, between Bandon and Clonakilty, in this county, but his isolation has not yet gone, in some respects, to the same brutal length as that of Mr Boycott. He is still permitted to receive and to despatch his letters; and car-drivers have, perhaps by some oversight of the "Boycotters," not yet been warned to avoid his house as if it were a lazaretto, and to refuse to carry his visitors within miles of his door. Perhaps he is considered by the mysterious persons who alone exercise authority in Ireland just now as only a "tyrant" of the second or third degree, and not as a first-class malefactor.

But, however this may be, I found none of the difficulty in reaching Lisselan which accompanied my second visit to Lough Mask House. When I started from Bandon this morning, that thriving town was wrapped in slumber, although the sun was shining brightly out of a deep blue sky, just flecked at the horizon with pearly-hued clouds. The ground was hard and crisp, and the hoofs of the horses rang out merrily as I sped in the direction of Clonakilty, through an undulating country mainly devoted to pasture, some of which was rough and sedgy. As I approached Ballinascarthy the quality of the land was visibly better.

Lisselan House lies in the midst of a charming pastoral scene. Beyond the clean-cut lawn flows the silvery flood of the Arrigadeen, its opposite bank is clothed with the bright green tops of white turnips in the midst of which is penned a flock of sheep (Shropshire Downs), and in the distance are green meadows and browsing kine. All would be soft, peaceful, and Arcadian, were it not for the helmets of the 3rd Dragoon Guards glittering in the sun as the patrol turns the corner of the wood, and the tall, dark figures of the Royal Irish Constabulary guarding the gate and doorstep. At present the house, the farm, and the neighbouring village are occupied by the police, and it has been thought necessary to increase the strength of the garrison in order to assure the safety of the servants who, to their infinite credit in such times as these, remain true to their master.

It is not pretended for an instant that either Mr W. Bence Jones or his son, who are as gigantic of stature as they are resolute of mind, need fear personal attack. They are known to be armed to the teeth, and the chances are that the weak-minded labourers who have deserted them are far more afraid of "the masters" than they are of them. The household of Lisselan consists for the time being of the Messrs. Bence Jones, father and son. Miss Bence Jones, their English house servants, two labourers - whereof one is English and the other Irish - Mr Law, the Scotch bailiff, and an Irish housemaid, who has remained faithful, and helps Miss Bence Jones to milk the cows and to attend to the dairy. The road is slippery on the high ground hard by, and it is debated at Lisselan House whether the farrier of the Dragoon Guards shall not be asked to "sharpen" the shoes of the animals employed there, for no local workman will touch them.

As I pass by the dairy, one of those in which collectively Mr Bence Jones makes £1,000 worth of butter yearly, I see the trim housemaid, dressed in cotton print, milking a cow, and am presently aware of "the master's" son and daughter, who have been up since the dawn feeding and penning cattle and sheep, and milking the cows. Since Monday the strike among the Irish employed on the house and the farm has, with the exceptions already mentioned, been rigidly maintained. The men, about forty in number, were "noticed" on Friday; on Saturday they announced their intention of working no more for Mr Bence Jones, and on Monday deserted the place as if it were plague-stricken.

On Monday morning Mr Law stood aghast at the sight of a farm of a thousand acres with nobody to work it; but he soon recovered himself, and with the help of his own work, that of a couple of labourers left, and the co-operation of the master's son and daughter, matters went on despite the strike. Mr Law is, of course, as a good Scotch bailiff should be, greatly distressed at the state of his cow-houses, feeding-stalls, and stockyard, now ankle-deep in "muck;" but the fine shorthorned bull seems none the worse, and the pigs have taken kindly to the new and disorderly condition of affairs. But things are not brought to a deadlock yet. Of the animals "Boycotted" in Dublin the sheep have since been shipped, and it is thought here that at the moment of writing the cattle will be on their way to Sir Thomas Dyke Acland, to whom they are consigned.

Byron wrote that "nought so much the spirit calms as rum and true religion;" but this dictum is hardly confirmed in the case of Mr Bence Jones's assailants, who number among them a minister of religion, as well as the irrepressible grogshop-keeper. I am informed that last Sunday the mutinous labourers - or, perhaps, it would be more correct to say the labourers who have been coerced by threats into mutiny - were addressed in the vestry by Father Mulcahy, and that either he or some other person assured them that they would receive their wages as if they were still employed. However this may be, the unfortunate families, about thirty in number, who have struck at the bidding of the anti-landlord party, are making a sorry bargain; for many of the men are getting on in years, and will have to seek work and house-room elsewhere when they are turned out of their cottages to make room for the strange hands who are coming to do the work they refuse to do.

The neat little dwellings of stone and slate that I observed to-day on the Lisselan estate are not let to the labourers, but are, with as much potato land as they can manure, thrown in with their wages, 11s. per week. They must now make way for people who will work, and are not afraid of "Rory of the Hills." Offers of help pour in upon Mr Bence Jones, and the first detachment of labourers is expected forthwith. One friend offers a phalanx of English navvies; but temperate counsels prevail, and it is thought better to get the really small number of men required brought in quietly. With police everywhere at Lisselan and Ballinascarthy, and cavalry patrols always at hand, it is hardly likely that violence will be attempted towards the newcomers or the present slender garrison.

There are, as in all such cases, conflicting reports as to the cause of the quarrel, if such it can be designated, between landlord and labourer at Lisselan. In his forthcoming book, *A Life's Work in Ireland, by a Landlord who tried to do his duty*, Mr Bence Jones will doubtless describe with characteristic accuracy the objects he had in view, and the means he took to accomplish them. He has also already made known his difficulties and disappointments through the medium of the Press. He has undoubtedly, had abundant opportunity of weighing the possibilities of Irish country life during the long period of his residence in Ireland. It is also clear to any unprejudiced person that he has striven, not only to do his duty by the land, but by the tenants occupying one part of it and the labourers employed on the other. In round numbers he owns about 4,000 acres, of which he farms 1,000 himself. Besides £1,000 worth of butter annually made, he sells £1,000 worth more of cattle, and £1,000 worth of sheep and wool, besides oats and various other produce.

While this one-thousand-acre farm was let to tenants, it yielded its proprietor an average rental of 17s. an acre. No person acquainted with farming would for an instant assume that a small tenant could make nearly as much out of his land as the farmer of a thousand acres; but allowing for all this, 14s. 3d. per acre appeared a very low rate to the landlord of the farm of fifty-eight acres occupied for the last half-century by the Walsh family. I gather that the grandfather of D. Walsh held the farm from the grandfather of the present landlord; that the original occupant was succeeded by his son; that on the son's death his widow retained undisturbed possession until her son was old enough to assume the management, and that then the landlord required 20s. per acre from him. To the landlord it seemed that the Walsh family had had a good bargain. He was informed, with what degree of accuracy I cannot at this moment ascertain, that the widow had given her four daughters respectively £140, £130, £130, and the stock of a farm, probably of equal value "to their fortune," and that she had also helped one of her sons to make a start in the world on an independent farm. From these circumstances he concluded that he was entitled to more rent than he had been receiving, and demanded 20s. from her son for a lease of thirty-one years.

To the tenant the case assumed a widely-different aspect. His grandfather, his father and his mother, had successively occupied the fifty-eight acre farm for fifty years. Two generations had been bred, if not born, on the holding at Ballinascarthy, just beyond the bridge. They had been decent people. They had paid their rent, and if his sisters had received good portions it was no more than their due, considering the respectability of their family. Was he, after his people had held the land for fifty years, to have it "raised on him" to nearly double Griffith's valuation? Was it just to increase the rent because his father and mother were dead? All these questions occurred to the tenant, beyond any matter of improvements and so forth. The landlord's position is quite intelligible. The value of farm produce had risen so greatly since the original rent was levied, and the farmer had prospered so well of late years, that the holding was demonstrably worth more rent than had been paid. On the other hand, the tenant held that the farm had done well by his people, because they had done well by it, and that to "raise the rent on him" because his family had behaved honestly and industriously was a monstrous exercise of arbitrary power. The upshot of the whole matter was a refusal on the part of the whole tenantry to pay the last "gale" or six months' rent. It is a noteworthy circumstance that none of the tenants are in arrear.

There are other accusations than that of raising the rent brought against Mr Bence Jones. The police barrack at Ballinascarthy was once a grogshop, given by the landlord to a dairymaid who had been long in his service. No sooner had she a groggery "to her fortune" than her hand was sought by a legion of admirers. It is not, I fancy, generally known in England that in this romantic country the warm-hearted, impulsive peasants almost invariably contract *mariages de convenance*.

It is said that a young man in the neighbouring city of Kerry was once sorely vexed in his mind as to his matrimonial choice. The "matchmaker" who arranges such matters had proposed two girls to him, one of whom had one cow and the other two cows "to her fortune." Now, the "Boy" liked the girl with one cow far better than her rival who had two, but the magnitude of the sacrifice he wished to make sat heavy on his soul. He consulted a patriarch renowned for his wisdom, and laid great stress upon his love for the girl with one cow. The oracle spake as follows: "Take the gyurl wid the two cows. There isn't the difference of a cow, begorra, betune any two women in the wor-r-ld." By similar reasoning a superannuated dairymaid with a grogshop is a very different person to the "pretty girl milking her cow" - sovereign lady of her presence, but of no groggery beside. Consequently the woman got married and died, and her husband having proved objectionable was evicted and the grogshop extinguished. This was another grievance against Mr Bence Jones, who is known to oppose the indiscriminate licensing which takes place in many parts of Ireland. I believe that in the neighbouring townlet of Clonakilty there are no less than forty-two whisky shops, a proportion to make Lord Aberdare's hair to stand on end. Furthermore it seems that after bearing with Mr Bence Jones for nearly forty years the people have dubbed him "tyrant" and "domineering Saxon," epithets certain to be applied to any Englishman who tries to do his own work in his own way in Ireland. Any insistence on anything being done in the master's way instead of the man's is "tyranny." Any curt command is "domineering." Irish peasants are accustomed to easier and pleasanter ways, and like to be coaxed and petted. It is only just to admit that under this treatment they display the utmost goodwill and pliancy. They will do anything to serve those who take them rightly, but they hate discipline. To the Saxon again it seems hard that he should be called upon to waste time in coaxing a mere hewer of wood and drawer of water, who, moreover, hews wood very badly, and draws water with exasperating deliberation. But a peremptory tone will not answer in southern and western Ireland.

It may be urged that it has taken the people a long time to discover that Mr Bence Jones was a tyrant. One thing is certain - they are likely soon to be rid of him. By living carefully he has been enabled to spend a large proportion of his income in improving his estate. He now announces his intention of throwing all his farm into pasture and leaving a country which has become uninhabitable.

It is curious, to say the least, that as he was correcting the proofs of the volume which embodies his experience, he was called upon to rise and welcome the resident magistrate and the officer commanding the patrol, considered necessary for the preservation of himself, his family, and the few dependants who yet remain steadfast.

CORK, December 20th

It is impossible to exaggerate the panic prevailing among the landed proprietors of Cork, Kerry, Tipperary, Limerick, and Clare. Within the triangle, which may be roughly described as enclosed by Galway town, Waterford, and Valentia Island, a reign of terror paralyses all those classes of the population owning any kind of property directly or indirectly connected with land.

Perhaps the agents whose calling is menaced with extinction preserve the most equable mind under the present arduous circumstances. They are to the manner born. They are accustomed to receive threatening letters frequently, and to be shot at now and then. Individually, therefore, they bear up very well, but it is far otherwise with their families, who look forward to St. Stephen's Day and its threatened meetings with undisguised apprehension. The men leave home in the morning bristling with double-barrelled carbines and revolving pistols, and, confiding either in themselves, their police escort, or both, keep, in the language of the country, a "good heart;" but it is far otherwise with their wives and daughters. As the "master" and the "boys" prepare to depart, and guns are being put on the car, together with the rugs and macintoshes, the matron's cheek grows pale, and her lips quiver as she bids farewell to the beloved ones, whom she may never see "safe home" again. This is no picture drawn by the imagination, with which flattering critics are pleased to credit me.

Such a scene as I describe was witnessed by me a few days ago, and I regret to hear that the brave lady, who bore up well for several weeks against ever-present anxiety, has broken down at last, and lies on a bed of sickness. In this struggle against a covert mutiny, women, as in open warfare, are the chief sufferers. There are many of the men who ask for nothing better than to be let loose on some visible mortal representatives of their intangible foe. But the general feeling is despondent. The unfortunate landowners, house proprietors, and many of the merchants, complain bitterly that they are delivered into the hands of a "convict," whose ticket of leave enables him to paralyse the industry of the country.

To a person unconnected with the landed interest of Ireland it is at first a little difficult to understand the almost insane terror of nearly all persons endowed with property. To the stranger the country is absolutely safe, and unless in the company of landlords or land agents he may go safely unarmed in any part of Ireland I have visited; but resident proprietors, and the representatives of absentees, are in very different case, and the farmers and labourers who have not yet joined the Land League are in a still worse position. So skilfully has this organisation been carried out that hardly a creature dare do his duty or speak his mind except the judges. In Court to-day the man O'Halloran, whose being sent up for trial at the Assizes here occasioned the riot at Tulla a few days since, was tried for appending a threatening notice to a chapel door. It will be recollected that the prisoner was brought before the magistrates at Tulla rather than at Ennis, in order to avoid a tumult, but that on its being known that he was committed for trial an uproar occurred, which ended in the bayoneting of three of the rioters by the police. The man was tried here to-day, and he will be tried again to-morrow before another jury.

I may not express an opinion on the evidence of the police; it will suffice that the jury of to-day did not agree, and that this absence of result provoked some severe remarks from the bench. Great blame is thrown upon Lord O'Hagan's Act[32] for frequent miscarriage of justice in this country, but the truth is that the outside pressure is too strong for any but a "packed" jury of independent, that is to say non-resident, persons to withstand.

That terrorism has prevailed not only over landlords who are flying from the country, and agents who are at least putting their families in the few places in which some semblance of order prevails - that is, within the shadow of a police barrack or under the wing of a garrison - but over merchants, as was proved the other day in the case of Mr Bence Jones's cattle. I hear of a similar occurrence to-day. Mr Richard Stacpoole, of Eden Vale, county Clare, wrote a few days since to a firm in Limerick for twelve tons of oilcake, not an insignificant order from a responsible person as times go. The answer was that the firm in question had not a pound of oilcake in store, but that the order could be transferred to a firm in Cork, who would direct the cake to some other person than Mr Stacpoole, "to be left till called for" at the Ennis Railway Station, and that if the purchaser would send somebody else's carts for it late at night or very early in the morning, he would probably get it home safely. It may be imagined that Mr Stacpoole declined to receive oilcake as if it were "potheen" or other contraband, and at once closed his account with the firm in question.

This instance is quoted out of many to show that the art of "Boycotting" is advancing from the proportions of a mere local strike to those of an almost national combination against any person who has incurred the resentment of the popular party. It is noteworthy that strict adherence to the "constitutional weapon" is mainly confined to the cases of those whom it is unsafe to attack by more violent means. His enemies dare not make an onslaught on Mr Stacpoole himself, for reasons well known and thoroughly appreciated; so they clip the ears of wretched hinds who are neither strong nor courageous enough to resist their violence, which is just now only

---

[32] Lord O'Hagan's Act had withdrawn from the sheriff the power of preparing jury lists, which had been used for political purposes. Some felt this enabled juries to be intimidated, [Clachan ed.].

employed against the defenceless; but such outrages are apparently quite sufficient to make the power of the Jacquerie absolute.

I am weary of hearing from panic-stricken interviewers that the "real Government of Ireland is that of the Land League;" but the facts adduced can hardly be passed over in silence. For the present, creditors have only two courses to pursue - to accept Griffith's valuation where they can get it, or to do nothing, await the action of Parliament, and go without money for their Christmas bills. "Weak holders," as they are called in the commercial world, must take what they can get, and stronger capitalists may wait for better times; for it is impossible to put the existing laws for the recovery of debt into effect. Evictions are out of the question. Neither Dublin writs nor "civil bills" can be served, except in a large town or its immediate neighbourhood, and seizure of goods for a common debt in country places is quite out of the question. The principal process-server in the town of Tipperary has retired from service, and addressed himself to "J.J." for several days past. That matters are going from bad to worse is proved by the calibre of the persons who are amply capable of paying their rent, but are afraid to do so. More than this, those who have paid before they received notices are threatened with pains and penalties if they do not join, publicly approve of, and subscribe to the popular combination.

Startling cases have just occurred in Tipperary. A farmer paying a very large rent even by English measure is leaving the country because he is threatened by vengeance if he do not immediately take back a labourer whom he dismissed for misconduct. Another large farmer is informed that all his labourers will be compelled to leave his employment unless he instantly joins the League. His farm includes a large percentage of tillage, and he must either undergo heavy pecuniary loss or submit, as he probably will do. A smaller tenant, who had been discovered to have paid on account a trifle more than Griffith's valuation, has been compelled to ask his landlord to give him the little balance back and a receipt in full. The request was acceded to, for the poor man declared that his life was not safe; that nobody would speak to him, and that nobody would work for him until he had righted himself with "the only Government which can carry its decrees into effect."

The 2nd Battalion Rifle Brigade has just arrived from Gibraltar, under the command of Colonel Carr Glyn, and will remain, together with the 26th Regiment, under Colonel Carr, and three troops of the 3rd Dragoon Guards, in Cork. The 37th Regiment leaves to make room for the Rifle Brigade; three companies go to Waterford, and the remainder to Kilkenny.

XVI - A CRUISE IN A GROWLER

CORK, December 21

Just before starting towards the scene of the last case of Boycotting I had returned from a tour in Kerry, undertaken mainly with the object of collecting facts and ideas concerning the fiercely-debated question of peasant propriety. There are other great estates in Kerry besides that of Lord Kenmare, which is twenty-six miles long, and covers 91,080 acres. There are Lord Lansdowne's still greater estate of 94,983 acres, and the large property held by Trinity College, both of which have given rise to considerable controversy of late.

In many parts of Kerry may be found townlands vying in wretchedness with Coshleen and Champolard, with Derryinver, Cleggan, and Omey Island while others give abundant evidence of improvement and enlightened management. On the north side of Dingle Bay lies the estate of Lord Ventry, a popular landlord I am told, for the reason that he has not "harassed his tenants" with improvements, nor sought to wipe out the effect of the old middleman style of mismanagement by reducing their number and forcing them to live in habitations better perhaps than they care for. The crowding of people into a few villages, brought about partly by the desire of middlemen to make a profit, partly by electioneering schemes, and partly by the natural gregariousness of the peasants, has been already too fully dwelt upon to need repetition. What was done by landlords and middlemen in many places has been emulated by squatters wherever they have succeeded in occupying free land like the Commons of Ardfert, the condition whereof rivals that of Lurgankeale, in Louth, and of the historic townland of Tibarney, in common, a map of which hung, if I mistake not, for some time in the Library of the House of Commons. This last-named spot consisted of 164 statute acres, divided into 222 lots among eleven tenants, who cultivated alternate ridges and patches in the same field. Whether held by small tenants or landlords or of middlemen or by small proprietors, the land was always in the same state of confusion.

On portions of the Blennerhasset estate previously spoken of, and on the Commons of Ardfert, the effect may be studied of influences against which the modern Kerry landlord has been in many cases striving for the whole of his lifetime. Half a century ago the advice to "neither a borrower nor a lender be," was systematically ignored. It is curious to hear that two eminent patriots of the period, Daniel O'Connell and the Knight of Kerry, were both middlemen, and in the case of Cahirciveen had one of the Blennerhassets as a co-middleman under Trinity College, and that the compact was only finally annulled by the resolution of the latter to have no more to do with it. The great "Liberator" considered as a middleman appears in an odd light, but he was a liberal specimen of the genus, and with his partners supplied Cahirciveen with previously unheard-of drainage and pavement. At the same time the ends of the Island of Valentia were leased by Maurice Fitzgerald, Knight of Kerry, the friend of Castlereagh and Wellington, to other middlemen, and it seemed that the work of confusion could go no further.

The Island of Valentia was, I was informed, a favourable spot on which to study the operation of paternal government. Sir Peter Fitzgerald, the late Knight of Kerry, had enjoyed unbounded popularity, and had employed his personal influence to raise the population under his care in the social scale. When he had retaken the lands leased to Sir James O'Connell or his ancestor, he found certain lowlands, notably that of Bally Hearny, among a number of small holders; but the patches held by each tenant were oddly distributed. Three men held farms of thirty acres each, made up of detached lots completely separate one from the other, and scattered broadcast over the area of the townlands; while another man's farm of the same area extended from the sea at one end to the top of the mountain at the other, measuring one mile and fourteen perches in length, with an average width of twenty perches. After some difficulties had been surmounted the fields were "squared," the odds and ends of lands consolidated, and the partnership in fields, with its absurd practice of cultivating alternate ridges, abolished.

In a speech addressed by the Knight of Kerry to his tenants, he distinctly put his foot down on the system of subdivision, to which the peasantry of Ireland are almost insanely attached. He determined to permit nothing of the kind in the future. To those who had already subdivided he offered new mountain farms, leaving the sub-dividers to decide who should remain and who should remove. To those removed for sub-dividing their small holdings, and to those whose still smaller patches made their removal imperative, reclaimed and reclaimable lands at Corobeg and Bray Head were offered, with brand new houses; and after much discussion and final casting of lots the extruded ones resigned themselves to the fearful doom of removal from the spots to which they had long clung like limpets.

To reach Valentia Island it is necessary to leave the railway track from Mallow to Tralee, and at Killarney commence what in London parlance might be called a cruise in a "growler;" for an unmistakable "growler," well built and comfortably lined, was the vehicle supplied to me as a "carriage," with a pair of excellent horses, by Spillane, the sometime guide and present postingmaster of Killarney. The postchaise assumes many forms in Ireland, but only once have I met the original coupe holding only two persons. It is a long drive to the ferry at the extremity of the peninsula between the bays of Kenmare and Dingle. Beyond, the Island of Valentia lies like a breakwater against the Atlantic, and the scene at nightfall is strange enough, with flashing lanterns, shouting ferrymen, and plashing oars. The ferryman is far from considering Valentia Harbour as a drawback to the island, and, like a fine old discontented retainer as he is, complains bitterly of the attempt made years ago by the late Knight of Kerry to establish a steam ferry. But ferrymen are always stern sticklers for vested rights. Doubtless Charon[33] claimed heavy compensation when the Styx Ferry was disestablished. Apart from the ferryman, however, the Valentians are by no means enamoured of their insular position. "That ould blackgyard of a ferry" is, in fact, just now a serious item of discontent.

It is urged by the islanders, nearly three thousand in number, including the villagers, the quarrymen, and the staff of telegraphists, presided over by the skilful and courteous Mr Graves, that the ferry is the cause of half their troubles. The peasants, who sell their stock at the thirteen fairs held yearly at Cahirciveen, declare that the cost of the ferry-boat for themselves and their beasts is a substantial reason for the reduction of the rent, inasmuch as they are put at a disadvantage with the people on the mainland. This is not the only grievance of that section transplanted to the hill side by Bray Head. They complain that they are afar off - a droll objection on an island six miles long - and have given their settlement the nickname of "Paris," in allusion to its remoteness from Knightstown and the ferry which leads to the grogshops and Fenian centres of Cahirciveen. I am told that the duty on the spirits sold in that cheerful townlet exceeds the whole annual value of the barony of Iveragh, and can bear witness to the convergence of the surrounding population on market day.

Beside the grievances already enumerated, and only felt in their full poignancy since the establishment of a branch of the Land League at Cahirciveen, the Valentians now complain that their land is "set" too high.

Amid the mass of conflicting evidence and the diverse methods of calculation, it is very difficult to arrive at any conclusion on this point. That the land is let above Griffith's valuation is certain, but so is much more of the cheapest land in the west and south. Moreover, the improvements made by the late Sir Peter Fitzgerald were not only considerable in the way of draining and fencing, but are visible to the naked eye in the shape of some fifty new houses, well and solidly built of stone with slate roofs, sleeping rooms up stairs, properly separated after the most approved fashion, a cowhouse, and other offices required by the Board of Works. These houses, which contrast remarkably with the old structures not yet improved off the face of the island, accommodate half of Sir Maurice Fitzgerald's agricultural tenants, of whom there are about 100 on his part of the island, as well as eighty-eight cottier or labourer tenants, who work for the farmers or at the

---

[33] In Greek mythology, Charon was the ferryman who ferried the dead to the underworld. [Clachan ed.].

slate quarry, and have little patches of ground attached to their cabins. Each new house built out-and-out has cost £80, and those put on existing foundations about £60 It seems to me wonderful that anybody should dream of building anything on the site of an Irish peasant's hut, but perhaps I am fastidious. So far as I make it out, about 6 per cent. has been charged for building and other improvements to the tenant, whose rent has thus in one case been raised by 2s. 6d., and in others by as much as 3s. 3d. per acre. As the entire rent in one case reaches 8s., and in the other 10s. 9d. per acre, it does not seem enormous; but it is no business of mine to decide on value. I only state facts as distinctly as I can, and whether the rent be light or heavy there is no doubt that the tenants have paid it with some approach to regularity even up to date, and that the local agitation is deprived of much of its effervescence owing to this fact. Against this fair side of the picture is the awkward truth that during the bad times of last winter the Valentians, including the tenants of the Knight of Kerry and those of Trinity College, received about £1,200 worth of relief among a couple of thousand souls.

It is equally worthy of remark that those tenants for whom new houses have been built are by no means enthusiastic about them, and apparently would rather save the rent of them and live in a rough stone cabin as of old. I am aware that in making this statement I am liable to a charge of prejudice against the ignorant people, of whom I can only speak with pity not unmixed with kindness. I may be told that pigs were thought to be dirty until people took to keeping them clean, and that the animals are known to prefer their last state to their first. I may also be told that filth is the outcome of poverty, and that the Irish peasantry are filthy in their habits because they are poor. Now, to speak out plainly, this is not true; for I have seen people with a round sum on deposit at the bank, and in one case paying as much as £250 rent for their farms, living amid almost indescribable filth. The dislike of soap and water, except for the visible parts of the human body on high days and holidays, appears to be part of the general indifference to beauty remarkable in the Irish peasant. His cottage is never adorned with flowers. Neither rose, honeysuckle, nor jasmine clings around his door. In a climate which allows fuchsia hedges to grow and bloom luxuriantly none appear round the peasant's garden. Myrtles, laurel, and bay there are in plenty at Valentia, but they are grouped near the gigantic fuchsia bush at Glanleam, or nestle among the houses of the telegraphic company. It is the same in other places. All is unloveliness and squalor, even when potatoes are plentiful and butter fetches a high price at Cork.

These thoughts were borne strongly in upon me during a visit to "Paris." A drifting rain obscured the Skelligs, and drove me to take shelter in a "Parisian" household. The house stood sound and square to the wind with its slated roof and thick stone whitewashed walls, whitewash being ordained by a Board of Works wildly striving for cleanliness and health. The exterior of the house itself was well enough, but alack for the approaches and the interior! Plunging through mud I reached the door, and, glancing through the window, descried the inevitable pig inside the kitchen. The people - to be just to them - seemed a little fluttered, if not ashamed, of the plight in which I found them. It was quite evident that since the new £80 house was built not a drop of water had been expended on its interior. The wooden staircase leading to the bedrooms aloft was in such condition that I shuddered to touch its sticky surface, the floor so filthy that I instinctively gathered up the skirts of my overcoat, the bedsteads filled up with blankets and odds and ends of unimaginable shades of dirt colour.

Yet this apparently poverty-stricken home was already subdivided in defiance of the conditions of tenancy. The eldest daughter had been married some little time without the landlord or bailiff finding it out, and there was the bridegroom established in half of the house and endowed with half of the farm. He was at home too; a huge black-browed fellow, doing nothing at all, after the manner of his kind. And this was the outcome of an attempt to distribute the Valentians in holdings of respectable size and to make them live in houses instead of hovels. Two families were already established in the place of one, and the house was already like unto a sty. The inhabitants, however, were mighty civil when they recovered from their surprise, and spoke well of their landlord and of everybody connected with him, especially of the ladies of his family, who had done much to find paying employment for the girls by getting them a market for knitted and other needlework.

Pursuing my cruise in a Growler round the coast I came past some magnificent scenery by Waterville, at the head of Ballinskelligs Bay to Derrynane, once the abode of the "Liberator," and now occupied by Mr Daniel O'Connell, his grandson, who gave me a curious instance of the profit to be realised on a dairy and grazing farm. He has leased the island of Scariff from Lord Dunraven for £60 per annum, has put a dairyman upon it, and sells off of it yearly produce, butter, cattle, sheep, wool, and pigs, to the value of £230, the valuation of the island, according to Griffith, being, including the dairyman's house £27 5s. Mr O'Connell also gave me an odd proof of the retribution which appears likely to fall upon the landowners of the barony of Iveragh.

When the Government valuation was first made public it was protested against by Sir James O'Connell, who succeeded in getting it reduced by 30 per cent., an unfortunate circumstance for the present proprietors if the Land League continue to have it all their own way. The League, however, has not yet troubled Derrynane; the tenants, who since 1841 have been greatly reduced in number by emigration and the consolidation of holdings, have paid their rent fairly up to this, that is to say fairly according to the usage of that remote part of Kerry. They average "the grass of six cows," with the run of the mountain, "for rather more" collops or young cows, not yet in milk.

Derrynane rejoices in many memorials of the Liberator, but the relic of "Ould Dan" that all visitors, and especially Irishmen, are most anxious to see, is in the oblong mahogany box lying on the tall desk at which he was wont to stand and write. It is that article of furniture without which no Irish gentleman's equipment was more complete than his house without an avenue. "My pistols which I shot Captain Marker," as poor Rawdon Crawley put it. There reposes peacefully enough now by the side of its companion, the weapon with which the "Liberator" shot Mr D'Esterre. It is a flint lock pistol of very large bore, and with stock reaching to the muzzle. One peculiarity about this pistol is worthy of note. Beneath the trigger guard a piece of steel extends curving downwards and outwards towards the muzzle, a convenient device, as I find, for steadying the weapon by aid of the second finger. On the stock is cut rudely a capital D., for D'Esterre. There are no other marks, although the pistols have a pedigree and a story attached to them.

One day an English officer stationed in Ireland found himself in the painful position of waiting for remittances. Knowing nobody likely to be useful to him he appealed to the most noteworthy Irishman of his day, and stating his pressing need, asked him to lend him £50 until his funds came to hand. Daniel O'Connell, who was a keen judge of character, lent him the money without hesitation, and was shortly repaid, with many expressions of gratitude. About a year afterwards the Englishman was ordered on a foreign station, and, unwilling to leave Ireland without giving some tangible expression of his thankfulness to O'Connell, called upon him and presented him with the duelling pistols in question, which were accepted as heartily as the money was lent. On taking his leave the Englishman said, "If you should ever have occasion to use these pistols you will find them very good ones; they have already killed ten men." The first and only time "Ould Dan" used them he killed Mr D'Esterre, to whose family, it must be added, he afterwards did all he could to atone for that injury.

Mr O'Connell also showed me a brass blunderbuss once the property of Robert Emmet. It has a revolving chamber, which, instead of turning automatically, must be adjusted by hand after every shot, a curious forerunner of Colt's invention, adaptation, or revival. Derrynane is delightfully situated at a spot called appropriately "White Strand," from the silvery sand washed by the Atlantic waves. Above it stands the celebrated circular fort of Staigue, built of dry stone, and with an inclined plane inside like those at West Cove and Ballycarbery. Opposite is the magnificent rocky peninsula of Lamb Head, the road across which much resembles parts of St. Gothard, plus the magnificent sea shining in the sun.

The crag of Lamb Head, broken into a thousand jagged slopes, is here and there overgrown with short sweet herbage. Wherever grass grows there will a Kerry calf or "collop" be found. How the pretty little black cattle cling like flies to those dizzy windy heights is marvellous; but there they are, night and day, for months at a stretch, giving no trouble to anybody, growing into condition ready for "finishing" on richer pasture, and giving life and beauty to a scene which would, without them, be but grandly desolate. The little Kerries are greatly prized as "milkers," and they yield good beef, but very little of it - not more than four hundredweight per beast. By the side of the superb shorthorns of the Ardfert herd they look like goats; but such cattle as Mr Crosbie's cream-coloured bull are only suited to richer pasture than the rocks of Lamb Head. It may also be added that for the purpose of dairy-farms the best commercial cows are all bred between the rough native cattle and shorthorns, or between Devon and Ayrshire, the latter cross being specially liked by Mr Hegarty, of Mill Street, county Cork, referred to in a previous letter, and by many other good judges. This fact, however, by no means detracts from the value of such a magnificent herd as that of Mr Crosbie. On the contrary it is held by many experts that first-class shorthorn bulls are a necessity for preventing the cross-bred animals from reverting to the original local type.

The improvement in cattle in Kerry, owing to the importation of shorthorns by Mr Crosbie, and in a smaller degree by other proprietors, is very marked; but despite this the thoroughbred Kerry still remains and is likely to remain lord of the mountain until mayhap he be displaced by the smaller Scotch cattle, as he has already been in some localities by the black-faced sheep, who leads an equally hardy and independent life until wanted for "finishing."

From Derrynane the road passes along the coast, and through Sneem to Derryquin, the estate of that typical landlord, Mr F.C. Bland, beyond whose lands lie those of Mr Mahony, of Dromore, the apostle of concrete and author of a pamphlet which has made a great noise in Ireland, and is accepted by "improving" landlords as stating their case perfectly. Mr Bland, whose domain lies on the north side of the embouchure of the Kenmare River, owns about thirty-eight square miles of territory, and is one of the most popular men in Kerry. Extraordinary stories are told of him. "Know 'um, begorra," answered a native to my query, "Don't I know 'um; and it is he that's the good man, your honour, and every man and baste will do anything for 'um, and he has got tame lobsthers that sit up to be fed, and a tame salmon that follows 'um about like a dog."

This, to say the least, appeared an ample statement; but I confess the temptation to see the man who owned contented tenants and tame fish was too strong to be overcome, and I therefore procured an introduction to Mr Bland, who with great modesty promised to show me his improvements on condition that I would also look over those of that arch improver his neighbour, Mr Mahony. To appraise the real value of the work done by these two gentlemen at Derryquin and Dromore - a region of some eighty-five square miles altogether - it must be understood that forty years ago this part of Kerry was, with the exception of the main track to Cork, absolutely without roads, an almost impassable tract of wild mountain and morass cut up by streams, which when swollen stopped all communication even for foot passengers. Yet it was inhabited by a considerable population paying rent, sometimes, for the mountain farms, to which they carried their store of meal on their backs.

It is said that the father of Mr Bland went to his first school in a pannier, a stone being put in the opposite one to steady the load on the ass's back. This was the "good old-time," when few of the people could speak English, none could read or write, all spun their wool and made their bread at home, and none dreamed of opposing "the master's will." Fortunately they were in good hands, for Mr Bland went to work, at first gently and afterwards more swiftly, at the task of making land and people more civilised than had been thought possible up to his time. During thirty years he has laid out £7,000 of his own and £10,000 of Government money in bringing his estate and people somewhat into consonance with modern ideas. He has made twenty-three miles of road, built thirty stone houses with slated or tiled roofs, and three schools. When the estate came into his hands there was not a cart upon it except at Derryquin itself. Now two-thirds of the tenants have carts and horses. Forty years ago the entire export and import trade was done by a carrier who came from Cork once a month and was looked for as anxiously as the periodical steamer at a station on the West Coast of Africa. Now there are carriers weekly in all directions, and steamboats calling regularly in Kenmare Bay. All this work has been compassed by the landlord, with the partial assistance of the Government, with the exception of one solitary house, which was built by the tenant.

The story of Mr Bland's tame fish, which "sat up, and followed him about like a dog," turns out to have had some foundation in fact. There is a fine pool of salt water at Derryquin (Ang. "Oakslope") Castle, which stands on the edge of Kenmare Bay; and this pool not long since held a number of tame fish, which came to be fed when anybody approached, just as carp do in many well-known places. Unluckily, however, a neighbouring otter found this out, and carried away the unfortunate fish at the rate of two every night till not a single fish is left. I hear that both salmon and pollock became equally tame, but that the former, although eating everything offered them, became miserably poor in a comparatively short time. The only denizen of the pool that I actually saw was a lobster, who came out from under a stone as I approached, in the hope, I was told, that I was going to give him a mussel.

Mr Bland, however, if he has not proved so redoubtable a fish-tamer as my original informant opined, has proved very successful in oyster culture. Having a little salt-water inlet, with a river running into it, he conceived the idea of breeding and raising oysters, but found the climate bad for "spatting," and now buys his tiny young oysters by the ten thousand at the Isle of Rhe, and puts them down in long perforated boxes on his oyster beds. When they are between three and four years old he consigns them to a correspondent at Ballyvaughan, who puts them in, I believe, deep-sea oyster beds for a while and converts them into the famous Burren oysters, which, like the Marenne oysters, are generally preferred by Englishmen to "Natives," while the "spat" of the latter is eagerly sought by the French for development into *Huitres d'Ostende*.

It rained so furiously at Derryquin that I hardly saw so much of Mr Bland's estate as I could have wished, but between the showers I was able to form a fair idea of his building and road improvement. It is a matter of pride to the proprietor that on a territory once impassable by a wheeled vehicle he can now drive to every farm in a carriage and pair, and that among tenants averaging "the grass of six cows" apiece; men and women at least speak English, and children go to school. The barbarous state of the country and inhabitants forty years ago may be gathered from the following anecdote. Two gentlemen were out shooting on the mountain and were driven by a "Kerry shower" - which is as much like a cataract as anything I know of - into a peasant's cabin. The man received them with all the dignity and self-possession peculiar to the best of his class, and when the storm cleared off invited them to eat with him on their return from the hillside. When they came back, expecting only potatoes and butter, they were astounded to see their host take several pieces of some kind of meat out of the pot and place them on the table, for there were no plates before them. It turned out that the mysterious meat was that of a newly-born calf whose dam was yet lying helpless in a corner of the cabin. The man was quite unconscious that there was anything objectionable in the dreadful food, and offered it to "the masthers" with perfect grace, and without the slightest pang at the costliness of the banquet. He had given the best and only meat he had to his guests. Like the Italian gentleman with his falcon, or rather the Arab sheik with his horse, who, my friend Mr Browning tells me, is the original of Boccaccio's mamby-pamby story, the Kerry mountaineer had fulfilled the rites of hospitality at whatever cost. For long after the date of the grim repast just recorded, in fact, even till to-day, the peasants on the Derryquin estate have been accustomed to refer their almost innumerable wrangles and squabbles to the decision of "the masther," who might be figured as a kind of Hibernian St. Louis, sitting under a tree, and adjudicating between his subjects. Sometimes it was not very easy to arrive at a decision. Not very long ago a man came with a complaint that his once-intended son-in-law had behaved shabbily and fraudulently. It appeared that the father of the girl had agreed with the "boy" that a cow should be killed "to furnish forth the marriage table;" that the father should provide the cow for the happy day, and that the cost of the animal should be shared between them. The cow had been killed, and the bride had been dressed, but the Kerry "county Guy" had not been forthcoming, that mercenary youth having married out of hand another girl with four more cows to her fortune than the one he was engaged to. Hereat the outraged parent demanded, not that he should pay damages for breach of promise, but his share of the cost of the cow. "And," said the masther, "you had the cow and the daughter thrown on your hands?" "Divil a throw, your honour," was the reply; "mee daughter got another husband in tin minutes, begorra, and we ate the cow, your honour; but Mike is a blackgyard, and should pay his half of the cow, your honour." This was a knotty case, but his "honour" decided that Mike should pay his share, and, to do that fickle bridegroom justice, he paid up with very little demurring. He was clearly three cows and a half the better by his bargain, and, I believe, lives happily to this day. It is needless to say that he has numerous children.

Mr Bland has under his paternal rule about 300 agricultural tenants besides the villagers of Sneem, who mostly have lots lying contiguous to, or at some little distance from, their houses. The holdings, albeit averaging the grass of six cows, vary very considerably in size and quality. Thus one farmer holds 803 acres, or "the grass of twenty-four cows," with mountain run attached, at a rent of £35, while another who has 1,493 acres is only charged £26 for "the grass of seventeen cows," with proportionate mountain. Even on holdings of this size, as well as on others of less value, such as 250 acres at a rent of £13 15s., Mr Bland has experienced great difficulty in inducing the tenants to bear any share of the cost of building and other improvements. Of course there are tenants and tenants at Derryquin, as elsewhere, but the general feeling has undoubtedly been averse to paying an extra percentage for improvements. Mr Bland has done what he could, but has rarely found anybody inclined to pay more than 2 per cent., and one irreconcilable actually refused to pay £1 a year extra to have a £70 house built for him. The "masther" appears to take a view of the subject which might have been with great advantage more widely distributed among Irish proprietors of the improving sort. It is not extravagant to ask a farmer with the nominal grass of twenty cows, and a mountain run on which he grazes twice as many bullocks, to pay 5 per cent. on £80 or £100 as the rent of a good and substantial house; but it is preposterous to ask the holder of a ten-acre lot to do likewise. Such peasants should, as I observed in one of my early letters, not be called farmers at all. Their condition is about equal to that of the English farm labourer. When the landlord can afford to build better cottages for them than they now have, he should certainly not expect more than 1, or at best 2 per cent. for his outlay, and carry the balance to his profit and loss account, after the manner of English landowners of the best class. The Derryquin houses or cottages are very well built and excellently planned; they are also very pretty with their whitewashed walls, red tile roofs, and doors painted red to match. These patches of bright colour give extraordinary cheerfulness to a landscape otherwise of green, brown, and grey, looking cold enough under a weeping sky. The walls are of stone, "dashed" after the Irish fashion with mortar or concrete, and slate roofs have now given place to red tiles in fancy patterns. Inside they are divided into two rooms on the ground floor, paved with concrete, and two sleeping rooms above, in order, if possible, to keep the people from huddling together at night. It is a fact, impossible as it may appear, that when the pretty and tasteful lodge at the gate of Derryquin was first built, the occupants, four in number, all slept together in one room rather than be separated at night, and were only induced to occupy the apartments built to prevent this habit by the threat of eviction. I might have doubted this amazing story had I not seen the condition of a cottage rebuilt recently on an old foundation at a cost of £60, for which a rent of £1 is charged. The tenant fought hard against the innovation, and yielded to the imposition of £1 a year, and a clean new house, only under fear of being turned off the estate. He and his have only been in the new building for a few weeks, but they have made wild work of it already. In the room to the left of the door a "bonneva," or half-grown pig of the size called a "shote," in the State of Georgia, was disporting himself by looking on at a girl spinning wool, a "boy" doing nothing, and two dirty youngsters wallowing on the floor. In the other brand new room, not long since left sweet and tidy by the builders, were piled an immense heap of turf and a great store of potatoes, over against which stood a bedstead and a pair of boots. There was nothing else in the room, not the slightest fragment of table or chair, not a sign of water or washing utensils; in the room above were also bedsteads, without anything that could be called bedding, and no other stick of furniture. Before the front door was a rough stone causeway, already ankle-deep in filth. Close up to the rear of the house was a dung-heap of portentous size and savour. Evidently this was a case of taking the horse to the water and being unable to make him drink, for the people thrust into a clean house were obviously doing their best to bring it into harmony with their own views. I heard also of a remarkable case of subdivision on the part of some labourers on Mr Bland's estate, higher up on the mountain. A couple or three years ago two "boys" received permission to occupy a cabin on a little patch of land. This spot has since grown into a colony. The "boys" have both got married, and have children. Their brothers-in-law also, with wives and children, as a matter of course, have built their cabins against the original one given to the two bachelors, and the holding has a population of forty-five souls. These poor people are surely the most affectionate in the world, and the uproar when any one of the colony is ailing is astonishing, and bewildering to more civilised and perhaps colder-blooded folk.

Mr R. Mahony's estate of Dromore (Anglice "Big Ridge") is the theatre of even more extensive improvements than those of Derryquin. Mr Mahony has 29,163 acres in Kerry, valued by Griffith at £3,071 In his pamphlet he states: - "In the year 1851 I came into possession of my estate. Old rentals in my possession show that for many years previous to that date there had been allowances made to tenants at the rate of about £1,000 per annum. Yet when I took up the estate there was not one drain made by a tenant, not one slated house, not a perch of road, not a yard of sub-soiled land. I then adopted the system of making all improvements myself, charging interest of the outlay upon the occupier according to the circumstances and increased value of the farm. The result has been that in five-and-twenty years I have built about eighty houses and offices slated or tiled, made twenty-eight miles of road, built nine bridges, made twenty-three miles of fences, thoroughly drained about five hundred acres, planted one hundred and fifty acres of waste land, and proportionately improved the condition and circumstances of the people."

There is abundant evidence of Mr Mahony's work on his estate, which is not only valuable in itself but as an example. The roads are admirably laid, and the employment of concrete made of Portland cement and the sand and pebbles of the seashore, since followed at Ardfert, was initiated at Dromore. Walls, floors, partitions, are all of concrete, and the roofs of the houses last built of handsome red tiles. The disposition of the apartments in the Dromore cottages varies somewhat from that of the neighbouring estate. The principal room, or kitchen, has nothing above it but the high-pitched roof, lined with wood tastefully disposed. The remaining three apartments are two on the ground floor, a tiny parlour and convenient bedroom, and one full-sized bedroom above. Separate cow-houses and pigsties are also appended to each cottage. So far as can be judged from a hurried visit, many of the houses are very well and tidily kept; in fact, so treated as not to destroy hope in the future of the Irish peasant cultivator, although this trimness is by no means so general as it might be. Mr Mahony has also, by way of showing his people how things should be done, a model farm and dairy, of such moderate size as not to be beyond the ambition of a successful tenant. The proprietor has also, like Mr Bland and Mr Butler, of Waterville, a successful salmon fishery, great part of the produce whereof goes, at some little advance on sixpence per pound, to the agents of a London firm, who also get an enormous supply of mushrooms from county Kerry.

There is a greatly-improved property in county Cork, lying west of Macroom and south of Mill Street. This is Ballyvourney, one of the estates of Sir

George St. John Colthurst, of Ardrum, whose father laid out an immense sum in reclaiming a portion of the 25,000 acres, which bring him in about £5,000 per annum.

There are other landlords in the counties of Cork and Kerry who, like Mr Bence Jones, have done well by their land; but there is no occasion to multiply experiences of a similar character. The purpose of my Kerry excursion was to observe the Kerry peasant when he had been left to himself, and where he had been looked after, and perhaps governed, by a landlord whose interest in him had not been diminished by recent legislation. My impression is very much the same as that produced by my visit to Connemara, that the peasant requires firm as well as gentle handling, and that his emancipation from the control of his landlord should be accompanied by some other authority representing the State, and interfering to prevent the tendency to local congestion of population.

The Kerry peasant's qualities are in the main good, and he is upheld under difficulties by hopefulness almost equal to his vanity and habit of exaggeration. A Kerry man's boat is a ship, his cabin is a house, his shrubs are trees, his "boreen" is an avenue, and, as a native bard declares, "all his hens are paycocks." He may be briefly described as in morals correct, disposition kindly, manners excellent, customs filthy. It is, however, despite his hopefulness, difficult to find any trace of that gaiety for which he was formerly famous, whether justly or not. His amusements outside the calm of Derrynane, Derryquin, and Dromore, appear to be cattle fairs, whisky, and sedition. At times he is unconsciously humorous, as in the story of the Duchess of Marlborough's Indian meal distributed for the relief of the poor during the hard time of last winter. A gentleman, who ought to know better, was buying some potheen, or illicit whisky, of the maker. "Now, Pat," said he, "I hope this lot is better than the last." "And, your honour," was the reply, "the last was but the name of whisky. Begorra, it's the Duchess's meal as makes mighty poor potheen." This was said quite seriously and with an injured air. For there is no merriment in Kerry. The old dances at the cross roads are danced no more. The pipe of the piper is played out.

XVII – "BOYCOTTED" AT CHRISTMASTIDE

KILFINANE, CO. LIMERICK, Christmas Eve.

The fox-terrier sits blinking on the hearth-rug in the pretty drawing-room as nightfall approaches, and a servant appears with a message that a woman has come with a big cake from Mrs O'Blank, a sympathising neighbour. There is no mistake about the size and condition of the cake; it is a yard and a quarter in circumference; it has a shining holiday face, like that of the fabled pigs who ran about ready roasted, covered with delicately-browned "crackling," perfumed with sage and onions, and carrying huge bowls of apple-sauce in their mouths. As the pigs cried, "Come and eat me," so does the cake appeal, but in more subtle manner, to the instincts and nostrils of all present. It has that pleasant scent with it peculiar to newly-baked plumcake. Huge plums, which have worked their way perseveringly to the surface, wink invitingly, and, above all, the cake is hot, gloriously hot, besides having with it a delicate zest of contraband acquired by being smuggled on to the premises under Biddy M'Carthy's shawl.

Biddy has watched the moment when the "boys" on the watch - scowling ruffians by the same token - had gone in quest of tea or more potent refreshment, and has slipped from the avenue which runs past the house instead of up to it, by the lodge gate and up to the door in that spirit-like fashion peculiar to this part of Ireland. When they wish to do so, the people appear to spring out of the ground. Two minutes before the monotony of existence is broken by a fight there will not be a soul to be seen, but no sooner is it discovered that some unlucky wight[34] is in present receipt of a "big bating" than hundreds appear on the spot, and struggle for a "vacancy," like the lame piper who howled for the same at the "murthering" of a bailiff.

This ghost-like faculty, however, has served us right well, for I need not speculate upon what would have happened to Mrs M'Carthy (whose real name is not given for obvious reasons) if she had been discovered carrying a huge cake to a house under ban. She would not have been injured bodily; no soul in Kilfinane would have touched the cake, much less have eaten the hateful food made and baked and attempted to be carried to the stronghold of the "tyrant;" but it would have gone ill with the brave little woman nevertheless. Her husband would have been compelled to seek elsewhere for a livelihood, for neither farmer nor tradesman would dare to employ either him or her. Her elder children would have been pointed at as they went to school, and sent to Coventry while there; and she would have been refused

[34] Living person – Old English, [Clachan ed.].

151

milk for the younger ones. Not a potato nor a pound of meal nor an egg could she have bought all through the hamlet; and if people at a distance had sold her anything, they would have been intercepted and compelled to take it back again. The carriers would not have delivered to or taken parcels from her; she would, in fact, have been very much in the condition that Eve, according to Lord Byron, thought she could put Cain into by cursing him.

Fortunately, however, the cake-bearer has escaped, and we fall with keen appetites upon the not very digestible banquet she has provided. The blockade has been successfully run, and we celebrate the event accordingly. We are not so very badly off after all, and in fact have passed a by no means dull time for the last two days. It is not quite so easy to frighten our garrison as a pack of sympathising peasants who attempt no kind of resistance against the mysterious leaders of the Jacquerie. The son of the house and his two grown cousins are here, the butler and gardener still remain staunch, as well as the coachman and a couple of bailiffs living outside, all "Boycotted" also. Moreover, we have a cook and housemaid with us, and two members of the Royal Constabulary. We have busy times, too. So far as turkeys, geese, chickens, and eggs, butter and bacon are concerned, we have enough and to spare within protecting range of rifle and revolver, but for fresh beef and mutton and flour we must depend upon Cork. Now the mysterious agent in Cork who sends us the supplies cannot get them carried nearer to the house than the railway station at Kilmallock, the interesting little town at which one of the county members keeps the inn and "runs" the cars, a fact whereof the citizens are not a little proud. When we receive the news, letter or telegram, announcing that meat or other stores will arrive by a certain train, we drive down to meet it, and without the slightest assistance, for not a single gloomy by-stander would do us a hand's turn, we carry it off to our own car, and thanks to the awe inspired by army revolvers, Winchester rifles, one constable on the car, and those officially at the railway station, bring our property away.

A day since there was great excitement concerning the arrival of a daughter of the house, who was coming down to keep house for the "boys" whose guest I am. Her brother and one of her cousins went down on the car to meet her, armed as usual, for although they would be comparatively safe with a lady on the car, they ran considerable risk until she was actually on board. The train came, but not the young lady, and as it was broad daylight her well-armed escort came back again. Towards the hour for the arrival of the evening train there was more anxiety. It was dark, but it was absolutely necessary to go down to Kilmallock again, on the off chance that she might have come later than was expected, and had forgotten to telegraph. If she had arrived and nobody had been there to meet her, the consequences would have been awkward. She would not, it is true, have been exposed to the slightest insult, for except in the case of Miss Gardiner, of Farmhill, I believe Irishmen have never forgotten their natural gallantry so much as to insult, much less shoot at and wound, a lady. There would, therefore, have been no fear of violence; but it is very doubtful whether anybody would have removed her trunks from the spot on which they had been laid down. Most assuredly no cardriver would have dared to drive her home, and I question if any house in Kilmallock would have afforded her shelter. However, she did not come by the train after all, and the "boys" drove back, not without an Irish howl to keep them company on the road.

Dinner over, the company being composed of the three "boys" and the writer, who among them made short work of a plump turkey and a vigorous inroad on a round of beef, besides disposing of soups, sweets, and sherry - not a bad menu under "Boycotting" rules - we, after seeing that the front door was properly barred, bolted, and chained, and the iron-linked shutters, relics of the Fenian time, made equally secure, adjourned to the kitchen for a smoke, a common practice in this part of Ireland. The kitchen, with its red-tiled floor, is a capital smoking room, warm and cosy, and while tobacco is leisurely puffed, and that eternal subject, "the state of the country," discussed, the eye reposes complacently on the treasures suspended from the hooks on the ceiling, plump hams and sides of well-fed bacon giving assurance that the garrison is far from being reduced to extremities. But there are in the kitchen other objects less suggestive of festivity. On the round table by the central column supporting the kitchen roof lie sundry revolvers, and nearer one of the windows a couple of repeating rifles and the double-barrelled carbines of the constabulary. Two members of that well-grown and well set-up corps are seated at a corner of the dresser, deeply engrossed in the intricacies of the mysterious game of forty-five, before which the mind of the dull Saxon remains bewildered in hopeless incapacity. Presently the well-thumbed pack is laid aside, and one of the constables addresses himself to the task of closing and barring up the shutters, thus shutting out all chance of any present being picked off by a shot through the window, as was done when Miss Gardiner was wounded under somewhat similar circumstances.

There is a great deal of gossip concerning the "Boycotting" of Mr Bence Jones, and that of the most recent victim, The Macgillicuddy of the Reeks, whose family is well known to all present; but even the one engrossing subject wears itself out at last. One cannot attain any wild pitch of hilarity among bolts and bars and Winchester rifles. Nobody appears to care for any stories but such as bear upon the present troubles and the Fenian affair in 1867. At Kilmallock there is no sign of song or dance; no talk of pantomimes, and what jokes are made bear grim reference to troubles actually endured and possible troubles to come.

By day it is by no means dreary. To begin with, the house is built on a charming spot six miles distant from a railway station; in front and beyond the lawn is a pretty little lake broken up by islands, making a tender foreground for the Galtee and nearer mountains. From the opposite side the view is equally delightful, the hills being crowned with trees and brushwood, an unusual sight in Ireland. Down the slope of the immense saddle-backed range lie fields of the brightest green, divided by banks and hedges delightful to look at after the grim stone walls of Mayo, Galway, and Clare. From behind these grassy slopes peeps the purple crest of the distant mountains, giving grandeur to a scene which might otherwise have been deemed tame. The climate, although chilled by recent heavy rains, is deliciously soft, and the breeze has none of that incisive quality common to the more northern hills. It is needless to say that at sunrise there is no chance of meeting any watchers of the "Boycotting" brigade. At seven o'clock any quantity of cargo might be "run" into the beleaguered citadel; but so for that matter can anything one likes be done at noon, under sufficient escort. When nothing is to be carried there is not the slightest occasion for escort in Kilfinane itself, although the attitude of the people is hostile in the extreme. Going for a stroll with the nephew of the absent "master," I am recommended to put a pistol in my pocket, and, much against the grain, do so.

I must confess that I draw a line at agents. Alone I should not dream of going about armed, although "indignation meetings" have been held to denounce me for speaking the truth and believing my own eyes, and I consider myself quite safe while in the company of many landlords. But agents are another matter. There is while with them always the off chance of something untoward turning up, and it is, perhaps, as well to be prepared for emergencies. Personally I must confess that I am favourably disposed towards the much vilified agents. They are in many respects the most manly men in Ireland. Nearly always well-bred, they excite sympathy by the position they hold between the upper and nether millstone of landlord and tenant. Perhaps they have made a good thing of it, but if so they have earned it, for their position always reminds one of that assigned by Lord Macaulay to the officers of the East India Company, such as Olive and Warren Hastings. To these founders of our Eastern Empire "John Company" said, "Respect treaties; keep faith with native rulers; do not oppress the people; but send us money."

This is exactly what easy-going Irish absentee proprietors preach - "Don't hurt my tenants; don't make my name to stink in the land; above all, let there be no evictions among my people; but send me a couple of thousand pounds before Monday, or remit me at least one thousand to Nice some time next week. - Yours, The O'Martingale." This, I take it, has been the situation for the last quarter of a century, since the younger sons of Irish families took to land agency as a profession because there seemed nothing else in Ireland for them to do. Nevertheless they are hideously unpopular, and I like to be armed when I take a stroll with them in a lonely country district.

So we walk down to Kilfinane to look after the progress made in arranging quarters for the soldiers presently expected, some fifty odd redcoats or rifles as the authorities may decide. It is instructive to observe the demeanour of the people towards us. My companion formerly lived at Kilfinane, and took his share of the work there, but he was the first of his family "Boycotted," and was obliged to take up his quarters in his uncle's house. Not a blacksmith could be found to shoe his horse, and not a living creature to cook his food; so a forge belonging to the mounted division of the Royal Irish Constabulary was sent down for the horse, and the master of that interesting animal went up to the big house to eat and sleep, and the "Boycotters" were, so far, brought to nought. But the good folk of Kilfinane eye us terribly askant, or, to be more literally exact, do not eye us at all; at least, their eyes betray "no speculation." Had I driven in from Charleville alone I might have gossiped with all the idlers of the village, but now that I am walking with a "Boycotted" person I seem to have become invisible. A few men are on the side walks - a few women at their doors - but they either look at us as if we were transparent as panes of glass, or suddenly become interested in their boots or finger nails, both which would be better for more regular attention. The children run away and hide themselves as if a brace of megalosauri or other happily extinct monsters had crawled out of the bog and come into Kilfinane to look for a meal. It is altogether a strange experience. It dawns upon me that the man who has driven me over from Charleville might issue from the hotel and ask for my orders, but he does not.

The edifice wherein he has established himself, his vehicle and horses, is of a bright salmon colour, rejoiceful to the eyes of the natives. My driver, on being asked at my arrival, greatly preferred the rude freedom and plenty of this pink hostelry to the supposed narrow rations of a house under ban. Possibly he loves the ruddy-faced village inn on account of its affinity in hue to that of his own visage, in which nose and beard contend fiercely for pre-eminence in warmth of tone. But be this as it may, he is just now giving warmth and colour to the interior of the establishment, instead of trying to catch my eye as I go past.

There is absolutely no sign of life or movement in the "Salmon Arms," or "The Rose," or whatever its name may be. Thus we stride down the street of Kilfinane in lonely grandeur till we come to the schoolmaster's house, to be presently converted with the schools into a barrack. Schoolmaster and wife are being temporarily evicted to make room for the military, in whose behalf a quantity of work is being done, not surely by the "Boycotters," who have already determined to "Boycott" the soldiers as far as they can by refusing to let a car carry a single article from the railway station. The military when they arrive and give that sense of security attached to a redcoat in Ireland, will be obliged to bring every kind of vehicle and transport animal with them.

In the cabbage garden of the school-house I meet an old acquaintance, Sub-Inspector Fraser, of the Royal Irish Constabulary, who seems to enjoy a monopoly of posts in which the roughest kind of "constabulary duty is to be done." Whether he esteems his "lot a happy one" I do not know; but at any rate, he looks hearty and healthy enough upon it, and is mightily cheerful withal. He has finished off one tough job, for it was Mr Fraser who was left at Pallas on the great day when horse, foot, and artillery smote the combined "Three and four year olds," or, rather, would have smitten them if they had been so misguided as to show fight. I have already recorded how the Palladians on that memorable occasion displayed a keen appreciation of the better part of valour, and I also marked my surprise that after it had taken "the fut and the dthragoons in shquadrons and plathoons," and "the boys who fear no noise" to boot, to bring the "makings" of a police hut from the railway station, where they lay "Boycotted," to Bourke's farm, twenty-five constables should have been judged a sufficiently imposing force to overawe the Palladians and to build the hut. But I hear that Mr Fraser's slender army proved quite sufficient for its purpose, and that the hut is not only built, but very well built, and likely to vex the souls of the Palladians for some time to come. There is plenty of work to do in getting ready for the soldiers. Masons and carpenters are hard at work - that is to say, as hard as anybody ever works in this part of Ireland.

On the dairy farms, which form the principal "industry" - save the mark! - of this rich part of the country, the life of the male kind is of the laziest imaginable. Employing girls to milk the cows and make the butter, the farmer appears to me to do nothing whatever except go to market and drink himself into a disaffected, discontented condition. He is rarely visible before ten or eleven o'clock in the morning, except on market days, and he appears to smoke and dawdle most of his time away. Just now he broods over his wrongs, and declares he "will have his own again," whatever that may signify. He says he is enormously over-rented. Perhaps he is; but I cannot forget that it is not many years since he and his neighbours in the adjacent county of Tipperary boasted that they had brought about an equitable adjustment of values by an ingenious process invented by themselves - that of "shooting down the rents." Have they gone up since under maleficent Saxon coercion? Verily, I do not know; for the faith I put in estimates and valuations, not excepting "The Book of Griffith," is but small.

Information in Ireland depends entirely on the person who "infawrrums" one, and is rarely complete. Almost everybody seems to think that an inquirer has some object to serve, and they either tell him what they think will amuse him or advance their own interest if it be repeated; but there are notable exceptions to this as to all other Irish rules.

Chatting easily, we stroll back through Kilfinane, bewailing the sternness of military rule, which keeps officers and men together, and will not permit of the principal coming warriors being quartered at Spa-hill. On one point we are most anxious, and that is, that the troops shall be in Kilfinane by Christmas-day, to the end that the gaiety proper to the British Army should enliven the "Boycotted" establishment at dinner time; while the imposing presence of Thomas Atkins should overawe the village mutineers, and bring grist to the proprietor of the Couleur de Rose Hotel. As evening gathers in we sit down drowsily to listen to the loud ticking of the clock and drink a glass of sherry to the health of "all poor and distressed Boycottees" within her Majesty's "sometime kingdom of Ireland." Soothed by sherry, incipient sleep, and the subtle influence of the season, the little garrison of Spa-hill gradually waxes benevolent, until one of its number actually suggests that a fat goose should be sent to the proximate cause of all its woes, Father Sheehy. Even as a big loaf of bread was once thrown into an enemy's camp, at one moment this spirited proposition is nearly carried, but it breaks down before the remark that the coachman, gardener, and two bailiffs are "Boycotted," bringing up the total number to about thirty-six, and that geese would be better distributed among these than flung away on the enemy; and the clock goes on to tick, the ticking growing louder and louder, and then comes the harsh, grating sound of shooting bolts and the clank of the chain on the front door.

There is some pretence on the part of one of my young hosts of going into his uncle's office and drawing a lease, until he is reminded that he will probably be performing a work of supererogation, that leases and feudalism and property are going out of date, and that the land agents of the future, if suffered to cumber[35] the earth at all, will be elected by the tenants, as the New York magistrates are elected by the persons whom they will be called upon to judge. And the clock ticks and the fox-terrier whines in his sleep. He is dreaming of rats, perhaps. It is pleasant to dream, even if one is a dog.

A sudden start. The long-looked-for telegram has come announcing the arrival of the daughter of the house shortly at Kilmallock Station. There is another skirmish for rifles, rugs, and revolvers, and a sally out of the fortress. No sooner has the brave young lady arrived, who with her brother and cousin, and perhaps the representatives of the British army, will form the Christmas dinner-party, than she draws up a bill of fare, which includes, as well as turkey, ham, and plum pudding, lobsters brought from afar,

---

[35] To weigh down; burden, [Clachan ed.].

thanks to feminine foresight. The retainers will feast on mighty joints of beef and on plum pudding galore. And now another telegram - The troops will arrive before the bells ring in Christmas-day.

As I approach the end of my letter, it occurs to me that although the place, events, and persons described would be recognised by anybody living in the counties of Limerick, Cork, or Tipperary, this account might appear to English readers rather as an imaginative and highly-coloured picture, painted for the Christmas market from a number of models, than as a simple sketch in neutral greys as exactly and faithfully drawn as is possible to the writer. To prevent any such misapprehension, I will observe that the events which I describe as occurring before me, have all taken place within forty-eight hours in and near the house of Mr Townsend, of Spa-hill, Kilfinane, county Limerick, and are telegraphed from Limerick city to the Daily News, because there was no nearer or more convenient office from which to send so long a message. Mr Uniacke Townsend is one of a large family mostly engaged in land agency, and has incurred the ire of the people of Kilfinane, Kilmallock, Charleville, and the surrounding country, in consequence of a difficulty with one Murphy, a fairly large farmer according to the Irish measure of farming capacity. Murphy's farm is known as Lisheen. It includes between 40 and 50 acres, and the rent, £240 per annum, has, I am informed, not been changed for forty-six years. When Murphy owed a clear year's rent and a balance on a "broken gale," he was sued for the whole amount. By May of this year he owed another gale of half a year's rent, and he was formally evicted and a caretaker put in possession on the 21st June.

It has been explained in a previous letter that after receiving any amount of credit an Irish farmer is again allowed six months' "redemption" after eviction. After paying up everything, including the additional "gale" incurred, less the proceeds of the farm, he re-enters on possession at any time within the margin of six months. Thus another "gale" fell due in November, and Murphy was still unprovided with funds. He did, however, very well without them; for the Land League, having become strong in the meanwhile in county Limerick, the caretaker was frightened away from the farm and Murphy reinstated. Mr Uniacke Townsend requested him to give up possession, and was refused, and it then became known that Murphy might expect imprisonment or fine for trespass. Thereat a meeting was held, and Mr Townsend solemnly adjudged worthy of "Boycotting." The lead in these disgraceful proceedings was taken by a Father Sheehy.

Whatever the merits of Murphy's case may be, and it seems that members of his family have held Lisheen for some considerable time, there is no doubt that Father Sheehy made an almost frantic speech against Mr Townsend, the agent, and Mr Coote, the owner of the property, declaring that "the very name of Coote smelt of blood." I am not aware of the sanguinary deeds of the Cootes in the past; all I know of them is that the present incumbent is a very old man, of somewhat clerical exterior, who, like "A fine old Irish gentleman, one of the olden time," lives in London, requests his agent to enforce the law against his tenants without delay, and, in order to encourage him to do his duty, sends down to Spa-hill the very best repeating rifles that money can buy.

The upshot of the matter is that Mr Townsend has been so threatened that he has yielded to the entreaties of his family and left Kilfinane for a week or two, at any rate. He is, however, like most of his profession, a very determined man, and declared that he would come home and eat his Christmas dinner in his own house, "despite of foes;" but Mrs Townsend, who, like the lady to whom I referred in a previous letter, has borne up nobly under her severe trial, was so scared at the thought of her husband's coming among a population banded together against him that she set off on Saturday and joined him, as the only way of averting some terrible disaster; for there is little doubt that the law will be put in force against Murphy now that his six months for "redemption" have expired; and nobody can tell what will happen at Lisheen any more than at Ennistymon if writs are issued against the tenants on the Macnamara estate, or on Mr Stacpoole's property, if he perseveres in his resolution to "Dublin writ" the people with whom he has to deal.

So the family at Spa-hill is broken up this Christmas; father and mother are both away - where I should hardly divulge, but assuredly where their Christmastide will be passed peacefully, if not joyfully.

Another gentleman of these parts is being severely "Boycotted," to wit Mr T. Sanders, of Sanders Park, Charleville, county Cork, just over the border from county Limerick; the Mr Sanders, in fact, whom I saw the Palladians roaring and yelling at on the occasion of my first visit to the classic battlefield of the "three and four year olds." On that occasion he had been vainly trying to get in rents for the charitable bequest known as Erasmus Smith's Schools, and Pallas was full of noisy and more or less drunken Palladians, who dealt with Mr Sanders in such wise that the police were obliged to see him into a railway carriage, and stand by the door till the train moved on. I would fain have called upon Mr Sanders as I drove to Charleville, but the civil and obliging landlord of Lincoln's Hotel at that place, who supplied me with an excellent carriage and horses, politely apologised for his inability to drive me thither. He could not possibly enter Sanders Park, nor would any of his men go near that abhorred spot. No orders concerning Spa-hill had been issued by the "Real Government" in the absence of the hated head of the house, and I might be driven there and welcome; but Sanders Park was another matter. I might walk out of the town, and across the park if I liked, and my informant would ensure that I went and returned in safety, as for that matter I knew very well; but not being fond of walking against time through the mud, I preferred going whither I could be driven in comfort. Moreover, the novelty of the thing is wearing off, and "Boycotting" is now only interesting when ingeniously evaded or boldly defied.

So long as a railway station is near him, the "Boycottee," if he have only two or three servants to stand firm, can practically bring the Boycotters to their wits' end. The railway companies being, I take it, common carriers, dare not refuse, like the cowardly shippers of Cork, to take the "Boycottee's" beef and plum pudding, wine and whisky, to the most convenient railway station, whence he, if well-armed and provided with an escort of constabulary, can bring in his supplies under the very nose of the infuriated peasants who stand scowling around the station gate and roar and "boo" their disgust at being foiled. There is not the slightest fear of the "Boycotters" running their heads against Winchester rifles and army revolvers, and the convoy need apprehend nothing hotter or harder than curses and groans, which, "like the idle wind, hurt not the mariner ashore."

This last quotation had the misfortune to displease one of my young hosts, who opined that he thought, on the contrary, we were all at sea in Ireland just now, and breakers were ahead. Perhaps he is over much of an alarmist, but his present situation is hardly calculated to inspire confidence in anything but conical bullets and cold steel. As we stand together on the doorstep, he remarks that it will be long before Christmas a la Boycott is forgotten in Ireland, and then he wishes me the compliments of the season. "Good bye," and "Safe home" - hateful valediction! I wish him and his a happier new year than the old one has been; but it would be a sorry jest to wish a merry Christmas to one whose greatest happiness and consolation are that at this time of gathered kindred, at the feast which comes but once a year for the re-knitting of the ties of domestic affection, the kindly voice of the house-mother is not heard beneath her own roof tree; that the chair of the house-father stands empty at the Christmas board.

XVIII - CHRISTMAS IN COUNTY CLARE

ENNIS, Monday

In a picture exhibited a few years ago, and since engraved, was powerfully and pathetically portrayed a scene of the early life of the Pilgrim Fathers of New England. It was wintertime, and the day was Sunday. Clad in raiment of quaint severity, the head of the house led his Puritan family and servants across the snow-clad fields to worship. Living in the midst of a hostile population, the little band of worshippers was armed to the teeth. The father carried his "plain falling band" and steeple-crowned hat with a stiff air, and also carried lethal weapons. His prim wife and daughters bare Bibles, and his serving men, muskets. "Like a servant of the Lord, With his Bible and his sword," the unflinching old soldier of the Commonwealth strode manfully from his homestead to his religious duties, not unprepared to deal with any foes who might turn up by the way.

As a glimpse of the remote past, as well as a work of art, this picture struck me as valuable; but it certainly did not occur to me that a similar sight would be seen within a short space in the kingdom of Ireland. Nevertheless, it may be witnessed on any Sunday in county Clare. Near Tulla, a spot of evil repute just now as the theatre of a recent attack upon magistrates returning from doing their duty, Colonel O'Callaghan, his wife and son, may be seen on any Sunday morning going to church armed with rifle and revolver, and protected by an escort of constabulary. The church is a long walk from Lismeehan (Anglice, Maryfort), and the way is not safe either for Colonel O'Callaghan himself, his wife, his child, or anything that is his.

I will not pretend for what are called "sensational" purposes that the stranger who ventures within the gates of Maryfort is in any danger so long as he remains within them, or that any weightier missiles than groans and hisses are launched at him as he goes to and from the house under "taboo." It is well known that an attack on Lismeehan would not be bloodless, and that the defence would be far fiercer and more deadly than that made at the Clare-street Police Barrack at Limerick. The little garrison is perfectly armed, and small as it is, would work mischief on any attacking mob; but the experience at Tulla the other day proves that safety is only purchased at the trouble and inconvenience of going everywhere armed to the teeth.

After my experience in the matter of Mr Sanders, of Sanders Park, Charleville, I did not think it worth while to go to a posting-house for a carriage and horses to reach Maryfort; but being fortunate enough to obtain the loan of a friend's victoria and servant I got a horse "sharpened" as to his shoes at Ennis; and drove over the frost-bound road to Colonel

O'Callaghan's house yesterday afternoon. It was a long drive to the most severely "Boycotted" house in Clare. It was also a drive of surpassing dreariness. The sun, which had made the hoar frost to sparkle on Christmas Day, barely pierced through the clouds on the afternoon of St. Stephen's. Leaving trim lawns, a forest of box-trees, budding roses and peonies, well-grown early brocoli and York cabbages behind, we drove through a country of eternal little fields and grey stone walls.

It is needless to say that Maryfort is a long way from Ennis. Every place is a long way from everywhere in this western part of Ireland - a fact, by the way, not infrequently forgotten by critics of the much-criticised constabulary. Where gentlemen's houses and considerable villages are as much as fifteen miles apart, the area of country to be watched becomes quite unmanageable. Only those who have incurred the fearful loss of time in getting from place to place in Connaught can form an adequate idea of it. Despite the discouraging remarks of its critics, this well-drilled, well-grown corps of Royal Irish Constabulary remains as staunch and loyal as of old, but it is absurd to expect impossibilities. Galway to a person sitting comfortably in his own library appears to be overwhelmed with constables. I believe that there is, in fact, one constable to every fifty adult males in that county - an enormous proportion judged statistically, but yet slight enough when the vast area of the county and the miles of actual desert which separate one partially civilised spot from another are considered.

A large percentage of the constabulary is also deflected from general to special service in affording downright personal protection, and that modified protection known as "looking after" individuals. A hundred and twenty persons in Ireland are now receiving "personal protection," amounting to the constant attendance of never less than two constables, frequently to the residence of four or more on the premises or the property. At least eight hundred persons are being "looked after;" so that it is no exaggeration to state that twelve or thirteen hundred men are detached from the regular force on particular duty of the most harassing and vexatious kind. Wherever the person under protection chooses to go, at whatever hour, or in whatever weather, his "escort" must accompany him; for their orders are "not to lose sight of him" outside of his own door. This is a troublesome duty, sometimes greatly aggravated by the conduct of the protected persons, who take sudden fits and starts, and fly hither and thither in the oddest kind of way. The constables get no rest; they are perpetually harassed and exposed, and they are quite superior to the consolation of a "tip."

I say this deliberately, for on three several occasions I tried to give a drenched and half-frozen constable a reward for service rendered, not for information to be given, and on each and every occasion I met with a dignified refusal, accompanied by one man with a friendly caution not to attempt that sort of thing, as some of the men might be rough. I say that I did not ask for information, because I generally knew more than the constables, for the excellent reason that I had wider and better sources to draw upon. From the country folk it is absolutely impossible to glean any scrap of information. A question immediately shapes their countenances into a look of hopeless simplicity and guilelessness bordering upon idiocy. Persons in quest of information in the remote parts of Ireland put me in mind of the hunter of the Rocky Mountains, who, while he was trying to stalk some antelope, became aware that a grizzly bear was stalking him. The people find out all about the person seeking for knowledge, but he discovers nothing.

After this it is needless to say that the constabulary must of necessity be the last people to learn anything from the country folk, and that a London detective would be as much out of his element as "a salmon on a gravel walk."

Between Ennis and Maryfort we only met two brace of constables on the road, but we knew there were others with Mr Hall, of Cluny, at Tulla, and other places within ten miles of Colonel O'Callaghan's house. There was a little gathering of people near the chapel at Bearfield, but in other respects the road was empty till we neared our destination, when a little crowd set up an Irish howl against us, followed by a shout of "Long live Parnell." Presently we came to Lismeehan gates, opened after a good steady look at us by an ancient retainer, in a grey frieze coat. I was told civilly enough that "the masther" was at home. Beyond a pretty park, full of well-bred cattle, lay the "Boycotted" house, tall and grey and grim, in the waning light. There was no sign of life in it. Under a handsome portico was the grand entrance, bolted and barred up, with shutters closed. There was nothing for it but to tug vigorously at the bell. Nobody came to the door, but around each corner of the house stepped an armed constable. A moment later a narrow slip of the shutter was moved, and we became aware first of a fur cap and then of a youthful face, which ultimately proved to be that of Colonel O'Callaghan's eldest son, home for the holidays from a great English school, and undergoing the "hardening" process of spending Christmas in a state of siege.

Presently came a maidservant, neat and trim, and after some wrestling with bolts the outer door was opened a little way, and our names and business demanded, after which we entered a great hall, apparently used as a refectory. Huge logs blazed on the hearth, and the room looked comfortable enough. We were next ushered into the drawing-room of Colonel O'Callaghan, who had just come in from herding his cattle and sheep, and was still girt with a brace of full-sized revolvers.

No whit dismayed by the attack made on him at Tulla, and holding his foes in very slight estimation, Colonel O'Callaghan is yet subjected to inconvenience and oppression of an extraordinary kind. The proximate cause of his being "Boycotted" was his action is serving four processes himself, because neither love nor money nor threats would induce a process-server to do his work. The country folk know quite well the difference between Land League law and the phantom which remains of the law of the land. The former is instantly enforced, the latter cannot be carried into effect at all, a fact which is telling upon its officers with discouraging effect.

Finding his writs could be served by nobody but himself, Colonel O'Callaghan started early one morning, attended by his escort, served the four writs himself, and then prepared to hold his own. Pigs were killed, barrels of flour and other stores were brought in, and the house provisioned to stand a siege. Recollection of old days in the Crimea, when Colonel O'Callaghan was in the 62nd Regiment, were revived under the provisioning process, which was by no means complete when he was formally "Boycotted," and left with 300 cattle and sheep upon his hands, with only one man to help him to look after them. Thirty odd herds, labourers, and other dependents have left Maryfort. Only three maid-servants, the old man at the gate, and another man now remain, and even the housemaid, who is Irish and a Roman Catholic, must be guarded to and from mass, amid the yells of the natives. It must be remembered that Maryfort is a lonely place, three miles from a post-office, and three times that distance from a railway station; that it is no light matter to send in and out for letters and parcels; and the emissary would, if unarmed, assuredly be stopped, if not maltreated. This difficulty of getting letters and fresh joints has been met in the latter case by falling back upon patriarchal customs. As Colonel O'Callaghan can neither sell his sheep nor buy mutton, he has taken to consuming his flock, albeit a sheep is a large animal to kill in a small family, and but for the winter weather the loss would be very great.

There is another annoyance - the risk of valuable cattle being houghed or otherwise mutilated; a risk calling for incessant watchfulness. That it is not of an imaginary nature is demonstrated by the fact that the tails were cut off of two of Mrs Westropp's cows a few nights since, and a threatening letter, savagely coarse and brutal in its wording, was sent to that lady. There is no doubt about this, for I have seen the letter, in which reference is made to the cows and brutal treatment promised to Mrs Westropp, a widow of small property.

The difficulty concerning letters, which it seems the postmaster at Callaghan's Mills is not compelled to deliver at Maryfort, is got over in another way. As we are discussing the question of supply, there enters to us a lady dressed in walking costume of studied simplicity. This is the terrible

Mrs O'Callaghan, of whom I had heard wonderful stories in Clare and Limerick; "And begorra," said one informant, "it's herself that's a divil of a lady entoirely, and she shoots rabbuts wid a rifle at three hundred yards and niver misses, and she tould 'um at the village that she'd as soon shoot one of 'um as a rabbut, and she is the sisther of Misthress Dick Stacpoole, of Edenvale. They was the Miss Westropps, your honour, out of county Limerick, and it is thim as makes their husbands the tyrants that they are." This account made me wonder at two things - firstly, at the astounding power of lying and exaggeration displayed by my interlocutor; and secondly, where the old Irish gallantry towards the fair sex has gone to. It seems to have gone very far, for one hears now of ladies being shot at. But, although not impressed with the truth of the information vouchsafed to me, I expected to see at least an Irish version of Lady Macbeth, instead of the graceful, well-dressed, thorough-bred Irish gentlewoman who had just come from a long walk to the post-office and back. Since the boy who used to carry the letter bag was frightened away, Mrs O'Callaghan has taken up his duties, and, armed with rifle and revolver, performs them daily.

With the case of Miss Ellard, and other ladies, before my eyes, I cannot blame Mrs O'Callaghan for going about armed, and maintaining a defiant attitude towards the people, who really go in bodily fear of her. There is, as I have observed, nothing to terrify in the look or voice of Mrs O'Callaghan, but I gradually gather from her conversation that it is not all romance about her wonderful shooting. If not at three hundred, yet at thirty yards she can hit a rabbit cleverly enough, and actually does go out rabbit shooting "for the pot" to relieve the monotony of everlasting pig and sheep. Mrs O'Callaghan is also nearly as good a shot with the revolver as her husband, and would certainly not hesitate to use that weapon in self-defence.

Such is the present personnel of Maryfort at this moment, affording a sketch of manners reminding one rather of a Huguenot family in southern France just after receiving the news of St. Bartholomew, than of any social condition extant in modern Europe.

As we drive out into the darkness and heavily-falling snow there is some debate touching the lighting of the carriage lamps. It is thought better not to light up, and to keep firearms handy until we get some miles from Maryfort.

A howl pierces through the darkness as we pass a clump of houses, and I remark that my friend's coachman drives very fast by any house on the road; but nothing occurs till we stop at a "shebeen" to light both cigars and lamps, for the snowstorm is increasing. Not desiring refreshment, I give the woman of the house a shilling for a drink for a man who is sitting by the fire. I explain the nature of the transaction to him, and wish him a happy new year. The sulky brute answers me never a word. Probably he knows or suspects where I have been, and if so would let me lie on the ground under a kicking horse till an end was made of me rather than stretch forth a hand. He will not speak now, and I observe that the woman, who has kept a tight hold on the shilling, has not poured out any whisky, although she has had the decency to ask me if I wished for any. It is a strange sight, this sullen silent savage sitting scowling over the fire; but *on se fait a tout*[36] in Disturbed Ireland.

Clachan Publishing

---

[36] There is everything, (Fr) [Clachan ed.].

Index

54, 64-70, 75, 86, 94, 95, 98, 112, 117, 121
McCarthy O'Leary, 116
Middleman, 30, 42, 49, 73, 75, 138
Millstreet, 116, 117, 118, 149
Monaghan, 65, 66, 67
Mountmorres, Lord, 20, 69
Mr Drinkwater, 80- 87

Nephin, 5, 6, 13, 26, 32
Newport, 11, 13, 21, 60

O'Callaghan, Colonel, 161, 162, 163, 164
O'Connell, Daniel, 35, 75, 79, 138, 143
O'Connell's duel, 143
O'Connell, Sir James, 139, 142
O'Donoghue, The, 121
O'Flahertys, 42, 44, 50
O'Gorman Mahon, The, 79, 80, 82, 88
O'Hagan's Act, - see Lord O'Hagan's Jury Act,
Old Irish Retainer, 107
Omey, 71, 72, 73, 138
Omey Island, 71, 72
Orangemen, 62-68
Oughbane, River, 119
Oughterard, 48
'Outrages', 38, 47, 95, 111, 128, 137
Oysters, 146

Pallas, 95, 96, 97, 98, 99, 100, 156, 159
Parnell, Mr, 24, 25, 36, 91, 121, 127, 163
Peace Preservation Act, 21
Peasant propriety, 138
Peat. See turf,
Poor-rate, 115, 126
Protestants, 37, 86, 88

Rakes of Mallow, 116

Rate of interest, 83, 102, 103
Read, Mr Clare, 117
Recess Valley, 40
Relief meal, 115
Repeal, 42, 102
Rifles, 21, 63, 64, 152-160
Rinvyle, 49, 50, 115
Rinvyle Mountain, 50
Robinson, Mr - Agent Ballinahinch, 47
Roman Catholic clergy, 39
Roman Catholics, 88
Rossturk, 10, 11, 15
Rossturk Castle, 10, 11
Royal Irish Constabulary (RIC), 6, 15, 21, 26-27,, 35, 37, 38, 59, 60, 61, 63-68, 79, 89, 91, 96-100, 113, 130-6, 155, 156, 159, 156, 162
Ruttledge, Mr, 65

Sanders Park, 159, 161
Sanders, T., Mr of Sanders Park, 159
Saxon, The (English men), 2, 14, 26, 40, 48, 57, 59, 70, 83, 86, 106, 107, 110, 111, 134, 153, 156
Scariff drainage works, the, 90
Scariff Island, 90, 142
'Sent to Coventry,' 129, 151
Shannon, 82, 84, 85, 95
"shebeens," 17 107, 119, 132, 133, 134, 165
Sheehane Hill, 35
Sheehy, Rev Father, 157, 158
Shillelagh, 15, 129
Skelligs, The, 141
Slob Works, 83, 85
Smallholding, 20
Sneem, 144, 147
Somerset Maxwell, Mr, 65
Spa-hill, 157, 159
St. John Colthurst, Sir George, 115, 150

Clachan's 'Historic Irish Journeys' series

Travels In Ireland - J.G. Kohl
   This is a very readable account by a German visitor of his tour around Ireland immediately before the Great Famine.

Disturbed Ireland – 1881 - Bernard Becker
   A series of letters written as the author travelled around the West of Ireland, visiting key places in the 'Land War'. We meet Captain Boycott and other members of the gentry, as well as a range of small farmers and peasants.

A Journey throughout Ireland, During the Spring, Summer and Autumn of 1834 - Henry D. Inglis
   Inglis travels Ireland attempting to answer the question, 'is Ireland and improving country?' using discussion with landlords, manufacturers and tenants plus his own insightful observations.

The West Of Ireland: Its Existing Condition and Prospects - Henry Coulter
   This is a collection of letters from *Saunders's News-Letter* relating to the condition and prospects of the people of the West of Ireland after the partial failure of the harvests of the early 1860s.

Highways and Byways in Donegal and Antrim - Stephen Gwynn
   If you take this wonderful account of a bike journey written at the end of the 19th Century with you as you travel around Donegal and the Glens of Antrim and you will journey not only over land, but also over time.

*   *   *   *   *

Clachan 'Local History' Series

Henry Coulter's account has been sub-divided for the convenience of local and family historians.

The West Of Ireland: Its Existing Condition and Prospects, Part 1, by Henry Coulter.
   This is an extract from the complete edition dealing with Athlone, Co. Clare and Co. Galway.

The West Of Ireland: Its Existing Condition and Prospects, Part 2, by Henry Coulter.
   This is an extract from the complete edition dealing with Co. Mayo.

The West Of Ireland: Its Existing Condition and Prospects, Part 3, by Henry Coulter.
   The final extract from the complete edition dealing with Counties Co Sligo, Donegal, Leitrim and Roscommon.

*   *   *   *   *

J.G.Kohl's account has been sub-divided for the convenience of local and family historians.

Travels in Ireland – Part 1, takes us through Edgeworthtown, The Shannon, Limerick, Edenvale, Kilrush and Father Mathew.

Travels in Ireland – Part 2, his journey continues through Tarbet, Tralee, Killarney, Bantry, Cork, Kilkenny and Waterford.

Travels in Ireland – Part 3, this section deals with Wexford, Enniscorthy, Avoca, Glendalough and Dublin.

Travels In Ireland - Part 4 –he goes north for the last part of his journey through Dundalk, Newry, Belfast, The Antrim Coast, Rathlin, The Giant's Causeway.

*   *   *   *   *

Henry D. Inglis' account has also been sub-divided for the convenience of local and family historians.

A Journey throughout Ireland, During the Spring, Summer and Autumn of 1834, Part 1 takes us from Dublin. Through Wexford, Waterford and Cork.

A Journey throughout Ireland, During the Spring, Summer and Autumn of 1834, Part 2 is an account of Kerry, Clare, Limerick and the Shannon and concludes in Athlone.

*   *   *   *   *

Stephen Gwynn's account has also been sub-divided for the convenience of local and family historians.

Highways and Byways in Donegal and Antrim Part One: Donegal

Highways and Byways in Donegal and Antrim Part: Two - Derry & Co. Antrim

*   *   *   *   *

Aghaidh Achadh Mór, The Face of Aghamore −edited by Joe Byrne.

This is a reproduction of a title originally published in 1991 and is of enduring interest to local historians and to those with ancestral roots in East Mayo. It covers such topics as Stone Age archaeology, family history, local hedge schools, O'Carolan's connection with the parish, the Civil War and townland surveys.

Lough Corrib, Its Shores and Islands: with Notices of Lough Mask - by William R. Wilde, first published in 1867. In the words of the author: 'A work intended to … rescue from oblivion, or preserve from desecration, some of the historic monuments of the country'.

A Statistical and Agricultural Survey of the Co. of Galway – by Hely Dutton

Dutton's survey has resulted in a detailed description of the agricultural conditions and practices of Galway in the early Nineteenth Century. He has added detailed chronologies of the leading officials of Galway town and its governance, as well as of the senior churchmen of the bishopric of Tuam and the abbeys, monasteries and convents, of the area.

A History of Sligo: Town and Country, Vol. I, by Terrence O'Rorke

This classic and well-loved history, first published in 1889, is the work of a man born and bred in Sligo. It remains a work of fascination for anyone with connections to Sligo, and is an important reference for anyone interested in the history of Ireland.

Captain Cuellar's Adventures in Connaught and Ulster, A.D. 1588,

by Francisco de Cuellar, Hugh Allingham and Robert Crawford

This is an extraordinary first-hand account of the survival of a captain of the Spanish Armada. Ship-wrecked off the Sligo coast he faces horrors and pursuit to the death. He finds sanctuary among two Irish chieftains before making his way to the North Coast of Antrim and final deliverance.

A Step Up – by Pat Nolan

This is the story of the one of the great Irish fishing vessels, the BIM 56-footers.

The book contains details on each boat, and recollections of individuals who owned and/or fished on them.

*   *   *   *   *

Poems, Ballads and Songs

Songs of the Glens of Antrim, Moiré O'Neill

Written by a Glenswoman chiefly for other Glens-people.

Away with Words by Michael Sands.

"It is truthful, thoughtful, touching and tender as well as being intuitive, imaginative, innovative and inspiring." Mickey MacConnell, Listowel, Co Kerry.

Clachan
Publishing

Clachan Publishing, Ballycastle, Glens of Antrim.
Buy from our site at clachan-publishing.com